FURIOUS GEORGE

FURIOUS GEORGE

MY FORTY YEARS SURVIVING NBA DIVAS, CLUELESS GMs, AND POOR SHOT SELECTION

GEORGE KARL

with Curt Sampson

HARPER

An Imprint of HarperCollins*Publishers*

FURIOUS GEORGE. Copyright © 2017 by George Karl. All rights reserved. Printed in the United States of America. No part of this book may be used or reproduced in any manner whatsoever without written permission except in the case of brief quotations embodied in critical articles and reviews. For information, address HarperCollins Publishers, 195 Broadway, New York, NY 10007.

HarperCollins books may be purchased for educational, business, or sales promotional use. For information, please email the Special Markets Department at SPsales@harpercollins.com.

FIRST EDITION

Library of Congress Cataloging-in-Publication Data has been applied for.

ISBN 978-0-06-236779-2

17 18 19 20 21   RRD   10 9 8 7 6 5 4 3

For my three coaches: Dean Smith, Bill Guthridge, and my father, Joseph Karl.
And for my three children: Kelci, Coby, and Kaci.

CONTENTS

INTRODUCTION

George needs to keep his mouth shut, first and foremost.

—KENYON MARTIN, DENVER NUGGETS FORWARD (2004-2011)

I *kicked a ball* at a referee once. Kicked it hard.

It was a cold night in a hot gym in January 1991. It was the last three minutes of a CBA game in Knickerbocker Arena in Albany, New York. We were playing the Oklahoma City Cavalry—remember them? Neither do I. Anyway—although we were up by about 20, I saw a serious problem, but the louder I yelled about it, the more I was ignored.

I've gotten a lot of techs in this situation, when at the end of a blowout, the refs just want the thing over with, so they stop calling anything. "Reffing the scoreboard," I call it. That annoys me a lot, because when I played in the NBA, "garbage time" was my time. For a bench player like me, here at last was a chance to show the coach how good I was. So while the arena emptied, I'd concentrate all my effort and skill into my two or three minutes on the floor. It made me mad as hell to get hacked but have the foul ignored because the refs didn't want to delay their postgame beer.

This wasn't one of those, not exactly. But a number of things were bothering me—and I snapped.

We missed a shot, OKC got the rebound, and our Ben McDonald

hustled back to play defense. Their Alvin Heggs got the ball, and took it toward the rim from half-court with all the subtlety and finesse of a bull running downhill. Ben had two full seconds to stand in the paint and brace for the impact. Bam! Both players hit the floor.

"Blocking," said Monty McCutchen, now an NBA game official. "Two shots."

What! I ran out on the court to put my face very close to Monty's while I told him that he'd just made the worst f'ing call I'd ever seen, but he interrupted my tirade, by putting one index finger on top of the other.

"Technical foul, Coach Karl."

I kept going. "This is crap," I said, "and not fair to players I'm demanding to play hard and they're not getting just calls from refs who aren't paying attention and—" McCutchen interrupted again.

"Turn around and shut up," he said.

I didn't do either.

While still screaming at Monty, I noticed the ball rolling very slowly toward us, and, without consciously deciding to do it, I tore into that orange Spalding Model 74 with a soccer-style kick, and I nailed it. *Whomp.* The ball flew over Monty's head and 12 rows deep in the upper deck. Our crowd cheered. I got my second technical foul and was ejected.

"It was forty-six-yard field goal, right up the middle," said Charley Rosen, the opposing coach, having fun with the writers afterward. "But it's easy to kick indoors. I want to see him do it with someone rushing and a little wind." Ha-ha.

At our practice the next morning, the coach of the local Arena Football League team showed up to offer me a job as a placekicker. Ha-ha again.

Okay, I know my goalie kick was childish, but it provided an instant of relief, it made my point, the fine wasn't too bad, and I didn't get suspended. As I mentioned, a few things had caused my temporary insanity: mail-it-in officiating; the sudden absence of Mario Elie and Vince Askew, our two best players, who'd left for the NBA (Mario) and a pro team in Italy (Vince); and an early, inconvenient tip-off in order to accommodate a college game later in the evening. That's the way it was in the minor league Continental Basketball Association, the home of the ten-hour bus ride.

There was also something deeper and darker going on with me back then. Twenty-five years ago, I was in my third year of being blackballed from the NBA, and I was moving my family all over the map so I could pursue my career. And even though the team I was coaching in '91 was in the midst of compiling the best record *in the history of pro basketball,* my phone wasn't ringing. I had a lot to figure out, personally and professionally. I needed to harness my passion for the game, a passion that had me kicking balls.

Obviously, I needed to evolve, to find a better way to get along in the world of games. But just as obviously, I needed to stay the same, because my emotional approach to coaching basketball worked. My teams won games. It was tricky. It's still tricky.

Maybe you've known someone like me, the maniac jock who's got to finish first, and maybe takes it too far.

At Penn Hills (Pennsylvania) High School, the University of North Carolina, and with the San Antonio Spurs, I dove for the ball, took charges, and started fights. I was still the same guy when I became a coach, and I gave up my body a second time.

How well I learned to control myself is a matter of opinion. A writer asked Ron Adams to analyze me in 2001, ten years after my field goal. Ron, a very smart man, was then one of my Milwaukee Bucks assistant coaches. "He's a little bizarre," Ron said. "But that helps him. In every culture, a crazy guy gets respect because nobody's quite sure what he'll do next."

I can't help it: I go after my team in practice and off the court. Nowadays I try to make my points gently, with happy sarcasm. "Hey, man," I might say in a cheerful voice. "You really sucked last night." But I haven't always been so thoughtful. In my first two NBA jobs, at Cleveland and Golden State, I took some pride in treating everyone the same, in being unafraid to yell at the star as loudly as I yelled at the last guy on the bench. I got fired from both those jobs. Given another chance—eventually—I learned that some people have to be handled gently, while others are secure enough to hear the truth without sugarcoating.

"JaVale," I said to my center in Denver, "in another world, I think you and I would be hanging out. But in this one, you don't play hard every night and you don't work on your game and I can't count on you."

Time will tell if JaVale McGee listened, but some players just can't hear you. Money in the ears.

What happens when you give a twenty-one-year-old $3 million or $4 million for his first job? He gets an entourage. He has less and less contact with people outside his group of helpers. He becomes less and less of a role model. And he thinks I can't tell him what to do because he knows I've been told to play him twenty-five minutes a game.

JaVale, by the way, was making about $11 million a year when we had our little talk.

I'm not saying that insulated, immature players have too much self-esteem. I think they hardly have any at all. They're fearful because they have so far to fall.

As my detractors perceive it, I have two big weaknesses. The first rap against me, the former garbage-time point guard, is that I can't coach a superstar. You may have read that I always fight with any player good enough for a Gatorade endorsement. True, over the years I've had some monumental public arguments with a handful of high scorers. But almost without exception, the All-Stars on my teams have had the best years of their careers when I coached them. I don't mind some tension; tension can be good. And the NBA coach who can't manage a working relationship with his best players is not going to win enough games to last.

Introduction

Yet there's always trouble when I have a player whose commitment is to his numbers or his money or his brand—and not to the team. Remind me to tell you about the time one of us kept the rest of us Nuggets waiting in a bus under an arena while he got a postgame massage. . . . When I call a guy like this on his selfish behavior, when his ego is threatened, he's got to show that *he* controls *me*. A guaranteed contract much bigger than mine is his power.

The other rap against me is that I talk too much.

There's a grain of truth in that, too. I've never been very good at hiding my frustrations or burying my opinions. Writers like me because I'm a good quote and clichés bore me (and them). This has led to trouble. When I coached in Spain, the more Spanish I learned, the less the club liked it. And I remember what the Milwaukee Bucks owner told me when he was firing me: "With all the media coverage we have, you're too honest." Senator Herb Kohl (D, Wisconsin) said, "Your openness has been used against you and against our organization."

I understand how I can bruise someone's ego by being too blunt, but when a player gets in trouble off the court, why can't we just say, "He got drunk last night and should take responsibility," instead of enabling him as if he's a victim? When I've got a player I'm not getting along with, management doesn't want me to say why. We won't let the world know he's got a bad attitude, he doesn't practice hard, and his teammates hate him. So we spin. And our game gets covered with layer after layer of PR, like too much frosting on a cheap cake. I'm not naive, but I think that by burying conflict, we're hiding the most interesting part of our personality.

Those two things—my insistence that even superstars must play basketball the right way, and my big mouth when they don't—have led, I guess, to a couple of periods of unemployment. Intervals of not coaching allowed me two stints with ESPN.

And that led to this book.

Introduction

I'd rather coach, of course, but I loved doing TV, loved having that platform. I like to talk, I know something about basketball, and I am opinionated, to put it mildly. Ex-coaches who do TV well—I'm thinking about Hubie Brown and Jeff Van Gundy—have tremendous influence.

In an average ESPN night, I'd analyze a few games, evaluate potential draft picks, comment on a trade, and weigh in on the rumors always floating around the NBA. A voice in my ear would say, "Nice job, see you tomorrow." It was usually about two or three in the morning when I limped out of there and into the snow of midwinter Connecticut. Someone would drive me the five hundred yards to the hotel.

On those dark, icy nights it dawned on me: TV is limited. It's a snapshot. I didn't get enough time to make you understand what goes on inside the NBA. TV and the Internet have exploded the amount of superficial information about our game but not the knowledge. I need a book—this one—to explain what really happens.

For example: I wasn't able to explain that dealing with egos that are like ostrich eggs—big and fragile—is the hidden reality of what NBA coaches do. It's even hidden from some owners—like the one in Denver—who don't appreciate the importance and the time and hard work involved. Before coaches can even begin to teach basketball or practice being a team, we've got to take care of Player A, who feels disrespected by Player B. And Player C doesn't think he's being used right; he wants more plays run for him. Players D and E had a loud argument on the plane because E thinks D won't pass him the damn ball. F is jealous of G's contract—and on and on.

For at least my last five years of coaching, the first ten minutes of every pregame or pre-practice coaches' meeting have been about smoothing over internal conflicts and how to handle those eggshell egos. Then my assistants fan out for one-on-one talks. "Really need your focus in practice today, E," they'll say. "We've got two new plays and a different way to defend Westbrook. And we're going to talk to D about how he distributes the ball."

Another example of insider stuff that TV can't get to: When other NBA coaches get fired, I take advantage, if I can. I wait a couple of weeks, then reach out to them. We have dinner and drinks. "Yeah, your owner is a dumbass," I'll say, and I agree that the GM can't build a sandwich much less an NBA team and the players are disloyal and the fans and the media in your city are idiots—whatever. Then I ask the money questions: How did you try to beat us? What are our weaknesses? Are we predictable out of a timeout or at the end of a game?

Whether it was my getting fired, or them, Larry Brown, Don Nelson, Del Harris, and a couple of others have given me good intel about my teams and my tendencies.

As you read this book, imagine I am on the next bar stool over and you've asked me what it's really like inside pro basketball. You seem okay, you're buying, and I want to say what I want to say. I don't mind a reaction and I don't mind pissing off twenty-nine teams: the only team I want to be happy is my own. So I'll tell you my strategy for beating Michael Jordan. I'll tell you why the Eastern Conference sucks. How, you may want to know, do I get a collection of individual stars to think and play like a team? (Sometimes I can't.) What's it like to coach a game? You might be curious about what it's like to get fired—does the owner do it, or the GM, and do they give you a cardboard box and order you to empty out your desk? Do they call security to escort you to the door?

From having coached a couple of thousand professional games and from having played 264 of them, I've been a part of the palace intrigues, the arguments, the despair, and the fun. I understand pretty well the psychology and atmosphere that produce winning.

Introduction

It's subtle, and luck is involved. The media makes out that there's this Grand Canyon between the genius coach who wins and the idiot coach who loses. It's not that way.

I guess I just want people to understand a little more about the game I've spent my life in.

I've got another reason for getting things down on paper (or on your electronic device). I'm sixty-four, not exactly old, but I've considered my own mortality a lot because I've had cancer twice. I remember when I got the biopsy results in May 2005, in the Westin Hotel in San Antonio, just before my first playoff game with the Nuggets. A few years later, when I heard the words "squamous cell carcinoma" I felt a chill that went right to my bones. I thought I'd received a death sentence. In a way, cancer never goes away. I admit that I'm scared as shit every six months, when I get the results from another PET scan. And that gets to my other motivation for picking up a pen and looking back. If I make any money from this book, it's going to my foundation, which helps cancer patients and their families navigate the ridiculously expensive, needlessly frightening, and stupidly complicated world of doctors, hospitals, and insurance: GeorgeKarlFoundation.org.

So: sorry, Kenyon. I'm not keeping my mouth shut. Not now, not ever. I've written a book about my life in basketball. Not that I've finished my coaching career, but I have been around long enough to take a look back.

Maybe I should have savored the wins more.

Maybe I should have had Gary Payton guard Michael Jordan in the 1996 NBA Finals.

For sure I should have given more time to my family.

And maybe I should have made nice with one or two of the superstars who tormented me and one or two of the owners and GMs who fired me.

I see now that I've evolved as a person and as a basketball coach

as I've gone from job to job. But my goal—to win a championship—
has never wavered.

I haven't done that—yet.

A few years ago, after I almost died, my outlook changed. So
did my diet and my beer intake and my weight. Basketball was my
life. Now life is my life.

But some things didn't change. I continue to have a crazy desire
to win—at anything. I still have a low tolerance for bullshit and
hypocrisy, and I continue to raise my voice and point it out when I
see it, because there's a lot of b.s. out there.

Basketball has given my life structure and meaning and a reason
to get out of bed. But I don't want to make it sound too serious
because, oh, my God, it's been fun.

So let's get started. I read a few memoirs to prepare myself for
this effort, and I've read a few reviews. The usual criticism of an
autobiography is that they're self-serving, too obviously written to
even old scores, or that their main purpose is to get the last word
in. Will that apply to this book?

Hell yes. Might as well admit it.

FURIOUS GEORGE

PASSION PLAY

George was tougher than barbwire, with this pay-you-back right now kind of temper. I didn't think he had the right temperament to be a coach.

—RED MCCOMBS, CO-OWNER OF THE SAN ANTONIO SPURS

When I put George in, he flat put the game on full speed. He turned the crowd on and turned the team on.

—BOB BASS, SPURS HEAD COACH

My coaching nemesis Phil Jackson burned incense and sage grass in his locker room. I burn brain cells.

Phil sold his teams on offensive rhythm and flow. I made my bones as a defensive coach committed to disrupting rhythm and flow.

Phil's ideal team is all quickness and finesse; I want contact and collisions.

Phil's style is cerebral and aloof. I'm pretty much the opposite. I want passion.

Most players understand the intensity I want and most of them like it, too. But not everyone is as fired up as I am. The season is long, the players are saving themselves, and the attack-first attitude

I prefer is at odds with the coolness a lot of NBA players try to project. Relaxed, nothing-bothers-me body language may be a cultural ideal but it's not my ideal. Cool is my enemy.

But after forty years in pro basketball, I've cooled off and calmed down a little bit. Now I'm known as an offensive coach who can help a team find rhythm and flow.

I'm not proud that in the past my passion crossed the line into anger. I used to think it was a good thing. It's not. Anger from the coach creates fear in the player. But what I want him to feel is commitment.

Maybe a little rage is okay, but it's got to be like garlic for the cook or the five-iron for a golfer. To be used when you need it and often not at all. Sometimes, of course, that white-hot feeling shows up on its own.

I once had a player who calmly turned the pages of the *Wall Street Journal* in our pregame locker room. Checking his portfolio, I suppose, while I'm pacing like an expectant father. Before practice, he'd read a book on the bench until the *instant* we were scheduled to begin.

That was Joe Barry Carroll, a seven-footer who was the first pick in the 1980 NBA draft. The emotionless JB had a high basketball IQ and was very advanced offensively; he had a big game that should have been even bigger. He made his only All-Star team when I coached him at Golden State. Not that I take any credit for that; maybe I deserve some blame that he made only one. But while I didn't bring out the fire in him, he certainly brought it out in me. His intellectual, above-it-all approach mocked everything I believe in.

I remember a playoff game against the Los Angeles Lakers. Adrenaline squirts like crazy into (almost) everyone's bloodstream during the playoffs but my stoic, businesslike center played against Kareem Abdul-Jabbar without any special urgency, or any that I could see. We lost a close game to go down 0-3 and JB made some mistakes at the end. But he was all right with it.

"Don't worry, Coach," he said afterward. "Just relax. We can't beat the Lakers." A defeatist thought if I ever heard one.

Another year, after another playoff season, I spoke to the media while the players showered and left. I changed into sweats and the locker room was empty and quiet except for me and my thoughts. That was when I tore JB's locker apart. The wood trim and his nameplate in front came off pretty easily but I had to work a little bit to yank out the insides. The next day, the players and a couple of writers saw the damage and put two and two together.

Suppressed rage is bad for you; I felt better afterward. I assume Joe Barry became even more convinced that his coach was a nut job. But did my sort-of out-of-control outburst inspire him, or the team? Who knows? We lost that series in four. But at least I made it plain how badly I wanted to win, and how badly I wanted *them* to want to win.

Of course, when anger escalates and people act like animals— showing teeth, staring, puffing up—fights happen. I didn't like fights but I wasn't afraid of them, either. I liked running and bumping and pushing and holding. The physicality of the game was fun to me. A court is only 94 feet by 50 feet and the ten athletes on it are big and fast. They're going to collide and someone isn't going to like it. And if there's a player on the floor who sees the value in a well-timed hip check the ref can't see, then that physicality can go beyond just playing the game. You see, a player like that *has* to win and will do what it takes. Someone like me, in other words . . .

Fights occurred. I fought in high school, on Pittsburgh playgrounds in the summer, in college at North Carolina, and more than once as a pro. Fines for fighting when I entered the NBA were only $500 to $1,000. Now the cost is so high, you'd be crazy to ball your fist. The fine for fighting now has a maximum of $35,000, which is plenty, but suspensions are *really* expensive. Each game the angry player must sit out costs him 1/82nd of his salary. And when you make $18 million a year, that's almost $200,000.

I played the way I did because, well, I was an insane competitor. I loved intensity and intimidation. And defense! I learned how to foul and get away with it; you can get away with murder while the ball's in the air. When my opponents were bigger and faster than me, which was often the case, I had to touch and bang to have an impact. I enjoyed that and I was good at it. And I was annoying. Most of my "fights" were just skirmishes, really. I'd shove or be shoved, scream a little bit, and it was over. Usually.

Then there was that game in 1975. Due to its unusual violence, a battle I more or less instigated earned an over-the-top nickname: the Easter Sunday Massacre.

I wore my favorite blue sweater that morning, then put on Marvin Gaye and a little heat in the blue Porsche for the drive to the game. March 30 was a cool day in South Texas, a high of 60. It was hot in HemisFair Arena, though, for the playoff game between the San Antonio Spurs and the New York Nets. I was the Spurs' backup point guard, in my second year in the league. At twenty-four, I was still young and strong and extremely willing to do damn near anything to win.

During warm-ups, I looked up at the Baseline Bums, the misnomer of a group of crazies seated fifteen rows above the visiting team's tunnel to the locker room. The Bums loved me. I sometimes drank beer with them after games in a big tent called the Lone Star Pavilion. Seems like all we ever drank was Pearl, the worst beer ever, but it was brewed in San Antonio. Just like the Bums.

Emotion peaked between the national anthem and tip-off. The coaches and players formed the usual circle. "Don't take any shit from them!" shouted our coach, Bob Bass. "Play hard! Stand up for yourselves!" The jaded professionals in the huddle may have thought, Yeah, right, but I listened.

The Nets had two All-Stars, Dr. J (Julius Erving) and Brian Taylor, their ball handler. I'd get Taylor if I got in the game. Bass put me in to spice things up in the first quarter and I immediately invaded Taylor's personal space, guarding him closer and more roughly than he liked. He threw some elbows at me. That was okay. In the second quarter, his elbow connected with my chin. Not okay. I saw blood, and I saw red, and I said, "Hell, I'm gonna hit him." I ran after him, jumped him from behind, and we both fell. Then we got up and squared off.

After that, it was crazy. The benches emptied. A cop came out on the court and his gun fell on the floor. Edgar Jones's teeth fell out. The wrestling and grabbing and shouting with occasional punching went on for twenty-two minutes. It was one of the longest-lasting fights in NBA history, resulting in a lot of bloody mouths and bruised fists. Taylor wanted to take another swing at me again after the game, out where the buses loaded. I just laughed at him, but not too loud, because we lost the game.

In a way, the fight with Taylor was business as usual for me.

Back then, I was regularly getting in little dustups with George Gervin, the Iceman, the best offensive player in the league. Our history started in the fifth or sixth game of my rookie year. I hadn't played a minute all season and we hadn't won a game. So it was in desperation that Tom Nissalke put me in against the superstar for the Virginia Squires. I got into kind of a physical match with Ice, which he obviously didn't like, and we won the game. It was the first-ever win for the Spurs franchise, by the way, and my friend Coby Dietrick and I were the high scorers. I played a little bit more after that.

A couple of months later, the Spurs bought Gervin's contract, so he became my teammate, and the guy I regularly guarded in practice. George didn't like my defense. He may have thrown a fist once or twice; he definitely extended his bony elbows and forearms toward my face.

Ice and I had different ideas about the correct intensity level in practice. Playing hard was my only way to show the coach I should be getting more minutes. Meanwhile, Gerv was expected to play thirty minutes every night and score 40 points. He did not like to sweat unless it was a game. I didn't appreciate that he wanted to save himself a little, and that I was taking his energy away. I respect his approach now, up to a point.

My willingness to play in-your-shirt defense and to dive for the ball led to a nickname in San Antonio: the Kamikaze Kid. Our fans liked me. But to others—like George McGinnis, the very powerful power forward for the Indiana Pacers—I was "the Gnat." George had a body like an NFL tight end, a muscleman similar to a more recent player, Karl Malone, aka the Mailman. George didn't like me. One night, he proved how much he didn't like me in a game in our arena.

That was the time I made this bull mad. I didn't guard him, of course, but I left my man whenever I could to swat, bump, harass, annoy, and take advantage of his relative lack of skill handling the ball. Late in the game, Big George got the ball on a breakaway, and I was the only one between him and the hoop. I retreated to the foul line, turned, and set my body to take a charge. It was a good strategy because he didn't have the handles to swerve around me, especially when he didn't want to. George didn't go sideways or stop as he got closer; he accelerated. And he hit me so goddamn hard with his right knee between my legs that my feet barely touched the ground as I flew from the free throw line to the basket standard. I hit my ass so hard that you could see the imprint of the pad in the bruise.

I got the call, and he got to beat the shit out of me. So it was a win-win.

Passion Play

———

The player I was is the coach I became.

Sportswriters often attached the word *combative* to my name, as in "Milwaukee's new coach is George Karl, the combative former North Carolina point guard."

The adjective probably fits. Still, I don't think basketball is war, or a metaphor for war. To me, it's a beautiful game with subtleties that reveal themselves with study.

At Denver, we developed an offensive flow as fun to look at as the Lakers in their Magic Johnson heyday. But other times my defense-oriented brand of ball has not looked so beautiful. We might be playing in harmony but appear to be in a five-on-five wrestling match. Either way, I think basketball has to be physical to be attractive. You've got to be able to hit each other. That's a bit of advice I often yell to my team: "Hit 'em!"

To win in the NBA, you need a minimum level of talent. Then it comes down to how you respond to getting elbowed in the neck.

I've never gotten into a real fight as a coach. But I came close more than once, in practice in the CBA and in my first few years in the NBA. I was an egotistical son of a bitch, and pretty strong, and the younger I was, the less fear I had of getting killed.

When I told World B. Free, who played for me in Cleveland, that his style of play was the most selfish I'd ever seen—he may have been the biggest gunner in NBA history—and World, né Lloyd, didn't like it. To take him down a notch, I put myself into a scrimmage so that I could guard him with a little more force than he was used to.

World was a great shooter with an incredible vertical leap. Like other clever scorers—Reggie Miller comes to mind—at the top of his jump shot he sometimes threw a leg out toward his defender, hoping to draw a foul. When he did exactly that against me, and kicked me in the shoulder, I tackled him. Pretty hard. We rolled around on the floor for a minute, then squared off, got into fighting position. Fortunately, the other players broke it up.

Good thing: just as you can't really win a fight with your wife, I don't think a coach can win a fistfight with a player. I also found you can't coach very well when you're playing, so I rarely bothered after that.

Away from the court, I laugh, I joke, I have friends, I have fun. On it, well . . . when I picked up one of Phil Jackson's books and read:

> *The joy they experience working in harmony is a powerful motivating force that comes from deep within, not from some frenzied coach pacing along the sidelines, screaming obscenities into the air.*

I wondered if he was talking about me.

I am not criticizing Phil, however, because he usually kicked my ass during our long, overlapping tenures as NBA coaches. I had dinner with him and a few others a couple of years ago in a fluffy L.A. restaurant. In a whisper, I asked Tim Grgurich—a great assistant coach and one of my oldest friends—if he thought Phil had any idea how many times I'd mf'ed him over the years, and how much I'd hated his guts.

And I wondered: did he win because he had Michael Jordan and Scottie Pippen, and I had Gary Payton and Shawn Kemp? And then he had Kobe Bryant and Shaq and I had Sam Cassell and Glenn Robinson. Or was his coaching superior to mine?

I've thought about Phil lately as I try to make the switch from NBA coach to NBA author. I've read his books and John Wooden's books and reread *The Carolina Way*, by my college coach, Dean Smith.

This book will be a little different. Other coaches with a pen find business parables in their sport. I don't. Yes, hard work and talent and responsibility are rewarded in the NBA and in real life, but if you find that one is just like the other, you're looking too hard. The NBA is a thing apart.

Do you, Mr. Businessman, or you, Ms. Biz Woman, travel half the year on your own plane with fifteen to twenty other employees? Do some of your worker bees have entourages and bodyguards and salaries that dwarf your own, and endorsement deals, and agents who call you to complain about how you're managing their clients? Does the media record and comment on everything you do and say? Do eighteen thousand people come out to watch you work? I think the only thing comparable to coaching a professional basketball team is coaching another pro sports team. Or being the pope.

CHAPTER 2

FUN, WITH ANGER

George didn't talk trash. He *played* trash.

—ART BARR, HIGH SCHOOL TEAMMATE

When they introduced him before the game, the Duke fans threw hot dogs on the floor.

—RON GREEN SR., *CHARLOTTE OBSERVER*

I didn't like the guy. I wanted to throw a basketball at him. But I love him now.

—WORLD B. FREE, CLEVELAND CAVALIERS GUARD

got off to a bad start.

After I had some success coaching in the minor-league Continental Basketball Association, a desperate team called. Would I be interested in interviewing for the Cleveland job? I would. I did. They hired me—first as a player personnel assistant, then as their coach. It was 1984. I was thirty-three, the youngest head coach in the league, and one of the youngest ever. The Cavaliers were not very good but I didn't care. I was in the NBA, exactly where I wanted to be, and I was sure I could handle it.

But any idea I had of turning things around by getting the

fans into it was going to be tough, because nobody went to the games, and I mean *nobody*. It was a perfect storm: bad marketing, an awful team, and the joke of an arena, a giant concrete barn stuck in a cornfield at the junction of two interstates thirty miles south of downtown. They called it the Coliseum at Richfield but we called it the Submarine because the damn thing didn't have any windows.

The Submarine at Richfield seated 20,000. We averaged 3,900, easily the worst attendance in the league, but that 3,900 was an official head count, and as inflated as a basketball. "A lot of people disguised as seats tonight," as one of our coaches would say.

I was used to packed houses as a player at North Carolina and in San Antonio. So coming out of the home team locker room three minutes before the tip gave me an unbelievable feeling, almost out-of-body. It was so big and empty and quiet that it could have been a church, but it wasn't a church. I'll never forget how clearly you could hear someone shout, "You guys suck!" Never before or since have I heard individual conversations or the boo birds so well. There were knots of fans way up in the smoky light in the cheapest seats at the top of the bowl. They were probably the happiest people in the building, partly because they couldn't see the game that well and partly because they smuggled in bottles of whiskey and blew out blue clouds from unlabeled cigarettes. So I'm told.

I would be coaching what the *New York Times* called "the worst club and the most poorly run franchise in professional basketball."

The problems started with Ted Stepien, the owner. He was a Pittsburgh guy in wraparound glasses who made his money renting billboards. Stepien tried to buy a championship but he was clueless about building a team. He made the horrible personnel decisions that caused the disaster but blamed his coaches, and fired, believe it or not, three head coaches in the year before I started with the Cavs.

But then, hope.

The Gund brothers, George and Gordon—they owned that awful arena—bought the team and Stepien's billboard business for $22 million in 1983, fired the coach, Tom Nissalke, at the end of the season, and hired me.

The Gunds, whose wealth came primarily from banking, already owned the local NHL team, the Barons. Gordon, the younger brother, who played hockey at Harvard, oversaw the Cavs. He was an impressive, dignified man with bushy eyebrows and an outgoing manner. In his twenties, he began to lose his sight due to retinitis pigmentosa. By 1970, he was completely blind.

Gordon tried to help me. If we had a conflict at all, it was with his belief in testing. Our owner saw great value in examining and analyzing the minds of our players, in part, I suppose, because he owned a testing company called Selection Research. "Now, George," he'd say to me, "we'd like to look at your management style with these guys. We think you'd get more out of them if you'd adapt to them better."

No, I thought but didn't say: that's too complicated. They've got to adapt to *me*.

Gordon wanted to meet with me and his psychologist from Selection Research, so we sat in one of the windowless rooms in the Coliseum. And the psychologist was blind, too.

I was a smartass, I didn't agree with the premise, and I'm sitting there with two blind men. *How do you guys know what's going on?* I thought but didn't say. *You can't even see the game!* A younger, crazier me might have made faces and waved his hands around because, obviously, they couldn't see me. Self-control was not my strong suit back then, but I sat there politely. Besides, we'd started the season 2-19. I had to listen.

The subtext of the meeting couldn't have been plainer: our rookie, and presumably our new star, Mel Turpin. Mel wasn't playing much and when I did put him in, he didn't show much.

He'd been the sixth pick in the previous draft, the group that in-cluded Michael Jordan, Charles Barkley, and Hakeem Olajuwon, but our new center was not destined for the Hall of Fame. Turpin was very talented but undermotivated, a combination that put my teeth on edge. I can close my eyes and see his moon face, and his beautiful midrange jump shot, and how, very gradually, there got to be more and more Mel. Eventually, everyone noticed, and someone, probably a writer, called him Dinner Bell Mel. The name stuck. His other nickname played off Karl Malone's handle: the Mealman.

My supersized problem child was addicted to fast food. I didn't see it, but we heard that he could eat two large pizzas at a sitting, or a dozen Big Macs. McDonald's sold its 50 billionth burger in 1984. Mel helped.

I started to resent him a little bit. After I saw Mark West knock Patrick Ewing on his ass in a summer scrimmage against the Olympic team, we pried him away from the Milwaukee Bucks. I pulled West aside before a practice. "If you hit that fat boy in the head during practice," I said, meaning Mel, "that won't bother me." Mark took the advice seriously, and it became a running joke on the team. World bought Mel a Cleveland Browns helmet.

We put a clause in Mel's contract that unless his body fat was 12 percent or less, his pay would be docked 10 percent. I'm pretty sure he never even took the test. His weight climbed and—big surprise—his knees began to hurt. Did I yell at him, did I call him fat and slow in front of his teammates? Hell yes.

"You can't go after him like that," Gordon said, or said through our GM, Harry Weltman. "You're emotionally abusing him." I might've been.

But Melvin Harrison Turpin was not my problem; 2 wins in the first 21 games was my problem.

Why were we so bad? Other teams had Kareem Abdul-Jabbar, Magic Johnson, Larry Bird, Michael Jordan, George Gervin, or

Julius Erving. We had John Bagley, Roy Hinson, Lonnie Shelton, Phil Hubbard, and Free. We didn't have a superstar.

But we shouldn't have been that awful. I should have been able to coach them up. Was I up to it? I thought I was. Even in the darkest days—starting the season with a nine-game losing streak, and losing four home games in a row in early December—I didn't doubt myself. But I doubted our best player, World B. Free.

I'd played against World so I knew his game, which was all offense, all the time. I tried to teach the habits and mindset of playing as a team but World's street-ball style undermined and contradicted every word I said. Ever play in a pickup game where the guy who gets the rebound on the defensive end is sure to dribble around and shoot? No matter if he's being guarded or not, whether or not a teammate has a better shot? That was World. He always thought he was open.

World's game *bothered* me. I don't blame him much now; he just thought he was better than any other option. Our relationship was awful.

Back then I saw World's MO as a series of cynical business decisions. He knew that the more points he scored, the more he'd make in his next contract. So he saved himself on defense and stayed ready to shoot. The GMs who paid him didn't seem to understand that winning is the point in basketball, not points. What good is a high scorer on a team that loses all the time? When it became clear that he would not play my way, I put his ass on the bench. We kept losing.

I knew World's jumper gave us our best chance to win, but between me being mad at him and a leg injury, he sat for about half of our first 21 games.

It's my book but let's hear from the players a bit.

"I'll never forget the first time George came in the locker room, all arrogant, like the world was his," World says now. "I thought

*the world was mine! George said we're gonna do it his way, but
I had a problem with it. I'm not gonna cut my shooting down
and I'm not gonna become a passer. He got in my face a couple
of times and nobody gets in my face, not my mother, not my
father—nobody. We had a players-only meeting because we were
not comfortable with his yelling. In the long run George helped
guys like me grow. But he had to grow, too."*

"World didn't buy in," says Roy Hinson, *our power forward.*
"He had an ego as big as the universe. And Mel was a pain in
the ass. He didn't take the game seriously, wasn't dedicated to
his craft. For the sixth pick in the draft, he should have brought
more."

Fun times.

So Free 'n' me fought for control of our team, and, as I said,
once or twice we almost fought. Two months into my NBA coaching career, I was shocked and furious to be 2-19, with our prize
rookie getting bigger and slower by the minute, and my relationship with our best player getting worse and worse. All I saw was
conflict and failure.

I didn't lose confidence but still I wondered: What brought me
to this crossroads? Why wasn't my stuff working?

My *sister Peggy* says I was born annoyingly competitive. And I
loved games. Basketball seemed perfect. A wonderful feeling
of angry fun came over me from the moment any game began.

In junior high school, we were up by two in an important game
with just a few seconds left. Thinking strategically, and acting a
little forcefully, I hip-checked their ball handler out of bounds.
The ref called a foul, which was okay, because I'd decided that the
other seventh grader wouldn't make both halves of a one-and-one
under pressure. He didn't. We won.

Fun, with Anger

I was born in Swissvale, Pennsylvania, a little town nine miles east of Pittsburgh in what was called the Mon Valley. We were uphill from the smoke and fire of the steel mills on the Monongahela; it was a typical suburb of the Steel City. On a *nice* day in those pre-EPA days, our air was light gray and the water was brown.

Our claim to fame in Swissvale was that Dick Groat lived there. Groat played short on the Pirates team that won the World Series in 1960, and he'd been an All-American basketball player at Duke, for which I forgive him now.

My fascination with games began in Swissvale. The walled alleys behind the houses in our neighborhood were perfect for handball, the first game I remember playing. My mother's father—Grandpa Patterson—showed us how to do it. We used a tennis ball. Stickball was big, too.

In the summer between third and fourth grade, we moved a few miles north up Rodi Road (aka Route 791) to Penn Hills. Like all of suburban Pittsburgh, our town was thick with trees and almost as hilly as San Francisco. But instead of the San Francisco Bay and the Golden Gate Bridge, we had the Ohio, the Allegheny, and the Monongahela rivers and at least twenty-nine bridges, including the Roberto Clemente. If you need to see the horizon to be comfortable, you wouldn't like Pittsburgh. Pretty cold, too. We could count on a few blizzards every winter. Snow tires were not optional.

I drove down my old street in September 2000 when I was back because the high school was retiring my number. There again was Rosemarie Perla, my high school girlfriend, whom I hadn't seen in twenty-four years.

Memories suddenly crowded my mind, and that strange feeling of time rushing by, like the scenery outside a speeding car. I lived in a small world back then, enclosed by the hills and rivers and high school sports. My sister and my parents and I lived in what might once have been a mill worker's house. Like the other houses on Southern Avenue, our narrow, redbrick three-one had a steep, short yard and an aluminum awning sheltering the front door. The years have stained those awnings and the shingles on the roofs, but everything looked shiny and new half a century ago, when Pittsburgh led the world in steel production and its population was twice what it is now.

The roots of our family tree were set in Germany and Wales. The Karls migrated from Bavaria to Wisconsin in the mid-1800s. They did about what you'd expect: they mined coal, steered freight trains, drank beer after union meetings at the German-American Club, and had babies.

Joseph Karl, my father, worked as a service rep and repairman for Bell & Howell, the audiovisual machine maker. My dad could fix anything, but his forte was the hand-cranked ditto machine, which readers older than age fifty may recall. Dittos—mimeographs—were a cheap way to reproduce images on paper. Schools used a lot of the machines. I can still remember the sweet smell of the purple ink on a dittoed history test.

Although my mother, the former Edith Patterson, was poorly educated herself—she dropped out of high school in tenth grade—she believed very strongly in the straight-A report card. My sister delivered them routinely, so I was expected to do the same. When I didn't, Mom didn't hide her disappointment. She had a shame-and-blame parenting style that I've tried not to imitate. Boys grow up trying to impress their mothers, but I could never do enough. I accomplished some things in athletics, and I know she spoke proudly of me to other people, but for some reason she couldn't or wouldn't give me a pat on the head. Her message: you can do better, you can do more. Maybe she thought withholding approval was good for me. I don't know. But I do know that I try to show appreciation, not leave it unspoken.

What kind of little brother was I? My sister put a padlock on the inside of her bedroom door to keep me out.

Fun, with Anger

I got B's in school and A's in sports. I ran track—sprints—but baseball was my best game. My ego would permit no other position but shortstop, and I had to bat third. I liked to wreak havoc with the other team. I was a pretty good spray hitter, so I'd get on base and steal another. My high school coach gave me a green light to steal home and that became a goal. When I finally did, I chose the wrong pitch, the wrong count, and our hitter swung and almost killed me. But I was safe at the plate.

Pennsylvania is football country. I was a strong kid with a taste for contact. So why didn't I put on pads? I did, for a year, playing quarterback on the freshman team. But then self-preservation took over: quarterback was more running than throwing in the wishbone offense the Penn Hills High Indians played. Since I didn't want to get hit fifty times a game by jacked-up defensive ends and linebackers who had a running start, I played volleyball in the fall and waited for basketball season.

I loved the Pirates. When the Bucs won the World Series in 1960, they owned our town. Roberto Clemente hit .314 that year and caught every ball in right field—my hero when I was nine. The Steelers were awful and I didn't care about them. As for college sports, the Pitt Panthers were a big deal, in football and basketball. But even though the Pittsburgh Pipers (later, the Condors) were an original team in the American Basketball Association (circa 1967) and had an incredible player in Connie Hawkins, for some reason pro hoops didn't catch on in my hometown. The NBA team I cared about was the New York Knicks coached by Red Holzman. Reed, Bradley, Monroe, Frazier, DeBusschere: their passing game looked like magic to me. The Knicks also had a forward on the bench named Phil Jackson. Yes, that Phil Jackson.

As basketball began to nudge out baseball as my favorite sport, my friends Artie Barr and Donnie Wilson and I made a pact to win the state championship by the time we were seniors. We planned to make it happen by playing every day in the summer. When my father asked about my summer job, I was able to convince him that by improving my jump shot, I'd stand a better chance of getting a college scholarship. Wouldn't that be just as good as caddying at Churchill Valley Country Club or mowing lawns? Dad agreed, fortunately.

Metal nets, double rims, white-painted backboards dotted with rust as if hit by a shotgun, cracked asphalt, rain-collecting depressions under both hoops: our court by Linton Middle School and the school administration buildings looked like a thousand others. Winter weekends I shoveled the snow in a twenty-foot semicircle under one hoop, and shot for hours with a glove on my left hand. Summer nights we'd go play the rich white kids in Mount Lebanon or the poor black kids downtown. I loved all of it, from the purity of the competition to the way a Regent black cherry pop (don't call it a soda) tasted after the game. Later—when we were of age, of course—post-hoops hops tasted damn good. The one brew to avoid was Pittsburgh's own Iron City. Pronounced "Ahrn City."

Our high school team played a three-guard offense. We played fast and pressed full-time. Although we didn't quite get that state championship, we won most of the time and averaged over 80 points, pretty good for thirty-two-minute games and no three-point line. I remember gyms overflowing with fans, and emotion in the air so thick it was hard to breathe. Caravans of cars followed our bus through snowy nights to our away games. Our coach, Dick Misenhelter, was a good tactician and he was a screamer. His intensity rubbed off on me. Almost all of our offensive plays ended with me taking a shot.

There were fights, too. One I remember involved me and Donnie and a football player named Skip Givin—who was on crutches—getting something started after one of their guys committed a hard foul on Artie. Everyone in the gym poured out on the floor;

Fun, with Anger

1968 was a good year for riots. The next year we had to play both our games with Wilkinsville during the day in an empty gym.

One time when we beat another rival, North Braddock, their fans pelted our bus with rocks as we pulled out of the parking lot.

We had a hell of a team. All five of our starters got Division 1 college basketball scholarships.

I got to choose from about one hundred schools. I didn't want to stay at home. Still, I looked carefully at Pitt, mostly because of the coach, Tim Grgurich, who oozed passion for the game. I felt as if he "got" me. As I mentioned earlier, I'd eventually get to coach with Gurg.

The others I considered were Princeton, Iowa, and all the Atlantic Coast Conference schools. The Ivy League and the Big Ten ultimately didn't interest me as much as the ACC, which I thought played the best college basketball in the country. Their games were on TV in the East, and their coaches were household names, at least in my household—Frank McGuire at South Carolina, Lefty Driesell at Maryland, and Dean Smith at North Carolina. And the league had one other distinction: its end-of-the-season tournament. A team could go 25-0 but lose in the sudden-death match play at the end of the year and not make it into the NCAA. The ACC tournament concentrated pressure and excitement and I wanted to be part of it. I headed south and east for campus visits.

At Maryland, Lefty Driesell slapped me on the back and told me I would be the key to winning the ACC for the Terps. Similar scenarios played out at a couple of other schools. I'd meet the team, see the arena, maybe the athletes' dorm, maybe go to a football game, and usually go to a party that night. Pretty girls at the party . . .

During my visit to Duke, I had a talk with Dick DeVenzio, also a Pittsburgh guy, who was a year or two ahead of me. DeVenzio, a 5'9" left-hander who was probably the best point guard in the history of Pennsylvania high school hoops, would go on to play professionally in Europe and to write five influential books on basketball. But his skill was wasted at Duke, which played a plodding, low-post offense. I was a little startled when he told me, "My biggest mistake was not going to North Carolina."

He was talking about Dean Smith.

UNC was my last stop. I went into His office, smiled, and extended my hand.

"Hi, Coach."

"How do you do, George?" he said. "How was your trip?"

Immediately I knew that Coach Smith had a different presence than anyone I'd ever met. There was something about him that was profound but hard to describe, some gravity or spirituality. He connected with people, deeply and almost immediately. I found this same vibe in John Wooden when I had dinner once with the legendary UCLA coach.

On my weekend at North Carolina I was treated respectfully, as a potential student, not as a 28-points-per-game high school star they were trying to seduce. No party, no football game; I visited school buildings and classrooms and met professors and mentors. This approach appealed to me because I thought of myself as more than just a jock.

But I was still a jock: I asked Coach Smith if I could play both baseball and basketball at UNC. He didn't encourage that idea but giving up baseball was not a deal breaker for me. It took me about two days to decide. I was going to North Carolina.

What happened when I got to Chapel Hill is very simple: like most freshmen, I was at sea. I knew who I was at Penn Hills High, but out in the world, away from home, who was I? It made a lot of sense to follow Coach Smith.

I learned pretty quickly that my arrogance and cockiness had to be worn down. I needed to become a quieter competitor, a team competitor.

What Dean Smith taught me could fill another book. It's not

easy to boil down one of the most meaningful relationships in my life, but I think I can at least outline it from a basketball standpoint: I learned the power of consistency bordering on redundancy; I developed an absolute belief in the team game; and I learned how to run a practice. It's a mistake-oriented game, Coach Smith said, with immediate opportunities for correction. How quickly you adapt is key.

I liked the subtlety of his approach. Coach Smith printed a thought each day on a chalkboard in the locker room. It wasn't some rah-rah crap from Vince Lombardi. It would be something profound or thought-provoking about life, from Jesus or Buddha or Shakespeare.

He created a brotherhood of current and former players, which gave hotshots like me some humility we needed badly. Some of us UNC basketball alums—the ones who've made the game our lives—have a reunion in Chapel Hill every summer, for golf and beer (vodka and Cran-Grape for Michael Jordan) and conversation. It's called the Doug Moe Invitational.

Mostly it was an excuse to see Coach Smith.

Dean Smith's college coach learned the game from its *inventor*. James Naismith was a highly moral man, and he had the virtues of teamwork and *not hitting each other* in mind when he invented the game at Springfield (Massachusetts) College in the winter of 1891. "Basket ball" was Naismith's answer to football, which was so violent and unpadded that a lot of schools banned it. In 1905, nineteen young men *died* playing football. But no one's life was on the line in Naismith's game. Basket ball (the two words eventually became one) could be played indoors, women and girls could play it, and subtlety and cooperation were more valuable than strength and controlled violence. Selfishness was not rewarded. It was nine-on-nine with a soccer ball, and you couldn't dribble— passing only.

Naismith went on to the University of Kansas, where he

coached a young man named Forrest "Phog" Allen, who coached Dean Smith, who coached me. The founding coaches saw basketball as a virtuous game.

Well-played basketball was Good. I loved that idea.

Another thing I loved about Carolina basketball: we played fast. Just like our high school team, we pressed and ran and took the first good shot. We averaged over 90 points per game, higher than almost all college teams nowadays, with no three-ball and no shot clock. I've won a lot of bets with that stat.

Six games into the season my freshman year, I got clobbered on a pick-and-roll and hurt my lower back. Traction was the state-of-the-art back then, so they tied me to ropes and pulleys for a week. When I got sprung from the hospital, I celebrated by playing in an all-night poker game. Stupid. I sat too long, my lumbar spine seized up again, and back I went to Chapel Hill Memorial, for most of a month this time. I couldn't play when I got out so I scratched my basketball itch by watching many hours of game film with the coaches and by sitting near them during games. This was the coaching staff being nice to me, and trying to keep me connected to the team.

It was fascinating to hear Coach Smith and his top assistant, Bill Guthridge—two old friends with nasal Kansas accents I liked to imitate—analyze the chess game on the floor or on the screen. During this time of convalescence, I learned the subtle stuff—strategy, game management, and substitutions—and latched on to a big idea. After the game, they analyzed film and gave every player a defensive grade. I began to see how a team could be simultaneously disciplined and creative. It comes down to the team having a *philosophy* more than a structure.

And an idea I already had—that point guard is the most important position on the team—got reinforced. Before games the coaches and the guards had what we called a "quarterback meeting" to discuss goals and strategy. We PGs listened carefully, because, among other things, we called the defense after every made basket.

For example: If I guarded the inbounds pass with my hands up it meant one thing—different traps, or a different rotation—while hands on hips or hands sideways signaled run-and-jump or whatever. I don't think the other teams ever caught on.

We won a lot of games in the last minute because we practiced end-of-game situations. In the huddle, with seconds left, on the road—say, at Duke's Cameron Indoor Stadium, with their fans screaming and calling you an idiot—Coach Smith was almost giddy. "This is fun!" he'd say. "Now, here's what we're gonna do."

We believed him and then we believed in each other. Coach Smith was no dictator. He taught, educated, and directed but he allowed us some free will. And his attitude about *team* was contagious. We forgot ourselves and our problems and thought only about North Carolina basketball.

With the talent he always got, should Coach Smith have won more NCAA championships? Maybe. But he would never change the Carolina way, that philosophy, just to recruit a player or win a game.

My mind (and my hair) grew at North Carolina. I was a seventies campus radical. I opposed the war in Vietnam and said so, and I developed a political philosophy that was not Republican. Our government has always helped people, I thought, and it always should.

My spiritual side developed, too. Although I don't consider discussing religion to be appropriate for a coach, I believe in God. At any rate, Bernard Boyd—a professor who taught the New Testament at UNC—encouraged me to apply for a postgraduate spot at Princeton Theological Seminary. I did and was accepted. But, as it turned out, I didn't go.

Not going to bore you with chapter and verse regarding my basketball career at Carolina, but, boy, did I have fun. You're probably aware that North Carolina is a basketball school. And you may assume that those of us on the team were automatically big men on campus, recognized in every class and at every party. Someone once asked me if I joined a fraternity in college. I did not. There was no need. I was in *the* fraternity.

I listened to the Rolling Stones and kissed the girls and drove a '69 Chevy Nova, dark green. The Nova remained on campus after I left, by the way. I sold it to a teammate, Mitch Kupchak, now the Lakers general manager. For fifteen years, the Nova got handed down or sold for peanuts from one basketball player to the next.

On the court, my years at UNC were a continuation of my fun run at Penn Hills High. I fought and dove on the floor and tried to steal the ball. Our big rivalry was with a school just seven miles away: Duke. I hated Duke.

"I don't get it," says Gary Melchionni, the Dukie who guarded me. "There's no rational basis for you hating us. I didn't feel it. Did you have a bad experience with a Duke coed or something?"

Very funny, Gary, but no. I hated Duke for its arrogance, its fans, and because it made our games even more fun. Remember: we were two basketball schools, so close together our campuses almost touched, and our rivalry resembled the famous annual football death matches, like Ohio State–Michigan or Army-Navy. Students camped out to be first in line for tickets—and still do. Excitement during the game was through the roof.

Duke beat us only once during my four years at Carolina. It was the day in January 1972 when they renamed their arena—it looked like an old castle—for their athletic director, Eddie Cameron. Ten thousand Crazies raised hell the whole game. They had a forward named Chris Redding who made free throw after free throw and a guard named Robby West who threw in a lucky last-second shot.

We didn't lose too often. Four of us went on to play in the NBA: Bob McAdoo, Bobby Jones, Mitch Kupchak, and me. Bill Chamberlain and Dennis Wuycik could really score and defend as well. We had Dean Smith, too.

We won the NIT when I was a sophomore, a big deal back when only sixteen teams qualified for the NCAA tournament. We came close to winning the national championship my junior year, when we made the Final Four, but we lost to Florida State in the semis. They had a third-place game back then, and we beat Louisville. (UCLA won it all.) I made All-America a couple of times, but even though there were two competing professional leagues then—the ABA and the NBA, and, therefore, more job openings for players—I wasn't convinced that pro basketball was in my future. I thought I might play for a few years in Europe, or, failing that, get a high school coaching job. Or go to seminary.

After I graduated, and was mulling my options, I was chosen for an all-star team that would play a Chinese all-star team—in China. China had been off-limits to the West for most of the twentieth century but a couple of random Ping-Pong games in 1971 represented a little opening. President Nixon went to China in 1972 and announced a formal "cultural exchange" for 1973. Our basketball games would be the first events on the list.

We went to Hong Kong, Guangdong, and Beijing and at each stop the people stared at us like we were from Mars. Lon Kruger and I liked it. The Kansas State guard and I would leave our hotel rooms to interact with the locals. We played Ping-Pong against eight- and nine-year-old kids who beat us with ease. One night we had dinner with George H. W. Bush and our Chinese "liaison"— who we all thought was a spy. The future president was an impressive man.

The first game—we played eight—took place on July 1, 1973, in Beijing. Capital Stadium didn't have the normal energy of a basketball arena. It felt and looked more like an auditorium, and it was filled to the brim with eighteen thousand identically dressed people. Weird. Mrs. Mao Zedong, the wife of their

Mr. Big, Chairman Mao—sat in the center of the front row. She wore a dress for the first time in forty years, which, I suppose, proves how big a deal this game was. I heard that she thought my hair was too long. The fans, if that's what you could call them, watched in silence for the most part, and applauded from time to time as if they were at a variety show.

We won all our games easily. The Chinese were pussies. Wait— that's a little unkind. I think the games were friendship first and competition second. They had some really big players but as for physical toughness, they hadn't gotten there yet.

—————

Which brings us back to 2 and 19 in Cleveland.

I felt supported by owner Gund and GM Weltman, but the newspapers and sports talk radio were crucifying me, and wanted me fired, the sooner the better.

Coach Smith followed my progress—or lack of it—as a rookie coach in the NBA. "Why are you coaching so much during the game?" he asked me more than once. "What are you doing during the week?" In other words, why wasn't my team more prepared and adaptable? He didn't think a sideline pacer and shouter helped a team much; his ideal was to coach not at all during a game. And Coach noticed when I told a writer something like, "I wanted more energy in the fourth quarter, so I put in Davis." I'd get a clipping of the story in the mail, with the I's circled. "Don't you mean 'we'?" he'd write.

My—I mean "our"—much bigger problem was figuring out a way to win some games. My assistants and I talked about it every day. Morris "Mo" McHone wanted to speed up our game; Gene Littles thought we should slow it down. I remembered that Coach Smith always simplified when things were going badly. But we added a bit of complexity, by making the center position a three-headed monster, with the heads belonging to Mark West, Lonnie Shelton, and Mel Turpin.

Then there was World, and the first time I asked myself the eternal NBA coach's question: do I change our concepts and hang with the player, or keep the concept and try to change the player? I guess I chose a blend. Since confrontation hadn't worked with World, I'd try cooperation.

We had a meeting. I told him we needed him to commit to defense—in part because it would give him more offensive opportunities. Steal the ball or help someone else steal it and you're out front in a breakaway situation. You'll score more points and make more money on your next contract. He'd said he'd do it.

Things started to turn around on a road trip in February, when we won 5 out of 6. "George is coming along fine—for a new coach," World told the media. I didn't react to the insulting praise. This sort of shit hadn't happened in the CBA, where the players were desperate for my approval, and nothing remotely like that occurred at North Carolina. Privately, I moaned about having to endure a power struggle with a mere player but it was a lesson I had to learn: the NBA is a player's league. On TV promos it's "LeBron James and the Cleveland Cavaliers against Kevin Durant and the Golden State Warriors." Versus the college game, where coaches provide the identity, as in "Mike Krzyzewski and the Duke Blue Devils go up against Rick Pitino's Louisville Cardinals."

Anyway: We won a few games and then a few more. I began talking to the team and to the media about the postseason, which had looked like an impossible dream in December.

Phil Hubbard, our small forward, was the key to our becoming competitive; he played the right way every game all the way to the end. Our point guard, John Bagley, came on strong at the end of the year. Free played offense and just enough D to keep me from going nuts. Edgar Jones had been a deep bench player but we put him in here and there for some crazy wild minutes. Hinson played consistently well.

We had to win the second-to-last game of the regular season at the New York Knicks to nose out the Atlanta Hawks for the eighth and final spot in the playoffs. "Play together!" I shouted in a time-out near the end of the game. "Don't give them any easy shots or easy rebounds." We didn't.

Ben Poquette hit a ten-foot jump shot, which is like saying Mel Turpin ran a marathon. Gentle Ben, a backup big, hadn't made more than three jumpers all year. We won 109–108 in OT. The Promised Land! We were a happy bunch of Cavs. We'd played nine games over .500 for the remainder of the season after our awful start.

Several odd things happened in our final game, in the Submarine, not least of which was that 10,185 fans showed up. The ten thousand were so happy and so unwilling to go home after the final buzzer that all the players and coaches came out for a curtain call, like singers after an opera. I'd never seen that before.

And I was shocked when the players picked me up and carried me out of the arena on their shoulders. As far as I know, that had never happened in pro basketball. Maybe the Celtics carried Red Auerbach and his cigar off the parquet floor of the Boston Garden way back when, but that would have been after winning a championship. And Red weighed a lot less than me.

"We didn't respect each other at first," World said after the game. "We do now. I play my butt off for George Karl." The writers and talk radio guys forgot they ever tried to bury me. Winning produces amnesia.

For the first time as a coach, I felt the incredible excitement of the NBA playoffs. I couldn't sit still. To blow off steam, I rolled a golf ball onto the floor of the long corridor outside my office. I swung hard with a three-iron and nailed it. I also nailed our ball boy, Richard Hofacker, who picked the wrong time for an office stroll. He went down like he'd been shot. But he was okay. And he later became the Cavaliers' podiatrist.

For the first round, best-of-five series, we drew the number one seed, the Celtics—*those* Celtics, the defending NBA champions, the team with Larry Bird, Robert Parish, and Kevin McHale. They barely beat us in Boston, winning the two games by a total of five points. The series resumed at the Submarine in Richfield. Near the end of our seven-point win in Game Three, our crazy happy fans chanted, "We Want Bird! We Want Bird!"—because Larry didn't play due to a sore elbow. We had an intoxicated group at Whitey's that night.

"They don't want no part of me," Bird said before Game Four, and then he played as if he'd been insulted. He scored 34 points to go with 14 rebounds and 7 assists. I coached my ass off, by which I mean I concentrated very hard on the chess match while 20,000 Cavs fans yelled and screamed. I wore a gray suit and a bouton-niere and I knelt a lot—my knees still allowed kneeling then. And I might have made a strategic mistake.

After Larry Legend made two free throws, we were down two, at 117–115, with about twenty seconds left. Should I call a timeout? The downside to stopping to draw up a play is that the defense has time to set up, too. So I rolled the dice. With about eight ticks remaining, Bags air-balled a three from the left side, which West caught. Under heavy pressure from Parish, Mark went up for the basket that would tie the score . . . it rimmed out. Parish swatted the miss out to the three-point line. Five, four . . . World caught it, shot it, missed it. Season over.

For the series, the Celtics and the Cavs had scored the same number of points. And given the way we started the season, we'd exceeded expectations by miles. Prolonged standing ovation as we left the floor.

A week later, on a pleasant May day in northeast Ohio, I stood in a suit on the steps of Cleveland City Hall with a crowd of several hundred watching from the street. "The Cavs' ability to bounce back from misfortune and perform as they did is an example for all of us," said Mayor George V. Voinovich. Then he handed me the key to the city, a little gold-plated skeleton key in a box.

I was a coaching genius.

Ten months later, the Cavs fired me.

I'd become an idiot.

CHAPTER 3

FERNANDO

We were driving through downtown Dallas after the game. . . . George stood on the seat of my Saab, stuck his head and shoulders through the sunroof, and screamed at the night. Golden State had beaten the Mavericks.

—PATRICK MADDEN

coached a game drunk once.

There were extenuating circumstances and "drunk" is a bit of an exaggeration. And I certainly don't recommend drinking a bottle of red before doing anything important.

On the other hand, in 1970 I watched on TV as Dock Ellis of the Pirates threw a no-hitter against the Padres while he was tripping on LSD. Dock said afterward that he had chewed his gum until it turned to powder, the ball kept changing size, and Jimi Hendrix hit for San Diego, using his guitar for a bat. A lefty, no doubt. I was nineteen when Dock threw his no-no. I was still impressionable but I wasn't tempted to try LSD.

In fact, until I started coaching, I didn't have an understanding of drugs other than alcohol. North Carolina was a pretty conservative school but a lot of wild things started happening on campus in the early seventies. From time to time, I whiffed the field-fire smell of burning marijuana at parties but I didn't inhale. I didn't even try it. I mostly avoided those parties because marijuana scared me to death and it was against the law. Using was grounds for getting kicked off the team, too. Besides, I was pretty damn happy without it.

I have no judgment against my friends who smoke. They say it's just about like drinking but with no liver damage or a hangover. I've had a massage above a medical marijuana clinic in Denver. But I'm not sure I like being in a state where weed is legal. It's just not me.

As for the really dangerous drugs like cocaine, LSD, heroin, and meth, I've never even seen them. When a cocaine scandal broke on my team in my third year as an NBA head coach, no one could have been less prepared to handle it.

I've learned a lot about the most popular vices and so has the NBA. Besides drug testing, the league's best weapon to keep guys out of trouble is the team plane. By flying to the next city right after a game, we arrive too late for anyone to go out.

Not that 3 a.m. arrivals necessarily prevent anything. Without actually seeing them in action, I know I've had players who used illegal drugs or excessive amounts of legal ones. I'm not the morality police; I care because their blood chemistry affects our team chemistry. A coach is always trying to find his team's pulse, to figure out its culture. Away from me, are they preoccupied with sex? Gambling? Bible study? None of my business. I just don't want anything off the court to be more important than the job on it.

I think the secret part of addiction leads to hypocrisy. The addict is pretending to be someone he's not. I'm really bothered when there's a big difference between how someone acts privately and the image he's trying to project. It keeps a team from uniting.

The addiction we see all the time in the NBA is not illegal, thank God. Lots of guys get hooked on women. The availability of good-looking women is surprising. Temptation is everywhere.

Players are celebrities. They're invited to every party and treated like kings when they arrive. On the road, you see party girls trolling in the hotel lobby, outside the locker room—everywhere. They're calculating opportunists and an NBA player is obviously a catch.

Some guys get caught more than others. "Shawn," I said one day. "*Vasectomy.*" Shawn Kemp, my power forward at Seattle, fathered many children with several different women. That's a distraction and it decimated his paycheck. (Shawn, incidentally, stepped up and took care of everyone. I'm proud of him.)

But I'm not against sex for the single guys: how could I be? In fact, I'm fine with them looking for euphoria before the game. There are obvious benefits to a good mood. On the other hand, having girls in every town undermines any chance at your supposedly real relationship back home. Drama screws you up and I don't want a screwed-up player on my team.

I'm not pointing fingers. I eat and drink and make love like a wuss now but I haven't always been so moderate. I used to drink ridiculous amounts of Diet Coke, maybe ten a day, and a few forty-eight-ounce containers of Diet Mountain Dew. I also ate too much of the wrong food. When I was young I thought I was athletic enough to work off anything I put down my throat, until I got slapped in the face. Combined with travel, stress, cheeseburgers, and ex-player knee and hip joints that make the simplest movement difficult or even painful, the NBA took a toll on my body. I'm sure it led to my cancer. My awful diet sure didn't help. I didn't understand the link between food and disease. The American Cancer Society says about a quarter of all cancers are caused by what we eat. And I was eating doughnuts and Ding Dongs.

As for beer, I used to order two Miller Lites at a time, using the theory that I would drink about twice as fast as the waitress could come by. I was much bigger then and I could drink a lot. A beer buzz made me happy and playful and sometimes too talkative. My friends and I drank enough beer to fill an Olympic-size swimming pool but these were always happy occasions, after golf or after the game. We weren't escaping anything. Seems to me that heavy drinking or drug use indicates you've got a monkey on your back.

I never figured out Allen Iverson's monkey. Late in 2006, when I coached Denver, we traded with Philadelphia for AI, and suddenly we had the two top scorers in the league—Carmelo Anthony being the other. Given the multimillion-dollar salaries involved, background checking in the NBA is pretty thorough. None of us were surprised that our new guard didn't like to practice—that was common knowledge—and that he liked to drink expensive champagne. But we didn't know what a nocturnal being Allen was. Sometimes he started a night out at 2 a.m.

The practice thing didn't bother me that much; a lot of players hate practice. But I didn't think we got all of Allen, his true personality. He'd been Defensive Player of the Year at Georgetown but with us he didn't commit to D. I think he'd aged more than we thought. Ten years of driving to the rim and taking hits on his little body—Allen weighed just 165 pounds—took a toll. The hits and his habits aged him. By "habits" I mean his night owl thing.

We were in L.A. that April to play the Clippers, a game we needed to win to improve our playoff position. In the morning our spy—the brother of our scout, Mark Warkentien—reported that our new, high-priced guard had left the Ritz-Carlton at 2 a.m. and returned to our hotel at about six thirty. He and his friends couldn't find anyone to pour any more Cristal. Our shootaround—NBA-ese for the light practice the day of a game—began at their arena, the Staples Center, at ten thirty, so Allen didn't have much time to sleep. Maybe he got a nap that afternoon. We won the game.

Fernando

―――――

Before I tell you about the incredible day I coached a game with wine in my bloodstream, and how I got unwanted crash courses in cocaine addiction and alcoholism, here's a little perspective:

When I came into the league, there was always a cooler of beer on the floor in the postgame locker room. I can remember guys loading up their travel bags in case they got thirsty later. My road roommate Louis Dampier kept his beer cool by storing it in the tank of the toilet in our hotel room. Sometimes he'd hang his Buds outside our window, holding them in place with white athletic tape. It took us years to figure out that beer was not good for us, and not just because of liver or driving issues. Beer does not rehydrate you. It's the opposite, a diuretic; you get a net loss of water. I drank a lot of Miller Lite for a lot of years and not nearly enough H2O.

Alcohol still has its place in the NBA but not on our airplane. It's not the beer or wine per se that I have a problem with; it's what it does to the rich, competitive young men who play cards on the flight. Add drinking to in-flight gambling and you get angry shouting from the back of the plane. Bickering teammates obviously don't help the team and I don't want to be a policeman. On the ground, management wants to know who drinks and how much, so some teams have placed PIs in the most popular clubs.

But I don't think that's necessary anymore, not when everyone's got a camera and a place to post the pictures.

I mixed basketball with adult fun at North Carolina—a little bit during my years as a player and a lot after my last game. Newly graduated Carolina basketball players hit the road to play exhibition games all over the state. Freed from the NCAA and Coach Smith, we all turned pro in a way. We each got a share of the gate receipts, with the host getting most of the money, of course, for whatever charity. We called it barnstorming. If we had a player or a former player from, say, Lumberton, we'd go to Lumberton High and pack the gym. Alums of the host high school were the usual opponents. Since there were no major pro sports franchises in the state, UNC basketball players were stars, and well known from TV, so the games were very popular. These were social occasions, naturally, with a beer or two or ten after the game.

Barnstorming money—and my $25,000 signing bonus from the Spurs—allowed me to buy a Duke blue Porsche 914. Late in the summer of 1973, I jammed all my stuff into my mid-engine two-seater and drove from North Carolina to South Texas. After twenty hours on the road I pulled up to the La Quinta by the San Antonio airport and met my new teammate and training camp roommate, Coby Dietrick. Coby was a 6'10" forward/center, start-ing his third year in pro hoops. He'd played college ball at San Jose State, where they've never heard of barnstorming. "You must have had an interesting scholarship," Coby said, obviously jealous of my little German sports car. We drove that thing fast all over Texas, and down to the border with Mexico.

A rookie is uncertain about everything but I'm not wired to hang back. I wanted to make the team—which I did. I wanted to make friends. I checked that box right away; the extremely talk-ative Dietrick and I hit it off. And I wanted to have fun. That was easily done in San Antonio. Besides the great weather and the un-usually friendly people, we were the community's team. It was North Carolina all over again: with no NFL or MLB or even any big-time college sports in the region, Spurs were celebrities, from our stars (Gervin and James Silas) on down. Everybody wanted to buy you dinner or a drink.

"You play golf, George?" asked Dr. Jerry Beckel. The Spurs' team dentist had filled my mouth with Novocaine and instru-ments and a suction hose.

"Argh," I said.

"Would you like to play Oak Hills next week?"

"Argh!" I said.

Fernando

Golf was huge. Day-off and summer headquarters for Spurs golfers was a great public course called Pecan Valley Golf Club, where they held the 1968 PGA Championship. The regulars in the Spurs group were Terry Stembridge, our radio guy; Doug Moe and Bob Bass, who were coaches; and me. We owned the place, or acted as if we did. We drank a beer or two during and after.

One day at Pecan Valley, I told the new pro behind the counter to give me a new glove—white, medium large—and a sleeve of golf balls—Titleist, 90 compression. Eighteen fifty, he said, or whatever it was, but I walked away, saying some bullshit like "Spurs don't pay."

A minute later, I was called back to the pro shop to take a phone call. While I sat on the counter and talked on the phone, the tall, goofy-looking pro literally picked my pocket. "Here's your change, Mr. Karl," he said. "Enjoy your day." A friendship was born—Dan Strimple and I have been tight ever since. I guess I like people who have some balls.

Coby's girlfriend was a Braniff flight attendant. She'd bring her best pal—also a Braniff "stewardess"—to games. So it seemed inevitable when the four of us started hanging out together. And that was how I met and would eventually marry Cathy Cramer of Boise, Idaho.

While I was doing well socially in San Antonio, I was also completely miserable. Coach Tom Nissalke hated me. I also know he was pissed at management for giving me a guaranteed contract. We were oil and water.

It was bad. One day after our third or fourth practice, I sat in the locker room and literally cried into a towel. I'd never felt so frustrated. "What am I doing here?" I moaned. Nissalke made the game so fucking slow it was like playing underwater. We spent entire practices shadowboxing. In other words, it was all walk-throughs of complicated offensive patterns—with no defense. We had a playbook as thick as a law book.

Slow ball shocked me and hurt me on some deep level. I wanted to get out and run, like I always had. Not Nissalke. His boring, hold-the-ball approach was about the coach controlling the game, not the players. Executing three screens and five passes before you even look at the basket made the coach appear to be a strategic master, but it was not a good system for me, a guy with a wide-open throttle. I'm sure Nissalke also noticed what a poor fit I was, and, as I said, he didn't like me anyway. He kept my ass on the bench. In our five exhibition games, I played zero minutes.

But I had my moments in my four-year career in the short shorts and high socks era. I was an instigator, a magnifier. I changed the tone of a few games and helped us win. For a while I owned the playoff game steals record (5). By asserting myself as a competitor, I influenced others to try as hard as I did. But given the way I played, it was not surprising that I didn't last. I kept blowing out my knees—three surgeries, two left, one right. Joint repair was not the subtle science it is now, so with each zipper, I lost about 10 percent of my speed. I didn't have that much to give up; no one does. As my playing career faded, my desire to coach grew more definite.

Both Bob Bass, who succeeded Nissalke as head coach my second year in San Antonio, and Doug Moe, a North Carolina guy who followed Bob, liked me and appreciated my passion for the game. Both of them played fast, thank God. So as I limped to the finish line as a player, and an entry-level nonplaying job came open—scout—my hat was in the ring. I was an attractive candidate, because not only would I accept the lousy salary—-$12,000—I'd save the team money on travel. As I mentioned, my wife was a flight attendant, so I could sometimes fly free.

Scouting was pretty simple: I'd go to college games to look at players we might want to draft and to NBA games to study our opponents. I was a spy but everyone knew I was there. There were a few GMs and player personnel guys I became friends with: Rick

Sund in Dallas, Wayne Embry in Cleveland, and Al Menendez in New Jersey. Some weeks I'd stay with the Spurs to talk about what I'd learned, and look at some video, and help Coach Moe however I could.

One of the stock scenes in the life of off-duty coaches is set at a table in a bar or restaurant: with pens scratching paper napkins and placemats, they draw up inbound plays and defensive and offensive sets. Beer or ketchup bottles represent players, which the scheming coaches use to set picks and so on. That's pretty much the way it was and still is for me, but mostly we just talk and laugh.

I especially loved sitting around with Doug. Within five minutes after a loss he'd be back to his social self. I'd be all wound up, ready to bitch about our bad luck or the referees or those *damn* players. "Relax, George, it's a long season," Doug would say. "Who wants another beer?"

I never forgot a couple of other bits of between-Budweisers wisdom from Doug. "A one-point loss should bother you a hell of a lot more than a loss by twenty," he said. "You could have done something to win a close game, but the coach can't do much about a blowout."

Another time, Doug drained his glass and confirmed what I think I already knew. "You've got to be a head coach in this league," he said. "You're a pain in the ass as an assistant."

Talking about the game is so important to me that I've always had an off-court headquarters. For example: at my first head coaching job, with the Great Falls Golden Nuggets of the Continental Basketball Association, our tiny office in the basement of a real estate office was beneath a bar named TJ's. So TJ's became our HQ. I spent many happy hours there yukking it up with my friend and most dependable player, Terry Stotts, and kicking the machine when I lost games of Donkey Kong, Missile Commander, and Frogger.

My home away from home in Cleveland was Whitey's Booze N' Burgers, a no-frills joint close to our arena in rural Richfield, Ohio. No windows, just like the Coliseum. You could lube a car with a basket of Whitey's french fries. In Denver, we spent a lot of time at Chopper's. Burgers, pizza, wings, beer, with walls covered by HD TVs: perfect. Robert "Chopper" Travaglini, the longtime trainer of the Nuggets, founded the place.

We made Ricky's Lounge in San Leandro our go-to at Golden State. Ricky's was the first sports bar that I know of: it had satellite dishes when the Warriors didn't. It was just a few miles from our practice facility, and it was on the way home, so if the traffic was bad on the 580, Golden State GM Don Nelson and I would pull in to Ricky's and watch the East Coast games until seven thirty or so.

For a couple of reasons, including that I had young kids at home, I didn't have a regular bar in Seattle. But once a year, I'd go out with our two best players, Shawn Kemp and Gary Payton, and take a taxi home. They taught me a lot about drinking. And if you think Gary can talk on a normal day, you should hear him after he's had a glass of something strong. The last couple of times we went down to the marina and drank on Gary's yacht. Which stayed tied to the dock, fortunately.

That was the nineties. Miller Lite in the night with Shawn and Gary was innocent fun compared to what had gone on in the NBA a decade earlier.

People my kids' age and younger have no idea that the league could have gone belly-up in the mid- to late eighties. Before Magic and Bird and David Stern came to the rescue, the whole thing teetered on the edge. It was drugs. In 1982, the *Los Angeles Times* estimated that 75 percent of NBA players were using illegal recreational drugs. I doubt that the percentage was that high, but as I said, I was really out of the loop on this. But I got in the loop in a big way, thanks to Chris Washburn.

Washburn's similarity to Mel Turpin strikes me now. Like Mel,

Chris was our number one draft choice (the third pick overall) and was expected to be a star. His potential (and mine; it was my first season with the Warriors) really excited the fans—Golden State sold its most season tickets in ten years. Like Turpin, Washburn was about 6'11", very agile for his size, a little passive, and could really score and rebound, at least on the college level. But both had a monkey. Turpin's was fast food and aversion to work; Washburn's was cocaine.

It was October 1986. Reagan was president, *Crocodile Dundee*, *Stand by Me*, and *The Color of Money* were the big movies, and I was going to put my bad ending in Cleveland behind me. A San Francisco sportswriter noticed when Washburn drove up to our first practice in a new black Mercedes-Benz 500 SEL—the big one—with red trim, darkened windows, and little wipers for the headlights. This was no big deal to me: I've always had nice cars and buying one when you win the lottery or get drafted in the first round seems reasonable to me. But I looked twice when I saw the little white basketball painted on the driver's side door next to the words "Grand Master."

He wasn't.

But I said he was or could be *before* the season started, because in our two preseason training camps, he was the best player on the floor. "I'm elated with his progress," I told the newspaper guys. "We're very excited. We think he's going to be a special player for us."

I had a lot to think about besides our rookie, of course. Early in the camp, I had to cut Phil Ford, one of the greatest guards in North Carolina history. (I've already communicated how much I love anyone and anything connected to my alma mater.) Our best scorer, Purvis Short, hurt his knee, and Greg Ballard, our first big off the bench, was coming off knee surgery. I wondered if I could handle the "enigmatic" personality of our star, Joe Barry Carroll. Enigmatic: the newspaper code word for "doesn't try very hard."

The season began. We won our first game, over Denver, which was coached by my good friend Douglas Moe. Three days later, the trouble started. Washburn showed up an hour and a half late for a two-hour practice. He had a sort-of believable story about picking up a friend at the San Francisco airport and the plane arriving late. Then he got lost on the way to our facility in Oakland.

Chris was twenty-one, the third-youngest player in the league. He'd rarely been away from his hometown of Hickory, North Carolina, and the Bay Area can be confusing for a newcomer. So we fined him, and I parked his ass on the bench and kept it there until he showed me something. Because the real hammer, the coach's ultimate weapon, is playing time. They all want to play. In December to early January, I didn't give Chris a minute in 8 of 14 games. In the stat line the acronym is DNP-CD: did not play—coach's decision.

Nothing worked. He still couldn't show up on time. Team buses from the hotel to the arena took off without him in Boston and Washington and he continued to show up late for practices. We asked Ballard to babysit. When Washburn was late three out of four days anyway—this was early December—Greg quit. Chris's agent hired someone to be the new nanny.

We fined CW nine times in the first three months of the season. The team voted to use his accumulated $10,000 in fine money for a new sound system for the locker room, a little irony, or an FU to Chris, because he had gotten in trouble for stealing a stereo at NC State. A real team is a tribe, or a brotherhood, and you have to prove yourself to get in. Chris stood outside.

He had a big smile, with a gap in his front teeth, but I wasn't smiling back. He tried to avoid me—he'd come to our facility in San Leandro in his practice uniform, then leave right after, staying out of the locker room, where he might have to talk to me or be teased by me. Chris reminds me now of all the pampered, entitled AAU babies I've had to deal with over the years. He was an only child, and I'm sure they didn't make him go to class at North Carolina State. Could I ever inspire the spoiled brat? I tried.

But we succeeded without him. The Warriors had their first three-game win streak in two years, and then the first six-game win streak in eight years. We built some belief and trust in each other. Purvis, JBC, Chris Mullin, and Sleepy Floyd were playing well together. Larry Smith was getting every rebound and the team was getting the hang of our trapping defense.

When we beat the hated Lakers at home, I was on a cloud. So it bothered me when our GM, Jack McMahon, told me to start playing Washburn more. Jack was preparing for the draft and needed to know if Chris could play. If not, we'd need to draft another big player. Jack was a great guy who really tried to help me but I said no. I wanted to stick with what we had going.

The same thing had happened at Cleveland, with Turpin, and I'd resisted then, too. Because I was being paid and evaluated on our record, not on how easy I made the GM's job. Besides, winning can be such a delicate thing. It's dangerous to mess with what's working.

That little conflict between McMahon and me disappeared in a cloud of white powder in late January 1987 when Chris left the team and entered a drug treatment center in Van Nuys. So *that* was why he'd been undependable and irresponsible and why he couldn't remember our plays. I didn't have much sympathy, but I was told to consider Chris's addiction an illness, not a moral failure. I told the media that I would read up on the subject and talk to the experts so that I'd have more understanding when/if Chris returned to the team. The most useful thing I learned was that wired-up cocaine users drink and drink and drink because nothing makes them tired. Then, of course, they don't sleep enough and get really awful hangovers. And they miss the bus.

I also discovered that drugs and whores were especially easy to get in Oakland, making it the go-to place for NBA players with those two bad habits. But I didn't really bother too much with drug education. I should have. All I really did was watch tape and coach, like always.

As Washburn's career and life went south, I kept returning to the day we drafted him. We thought we needed a big guy, But, as I told Nellie the next day, in my heart I wanted Ron Harper, the 6'6" guard who went on to win rings with the Bulls.

Why are we drafting big guys, anyway? I think big low-post players just slow us down. All I want out of a big is to defend, rebound the ball, run the court, set a screen, roll to the hoop, and dunk. The modern NBA is about getting as many fast, versatile decision makers as you can.

In mid-April, I won my hundredth game as an NBA coach, the Warriors qualified for the playoffs for the first time in ten years, and our fans were over the moon. And right about then, the league came close to going out of business.

A grand jury in Phoenix indicted three current and two former Suns for using cocaine, and their rookie William Bedford was subpoenaed to tell what he knew. Unbelievable: a drug was destroying an NBA team. It could have taken down the whole league and not just from bad PR. The press didn't really pick up on the possibility of gamblers and dealers pressing addicted players into shaving points or throwing games. If that had happened, not even Bird, Magic, and Stern could have rescued the league.

We could see how bad our problem was just by looking at the "drug draft" of 1986. Len Bias died of a cocaine overdose in a University of Maryland dorm room two days after Boston selected him second overall. We had the useless Washburn at number three. Bedford was number six—another monumental bust, and for the same reason as the others. At number seven, Dallas took Roy Tarpley, whom the league eventually expelled for repeatedly failing drug tests. Although Tarpley had a couple of good years, four of the seven best college players of 1986 had little or no impact as pros because of what they put in their noses. A lot of us acted totally surprised but some of these guys had problems in college and we drafted them anyway. The thinking was that they would mature and get past it. I'd totally supported taking Washburn third at Golden State despite his "problem," which we thought was marijuana, a minor thing compared to cocaine.

Chris surfaced in 2015 at a homeless shelter in Dallas, as a part-time counselor, not as a resident. He gave don't-do-what-I-did speeches. His rough life has included prison time, poverty, and homelessness. He's back in Hickory now and he says he's been clean for more than a decade. His son plays basketball for TCU.

Turpin, who worked as a prison guard after his basketball career ended, committed suicide at age forty-nine in 2010.

Drug problems are treated a little differently in the modern NBA. The coach doesn't even hear about a player who tests positive and gets his first strike. Management or the league handles it. We've got a more thorough drug-testing program than the NFL or MLB, which we always brag about. But we've still got a drug issue, though a different one than thirty years ago. And this one bothers me more than the dumbasses who got in trouble with recreational drugs.

I'm talking about performance-enhancing drugs—like steroids, human growth hormone, and so on. It's obvious some of our players are doping. How are some guys getting older—yet thinner and fitter? How are they recovering from injuries so fast? Why the hell are they going to Germany in the off-season? I doubt it's for the sauerkraut.

More likely it's for the newest, hardest-to-detect blood boosters and PEDs they have in Europe. Unfortunately, drug testing always seems to be a couple of steps behind drug hiding. Lance Armstrong never failed a drug test. I think we want the best athletes to succeed, not the biggest, richest cheaters employing the best scientists. But I don't know what to do about it.

was in Europe myself a year and a half later.

Madrid is a beautiful, ancient city with a look and a feel unlike anything in North America. When we moved there in 1989, I felt like a fish out of water for a while. In Spain, they drink wine at every meal but breakfast, they eat dinner when I usually go to bed, and they take siestas. Sometimes they tack your mother's maiden name onto your last name, making me, for example, George Karl-Patterson.

Soon after arriving, and looking for a little piece of home, I went through the drive-through at a Burger King for a *hamburguesa*. A mess: the rapid Spanish words and numbers coming out of the little speaker sounded nothing like the Mexican Spanish I was vaguely familiar with, and they couldn't understand me, either. Somehow I got my burger, *con queso y tomate*.

Car travel in the city was also tough because their road signs are tiny tile squares embedded in the sides of buildings. I didn't even try to drive to my first practice as the head coach of Real Madrid. I took the train, went forty-five minutes in the wrong direction, and showed up Chris Washburn–late. Even the basketball court looked unfamiliar. The three-second lane was wide on the baseline and narrow at the free-throw line—a trapezoid. But I could handle that part. Basketball is an international language. Blocks, rolls, screens, defense—the fundamentals are universal.

With the help of bilingual assistants, I could teach and coach. I proved very poor at picking up the new language. My Spanish was confined to *digame* ("talk to me"—an alternative to *hola* when answering the phone), *gracias*, and *otra cerveza, por favor* ("another glass of buttermilk, please"). I caused some laughter among the waitstaff at a restaurant when I ordered *polla* (penis) when I really wanted *pollo* (chicken). And I got in trouble for confusing *mierda* (shit) with Miera, which is a river and a town in Spain.

Fernando

My best communication moment came after a loss, when I told the press *jugamos como mujeres* (we play like women).

We took a bus to any game we could reach in four hours or less. For some reason, our players loved the bus. Those long drives gave me a lot of time to think. I remembered that I'd been in Madrid in 1972, for one of the special trips Coach Smith organized every year. There was a tournament, and we beat Real Madrid in the finals. I also thought about the twisted journey (more on that later) that led me to coach one of the world's best-known athletic clubs and about how we—the United States—helped make our game the second-most-popular sport in the world (after soccer, of course). We're not given enough credit for that. I loved coaching in Europe. I'm glad I did it. I'd do it again.

Our star at Real Madrid was Fernando Martín Espina, a skilled big who could shoot and run. Fernando caught everyone's attention at the Olympics in Los Angeles in 1984, when Spain made the finals against the United States. In 1986–87, he played for part of a year for the Portland Trail Blazers, making him the first Spaniard and only the second European to play in the league.

But he was injured and homesick, so he didn't last long in the Asociación Baloncesto Nacional and they welcomed him back to Real Madrid like a long-lost son. A national hero, Fernando was twenty-seven in 1989, the year I coached him, a handsome guy with a full head of dark hair. The U.S. equivalent in that era would have been Magic, Bird, or Michael Jordan. Maybe James Dean gets closer to the impact he had.

We had a six o'clock home game against CAI Zaragoza on December 3, a Sunday, a month into the new season. Fernando was injured and wasn't going to play. He left his home a little before 3 p.m. in his Lancia Thema, a plain-looking sedan but with a V-8 Ferrari engine. He crashed it on one of Madrid's main highways, the M-30. I rushed to the hospital with several of our players. I remember a waiting room filled with people hugging, praying, and speaking in soft, rapid Spanish. A doctor came out. Fernando had died.

The grief that followed was so intense and widespread that it overwhelmed me. The next few days contained some of the most emotional moments in my life. Every detail is frozen in my mind, including that a cold rain fell all day the day of the funeral.

We called off that night's game. The next morning there was a private church service. Then, following an 8 p.m. mass, Fernando's body lay in state on the jump circle in the center of the Palacio de Deportes, our arena on the Real Madrid campus. People filed by until dawn. Our usually noisy arena was quiet except for the sounds of hard shoes on hardwood and crying.

No one could figure out a way to get the dark, wooden casket to the hearse. So our red-eyed players put Fernando on their shoulders and carried him up the arena stairs and out into the rain. The hearse drove slowly through Madrid to the Basilica de San Francisco El Grande for the funeral mass. People bowed their heads and wept by the side of the road. It was the saddest sight I've ever seen.

I counted twenty buses from around the country at the cemetery, including groups from other European league teams. But a big concrete arch near the entrance prevented the buses from parking anywhere near the gravesite. Hundreds of people dressed in black had to walk hundreds of yards through the drizzle.

I'd met with the team at the church. "We've got a game tonight," I said. "We can play or we can forfeit."

"Damn right we're playing," said Fernando's brother, Antonio, who was also our second-best player. "Fernando would think we are a bunch of cowards if we don't play." Everyone agreed.

After the burial, we went to a hotel restaurant to eat and drink and to hear and tell stories about Fernando. It was emotional. There was crying and there was wine. It went on much too long for a team with a game that night. And that was how I came to coach—for the only time in my life—while trying to fight off the effects of alcohol.

There were a bunch of goose bump moments. Fernando's jersey—white, blue lettering, number 10—was draped over a chair on our bench and players on the opposing team dropped roses on it. Before the game, our players spontaneously ran up the aisles and through the sellout crowd to the president's box to give Fernando's mother a group hug.

Maybe the players were a little buzzed, too. We were clearly exhausted emotionally. We played extremely poorly in the first half and fell way behind.

They didn't get a lot of fire from me during the timeouts and I wasn't going to make a big deal out of a loss under the circumstances. But Antonio was angry. "You're a bunch of *putas*," he said at halftime. "Fernando wouldn't like this."

We went crazy in the first six minutes of the second half and caught up. Each basket we made and each defensive stop received unusually fierce yelling and applause. Near the end of the game, after we'd come back from 19 down to a 15-point lead, the emotional crowd began to chant: "Fernando esta aquí! Fernando esta aquí!"

Fernando is here. Fernando is here.

CHAPTER 4

GEORGE KARL HAS LOST IT!

His players look like they believe in the plan. They bring it to every game. His teams are not hard to watch.

—COBY DIETRICK, FORMER SPURS TEAMMATE

I hit someone before every game.

It happens like clockwork. While the players are on the floor warming up, the coaches mill around the big digital timer that's in every NBA locker room. Sometimes the conversation is "Let's not double LeBron until he hits three jumpers in a row." Sometimes it's "That's the ugliest tie in the history of ties." We're excited and a little nervous, as if we're in line for the roller coaster. My heart rate is the fastest it will be until the final minute or two of a close game.

When the countdown to the tip hits four minutes, we're ready to enter the bright lights and loud rock music in the arena. One second later someone screams "Three fifty-nine!" And then—BAM!

I throw a hard elbow at the shoulder of anyone within reach. The response: BAM! an equally hard pop to my shoulder or chest, and "We're gonna kick their ass!" There are three or four of us and we all bump and check and even punch each other randomly for about thirty seconds. These aren't love taps, either. We've had guys hit the floor. When I weighed 295, I could hit pretty hard. I've done this for twenty years.

Some people will wonder about the mentality of a person who acts this way. Well, it may seem juvenile or caveman from the outside but these little bursts serve a purpose. First of all, I've never lost the pregame feeling I had when I played. I'm pumped up and adrenaline is flowing fast into my bloodstream. But I can't run or throw an elbow or dive on the floor. I've got to let it out somehow. Also, the punch reminds us coaches that our game is physical, and that we have to stay on our guys to hit and hit first.

Also, I kind of like it.

Like anyone who does a job with repetition, habit takes over in the NBA. Coach Smith taught us the stress relief and comfort of repetition. (We'd all recite the Lord's Prayer with Coach Smith before a game, for example, a ritual I obviously didn't copy.) So I try to bring routine and consistency to our crazy NBA lives. Counting exhibition, regular season, and playoffs, we play about one hundred games a year. The challenge isn't the sameness of airports, hotels, and arenas. It's the disconnected feeling of being on the road so much. Add the superstition athletes and coaches are prone to, the pressure everyone feels, and you can see how we find comfort in ritual.

A lot of it—when the game starts, when the plane takes off, our hotel—is just imposed on us. But I decide a lot of other things, such as how we play, who plays, and when and how we practice (my teams practice harder than any other in the league). I'm not trying to control the culture so much as make everyone comfortable and certain things a little more predictable.

After a year with me, everyone knows how many fire-and-brimstone speeches I'll deliver during the year—not many. "You only have a six-shooter," Jack McMahon told me once. "You can't go after your team after every bad loss." When I drew near the end of my allotment, Jack would say, "You've got one bullet left." My GM at Golden State was a very smart man.

I have a system of bribes called 30-30-30, and each of my players knows what it is. Everyone knows our rules for shot selection, our basic substitution pattern, and how we run timeouts.

The only unpredictable thing is the game itself.

What's it like to coach one? I'll tell you.

———

invented the pregame mosh pit that I just described to you. Most of the rest of my stuff I stole from Dean Smith, Bob Bass, Doug Moe, Larry Brown, Don Nelson, Gene Esplen, Don Bassett, and Dick Misenhelter.

Before I tell you what happens on game day before and after my assistants and I beat the shit out of each other, I will describe the steps in my evolution as a coach.

The first step occurred in June 1973, when I got drafted to play professional basketball. (As I mentioned, I had briefly considered the seminary as well.) Actually, two teams drafted me, the New York Knicks and the Memphis Tams of the ABA (the Spurs of the ABA got me when the Tams missed the deadline to send me a contract). Money was discussed, obviously, but I didn't immediately grasp the most important thing about professional basketball: it's a business. Put away the Carolina blue pom-poms. It's not a game anymore.

I got my first good look at NBA front-office hardball during my second year playing for the Spurs. As his slow-mo offensive game demonstrated, coach Tom Nissalke liked control. His control of the team would be more or less complete if he were also the general manager. The Spurs already had a GM, Angelo Drossos, one of the thirty Spurs co-owners. Angelo would be the key to getting San Antonio from the ABA into the NBA. Good guy; I played tennis with him at San Antonio Country Club.

But Nissalke worked the other owners and got enough support so that they had to have a meeting in a high school classroom to decide if Angelo should go. And Angelo was going, until Red McCombs, the majority owner, switched his vote at the last minute. Nissalke came into the room expecting to be told he now had two jobs. But he left with one and soon he had none. They fired his ass a couple of days later.

Things like that didn't happen at North Carolina, and it shocked me a little bit.

Then *I* got the ax. As I mentioned, after four seasons as an increasingly injured Spurs point guard, I spent two years in San Antonio as a scout and assistant. I was a good soldier, I thought, doing a good job, and I was loyal to the team.

But in the summer of 1980, when I was running a Spurs-sponsored basketball camp at Cole High School in San Antonio, Bob Bass came into the gym. Bob had gone from coach to GM, and he had news for me. Doug Moe had been fired. The new coach, Stan Albeck, would not require my services. I hadn't planned for this.

While I came to grips with my new reality, I played a little tennis and a lot of golf. One fine morning at Pecan Valley, I shot 73, which is still my best-ever round. *I've got it now*, I thought. I decided to tee it up again that afternoon, and give my friends a chance at winning their money back. They did. I shot 86. Fucking golf.

Meanwhile, word of my unemployment was making the rounds—I hoped. I didn't have an agent to spread the word. But—as you might expect—scouts get to know people around the league. Everyone's a potential employer, and sometimes you establish real friendships. My allies in the league were Embry, Sund, and Menendez, as I mentioned, plus Del Harris, an underrated basketball genius and the head coach at Houston; and Don Nelson. Nellie, then the Milwaukee head coach, became a big part of my life.

Many times I'd had meals with these guys at the media buffet before the game, sometimes beers after. Hey, Wayne, Rick, Al, Del, and Nellie: you got a job for me?

They didn't. I worried a little bit. I spoke with another guy on my side—Marty Blake, the NBA's director of scouting. Marty made a phone call that changed everything for me.

He'd called a very distant outpost in the world of pro basketball: Great Falls, Montana, home of the Montana Golden Nuggets of the Continental Basketball Association. The who in the what? Neither the team nor the league exists anymore.

The CBA, the oldest league in the United States, was organized right after World War II, in 1946, two months before the NBA got started. The Continental evolved from the Eastern League, which fielded teams in northeastern factory towns. The Allentown Jets, the Wilkes-Barre Barons, the Berwick Carbuilders. Over the years, the Eastern League expanded, changed names, got a little classier, and became the official feeder system to the NBA. Think AA or AAA minor league baseball. *Bull Durham* stuff—a lot of bus travel, bad food, cheap hotels, no money.

Following Marty's recommendation—and another one from Nellie—Golden Nuggets GM Ray Dobbs called me. We know you've never been a head coach before, but we've heard good things, he said. Something like that. But I remember his exact words regarding the head coach's salary: $18,000—a minor raise from what the Spurs had been paying me but a long way from the $55K I made my last year as a player. My income was obviously going in the wrong direction. But I wanted this; I knew I wanted to coach. I conferred with my wife. Cathy was the adventurous type, fortunately, and saw that this job could be a stepping-stone—if I won. I'll take it, I said.

But could I take Great Falls? It's desolate or beautiful, depending on your point of view (I came down on the desolate side). I remember getting off the plane and seeing my new home for the first time. The Rockies looked dark blue in one direction and the high plain seemed endless in the other. This was either the end of a line or the beginning of one. In December, when it was 50 below zero, my nose almost froze. The ground around the iced-over Missouri River was dry and brown and as hard as concrete. I quickly learned that everybody ran an extension cord to their cars and placed a heater on the engine at night. The oil froze if you didn't.

"I like to play this game fast," I told the players. "If we can rebound the ball, and you can defend, we will play fast." I was looking at a 6'9" lefty named Rich Yonakor. I knew his game, and I wanted him to succeed, because he'd gone to North Carolina.

But the one guy whose attention I had to have was our point guard. At San Antonio, Bob Bass had James Silas and he ran the team. It was the same thing with me and Coach Smith at North Carolina. Fortunately, our "one" was Robert Smith, a fantastic guy with tremendous positive energy. The Spurs called him up one Sunday, but Robert asked for permission to delay reporting so he could help us win a playoff game against the Wyoming Wildcatters. Ninety-nine percent of players would not have risked injury to play another minor-league game; they'd have been on the next plane to South Texas.

I basically taught Carolina basketball at Great Falls, and I didn't delegate. There was no one to delegate to. But despite all the hardships, coaching felt right, like it was my calling. And it felt powerful, like the first time I rode a motorcycle.

———

We played our games in the Great Falls High School gym, the home of the Mighty Bison. We practiced on a splintery floor in the dimly lit basement of the Salvation Army. Road trips meant endless bus rides through the Badlands to Billings or Casper or Yakima, and exhausting trips to play games in the East.

Player salaries were standardized. Two hundred fifty dollars per week. Take out taxes, rent, gas, and food and there's not much left. It was essentially poverty. We had a forward named Kenny "Dog" Dennard who played at Duke but I liked him anyway. He often brought his wife, Nadine, over to our house for dinner. We'd watch a movie on Showtime and then they'd sleep on our couch. "A lot better than the Salvation Army mattress on the floor in our apartment," Dog would say.

Yes. That was a rough basketball life.

I remember once playing seven games in ten days in four time zones. We played the Anchorage Northern Knights, the Alberta Dusters, and we were off to Fargo and Flint. On planes, it was tall guys who had just run their asses off squeezing into coach seats.

Despite the conditions, attitudes were pretty good and bitching was pretty low. There were only twenty-three NBA teams at this time so competition for a call-up was fierce.

For example, Dog dove for a loose ball and hurt his hip just before the CBA All-Star Game. He was hoping to get noticed that night. But the doctor told him to rest. That wasn't going to happen.

When the doctor left the exam room, Dog swiped a bottle of lidocaine and then got some needles at a drugstore by pretending to be diabetic. He injected himself in the hip for the next week or so. No one knew but Kenny and Nadine. He told me much later. But this dangerous self-doctoring worked. The Kansas City Kings called him up.

Our practices in the Salvation Army gym were crazy cold because we were always the first ones there. I tried to arrive early to turn on the damn boiler. The players wore two or three warm-up suits and looked like Michelin Men. But worse than frozen toes and seeing our breath on our practice court, our underfunded owner stopped paying the rent for our games at the high school. And then he just bailed. We didn't see him again after late January. Several times I had to go before the Great Falls Board of Education to convince them not to kick us out while we tried to regroup. For a while, no one got paid, including me.

Cathy and I dipped into our savings to make payroll—more or less—and we invited a few players to share our house.

As so often happens, a chicken saved us. Management scraped together $5,000 to pay Ted Giannoulas—aka the San Diego Chicken—to entertain at one of our games. The Chicken Game, as we called it afterward, was a big hit and infused the team with some cash and a boost in popularity. Such a hit that the new owner tried three more Chicken Games the next year, but the novelty wore off pretty quickly.

Speaking of chicken, we always controlled the backboard pretty well at home because the leading rebounder in any game got a coupon for a McChicken sandwich at McDonald's.

The CBA was willing to be inventive to put asses in seats. For a short time, we had sudden-death overtimes, believe it or not. We had the first million-dollar shots (from three-quarter court) for fans at halftime, and "quarter points." Each game was worth seven points in the standings. You'd get four points for a win, but up for grabs was a point for "winning" a quarter. This supposedly kept fan interest up, even in a blowout.

All of us regarded the CBA as our best chance (or our last chance) to make it to the big league. We were players who got dropped from NBA teams (or never made it on a roster), a few refugees from overseas leagues, and coaches and referees trying to move up or get started. There was some desperation. There's no question it was the most physical basketball I've ever seen, and it got out of hand sometimes.

A couple of years after Kermit Washington shattered Rudy Tomjonavich's face with his fist, I witnessed a punch that must have been just as hard. It was my second year in the CBA, and we were in Billings, playing the Volcanos (their misspelling, not mine). Current NBA referee Bennett Salvatore called the game. We had Ronnie Valentine, whom we picked up after the Denver Nuggets dropped him, and he was playing great, averaging 25 points per game. They had Sam Clancy, a big man from Pitt, who played pro basketball only this one year before he began a long career in the NFL as a defensive end. Ronnie and Sam got tangled up, got mad, and squared off. Clancy swung a vicious right cross that dropped our guy and broke his cheekbone. Big Sam got suspended for three weeks. It'd be three years to life if it happened today.

One detail about that Billings team: one applicant for the head coaching job there was Phil Jackson, a recently retired New York Knick trying to break into coaching. They couldn't get the money right, so Phil went elsewhere.

We made the finals my first year in the CBA. Willie Smith was our point guard and the league MVP. He was also a jackass because he decided his back hurt too much to travel to New York for the playoff games against the Rochester Zeniths. We lost in four games. I was about 2-10 overall versus the Rochester coach, Mauro Panaggio. Couldn't beat that guy. He always had better players. And they showed up for games.

After playing for a few years in France, Spain, and Italy, Terry Stotts joined our team for the 1981–82 season, the beginning of a long association. Terry—now the Portland Trail Blazers' coach—played mistake-free ball, and he was the best inbounds passer I've ever seen. We made the Western Conference finals, but lost.

We made the finals again in my third CBA season. In Game Seven—which we lost to the Detroit Spirits—Phil Jackson showed up to watch. I coached in a tuxedo. I have no idea why either occurred.

Criminal assault, poverty, and a frozen gym . . . I could go on and on about how Great Falls wasn't the University of North Carolina or the San Antonio Spurs. But I loved it. All the inconveniences we faced off the court made us a tighter team on it—as much as that was possible, given the constant turnover of players.

For the coach, frequent call-ups were a good thing: it meant that you knew how to get players ready for the NBA. Enough player promotions meant—maybe—that the coach should be called up, too. Constantly losing your best guys made it a lot harder to win, of course, and every coach wants to win. But I did both. I was named CBA Coach of the Year the same two seasons we made the finals, in 1981 and '83.

It was obvious to me and to everyone else: I could coach. My ego and will and knowledge could dominate players in a good way. I didn't cajole or appeal to reason: I challenged my team, questioned their manhood and their intellect when they screwed up, and dared them to play better than they ever had. The coaches I'd been exposed to affected me, of course, but I had my own style. It worked. I've never really changed it.

I got called up by Cleveland, as you know if you're following along. I was the player-personnel guy at first. I worked my ass off. Although I got a nice bump up to $45,000, I was hurting financially. I had two houses because the one in Montana wouldn't sell. I'd go on the road and live cheaply—the pregame media buffet was a big help—so I could pocket the per diem money to pay the bills. About twice a month I'd compare our income to our outgo and say, "How in the world are we gonna do this?"

Not for the last time, Nellie intervened. He made it clear that he wanted me on his bench in Milwaukee, so I made it clear to Harry Weltman, the Cavs GM, that the Bucks wanted me and that I was tempted. I wanted to coach and I needed the money. "Why don't you wait to see what we do here?" the Cavs GM said. I did. They fired my old nemesis Tom Nissalke. Suddenly thirty-three-year-old me was running an NBA team.

Weltman showed a lot of courage by sticking with me through our disastrous start. He could easily have said he'd made a mistake and punted me out the door. I never thanked him, even through his son, Jeff, who was our assistant GM in Denver—so I'm doing it now. Thanks, Harry.

Starting a season 2-19 and then making the playoffs—then playing Boston so well in the first round—delivered a powerful message. It showed how quickly a team could go from bad to good. But in year two, we went from pretty good to very bad.

About the only good thing I can remember about that second year in Cleveland was winning at Los Angeles early in the schedule on the night the Lakers got their championship rings for the previous season.

"Come on! We're celebrating!" I said to assistant coach Mo McHone and trainer Gary Briggs when we got to the Marriott on Century Boulevard. The hotel bar had the usual business travelers and low-key vibe. But then I started buying drinks for everyone and soon we had a party going on. And eventually a five-hundred-dollar bar bill.

"Take care of that, Gary," I said.

"What the hell is this?" said Weltman when he got the bill.

I was a cocky dude, that's for sure. Possibly because Ray Dobbs at Great Falls left me alone for three years, I could not get used to taking orders from a general manager. And I didn't want to. Almost anything I heard from our GM got on my nerves a little bit. "You need to give more minutes to Mel in the first half," Weltman would say. I'd ignore any suggestions, which shows you how clueless I was.

Yes, thirty-five-year-old me was an egotistical asshole but I felt like I was out on a limb. My contract was up at the end of the year and I hadn't been renewed. Because I'd been one, I already knew that NBA players know each other's salary and length of contract as well as they know their own phone numbers. And they're especially clued in to the coach's situation. I don't blame them. This year's coach may like him, may have drafted or traded for him, but next year's guy might cut or trade his ass. Money is involved.

And power. In any business, if you know your boss is on shaky ground, you probably don't listen to him too much. Strong-willed players—Kobe Bryant and LeBron James come to mind—try to take over when the coach is weak. But that didn't happen with the Cavs in 1986 as far as I knew. Then again: "I saw guys tuning you out, not even paying attention," World Free told me recently. "It got ugly in that locker room."

Injuries to Phil Hubbard and Lonnie Shelton, two of our best players, hurt us and amped up my frustration.

I bitched about Weltman at Whitey's Booze N' Burgers. The hell does he know, I'd say, and why can't he get me some players? Sports radio WWWE and the newspapers attacked, had me fired this week or next at the latest.

We were losing more games than we were winning, certain players were growing sullen, and I was battling our GM. Still, I was getting job offers.

But not from Cleveland; they wouldn't commit to giving me a new contract. The University of Pittsburgh called to ask if I'd consider coaching there. The Cavs reluctantly gave me permission to talk to them. I drove the one and a half hours to my old hometown on a day off. At lunch, the Pitt athletic director put a million-dollar deal on the table. The papers printed that I was talking to Pittsburgh about a job; I denied it.

"George is disloyal," Weltman told Cleveland's *Plain Dealer* and the *Akron Beacon Journal*.

Meanwhile, Nellie was whispering in my ear. "If you don't get a new contract in Cleveland," he said, "I've got a head coach job for you."

You do? Where?

Even though I was about to endure some hard times in professional basketball, I'm glad I didn't take the position at Pitt. I'm just not a college coach.

"Karl, you suck!"

You should have heard the insults and the boo birds when I came out into our echo chamber of an arena for the last time. As

I walked to my seat, a ball from the warm-up bounced to me. For the hell of it, I turned, shot, and swished it from forty feet. Our nasty little crowd went silent for a minute.

Despite all our problems on the floor, and fans carrying pitchforks and flaming torches, I didn't see it coming when Weltman phoned me the next day and said the magic words: "We're gonna go in a new direction." A new direction without me, that is.

Well, I didn't take it well. I went underground; I was too emotional to talk to the media. Cathy handled the reporters for a few days, but she was just as pissed off as I was.

I called our owner. Gordon explained that it came down to communication. To start with, he'd made it a rule for himself to always respect the chain of command; except for very rare occasions, he would not talk to me. Harry had to do it. And he'd told Harry to tell me to play Keith Lee in a game with a team that wanted to trade for him. I didn't hear the request, or I ignored it, or a little of both. Anyway, I didn't play Lee a minute in that particular game. Gordon, looking like he had no control over his own team, reacted angrily. I have to admit that it made me feel slightly better when he told me he was firing Weltman, too, as soon as the season was over.

Lesson learned, more or less: get along with your GM.

About a day after I left Cleveland with fifteen games remaining in the season, I agreed to consult for the rest of the year for Milwaukee. That spring Milwaukee Bucks co-owners Jim Fitzgerald and Dan Finnane sold the team, bought another team, the Golden State Warriors, and hired me as coach. Nellie, the Milwaukee coach, was in the loop on all this, of course, and endorsed me for the job.

"George is a hard worker, a disciplinarian, and a very knowledgeable basketball man," Nellie told the media. "He's totally dedicated and consumed by the sport, like most of us wackos."

Consumed wackos—that seemed about right. Nellie and I looked at basketball the same way, in that we could hardly see anything else. We both liked to play fast and small and unpredictably. We both liked to hit the golf ball in the off-season. We both had starter beer guts.

Just before my second year with Golden State, Nellie was at the center of some very big and very unusual NBA news. He would be leaving the Bucks after coaching ten mostly successful years there to become a co-owner and vice president at Golden State. My new boss had my respect—he'd played on five championship teams at Boston, they'd retired his number, and he may have been the smartest, most strategic coach in the league. And he was my friend. What could go wrong?

Not much had gone wrong my first, pre-Nellie season at Golden State. It was a great year, smooth and successful, and it felt like redemption after the way things had ended in Cleveland. Since we had no GM, I had a lot of responsibility. Finnane and I made all the personnel calls. Yes, Chris Washburn distracted us for a while, but the other guys bought in. The aloof Joe Barry Carroll figured out how to deal with me and I with him. It wasn't easy. JB just antagonized my soul. He was a great player, but nothing that motivated me motivated him.

The Warriors had finished 30-52 the year before I got there, and fans stayed away from Oakland Coliseum Arena. But our arena filled up with very happy people when we improved to 42-40. Sleepy and JB made the Western Conference all-star team, and, as I mentioned, the team made the playoffs for the first time in a decade. It was my first year at Cleveland all over again, except that I had a great relationship with our GM, Jack McMahon. My assistants and I hoisted a few at Ricky's and discussed how we were going to beat the Utah Jazz in the first round of the playoffs.

Yes, *that* Utah, the one with John Stockton and Karl Malone, the best pick-and-roll guard and best forward ever. And they had a 7'4" center named Mark Eaton, who blocked every shot. They had the home court advantage. We were not favored. We lost Game One, we lost Game Two, and then I lost it.

"George Karl is going at a fan! George Karl is going at a fan! George Karl is going at a fan! Now George knocks him over!" shouted our TV play-by-play guy to the viewers back in the Bay. "George Karl has lost it and he has attacked a fan!"

Perhaps I should explain: our Greg Ballard and Malone got into it a little as Game Two ended. Karl threw the ball at Greg, and Greg threw it back, harder. Security wasn't very good, so a bunch of fans spilled out onto the floor along with every player and coach. Lots of shoving, a crazy, disorganized scene, including rehabbed Chris Washburn trading insults with Mark Eaton and having to be held back.

While I was trying to break up a scuffle, some dumbass in a backward white ball cap and a white golf shirt punched me in the back. I was already unhappy at the final score and now this! I turned around and charged. White hat guy backpedaled through the confusion of bodies and then Chris Mullin—not me— knocked the shit out of him. I didn't really lose it.

Now our team and our fans had emotion to burn—I stirred the pot a little bit in the media—and we won the next two games at home to tie. But no way could we win Game Five back in Salt Lake City. No NBA team had come back from two games down to win a five-game series since the Fort Wayne Pistons did it in 1956.

Our GM and I took in an Oakland A's game—their coliseum was across a parking lot from our arena—to talk about how we could do it. I told McMahon that I thought we should play slow and sloppy, to hang on them, to try to take away any crispness they might have in their offense.

The baseball game droned on. I think Jose Canseco or Mark McGwire hit a home run.

Then McMahon gave me a different idea. What I think you

should do, Jack said, is get our guys to feel that they can play *great*. I started pitching that idea to the team in practice the next day.

We flew to Utah. About an hour before the game, I saw their coach, Frank Layden, in the hall outside the locker rooms. Frank was a big, beefy man with a pink face and black-framed glasses and a head of thick, gray hair. He always had a New York–accented story or a joke to tell, and he was funny enough to do stand-up. People loved him. But now, as we shook hands, he made a little mistake.

"Don't worry about it, George," he said. "You guys had a great year."

I went straight into our locker room and told the team about Frank's condescending attitude and his verb tense.

"'*Had* a great year.' Those motherfuckers think they've already beaten you!"

I also told two of our older players, Purvis and Ballard, that they had earned the opportunity to make a little NBA history, and that they should "go playground" if that's what it took to make them feel relaxed. This was not a difficult speech to deliver, and it worked. We raced out to a 67–51 lead at the half and held on at the end. Move over, Fort Wayne.

Layden, incidentally, was very upset with me when he heard he'd supplied my motivational speech. He called it "high school-ish," and he didn't talk to me for two years. But I certainly don't regret it. It was an elimination game and what Frank said angered me and my players.

Not incidentally, Sleepy Floyd, Larry Smith, Purvis Short, and Joe Barry Carroll had played smart, passionate basketball. *That* is why we won.

Back in the Bay, we were heroes, at least until the next series. My assistants and I met again at Ricky's and drank happy beers while we plotted how to beat our opponent in the Western Conference semifinals. The Lakers.

George Karl Has Lost It!

Yeah, *those* Lakers, aka Showtime, the team with Magic Johnson, Kareem Abdul-Jabbar, and James Worthy, all three of whom are in the NBA Hall of Fame, and Byron Scott and Michael Cooper, who were damn good. The glitzy Lakers also had a Hall of Fame coach in Pat Riley. His playoff record after Game Three of our series was 63-27. Mine was 4-9.

We lost the first three, but we won Game Four: the famous Sleepy Game. Eric "Sleepy" Floyd went crazy, with 29 points in the fourth quarter and 39 in the second half. Fifty-five total.

Watching a tape of Game Five recently, I noticed how young and angry thirty-six-year-old me looked; how few threes we shot; that Bill "Mumbles" Russell was the TV color guy; and that the Laker Girls wore little purple skirts.

I started this elimination game with a carnation in my lapel but ended it flowerless, with my tie loosened and sideways, my shirt wrinkled, and my hair (I had hair) all over the place. The Lakers made everything and we fell behind by 20. They shot more than 40 free throws; we shot about 10. We had to press and trap to get back in the game, which gave Magic lots of open court to be magical in.

With the game out of reach and three minutes left, I put Washburn in. He'd been back from rehab since March but he was not in great shape. His shorts were so short and tight they looked like hot pants. We tricked Atlanta into taking him the next year. By which I mean we were willing to give him away. And we did, getting in return only the rights to Ken Barlow, a Notre Dame grad who never played in the NBA.

The only other highlight in the game was a fight. Purvis and Michael Cooper got tangled up under our basket in the second half. Coop got up off the floor and walked toward Purvis, who sensed a challenge and shoved their skinny guard in the shoulders. Cooper threw a right hand. Zing: a spike of adrenaline and rage made me the fastest guy on the floor. I was off the bench and in Cooper's face in about two seconds. In a different time and a different place, there's no doubt I would have popped him one. But all I really wanted was to tempt him to throw a punch at me and get thrown out.

He didn't.

———

Which leads us back to my sort-of violent pregame ritual, and my ritual and habits within the game.

I don't remember exactly when I started the mosh pit—I didn't do it at Cleveland or Golden State but I know the coaches hit each other in the early nineties in Seattle (although with a couple of the older assistants, I had to be careful). The tradition evolved from the pregame hip checks and elbows I've always given to my players. "You gonna rebound the ball tonight?" I'll say, and give my man a friendly forearm to the neck. I want our players to feel my excitement—and I just like being physical. The bumps and shoves in the scrum feel good, like they're a ground wire for all the electricity in my body.

A couple of times a year, I just don't feel anything before the game. That's when I'd turn to Tim Grgurich or Chad Forcier—two of the great assistants I've had—to pep-talk *me*. "We've worked our ass off to get here," Gurg will growl. "We're gonna play great! You're gonna coach great!"

Flushed and usually laughing, my assistants and I walk out into the arena. At home or on the road, I act like I own the place, but it's no act. The competition that's about to start turns me on, puts a little smile on my face. It's a game—in the playful sense of the word—and I love games. I'm also aware that I'm communicating with my team *every minute*. I want them to see a confident, competitive leader, not a frightened or concerned wimp of a coach. I guess I want the other team and its fans to see the same things.

There's loud music: "Rock and Roll (Part 1)" by Gary Glitter—the "Hey Song"—has been the pump-up-the-fans music for years.

I scan the arena for a moment, from the floor way up to the cheap seats at the top of the bowl. I'm observing in a sort of general, unfocused way; I don't look for friends and family I've gotten tickets for. I don't sit. I watch both teams shoot jumpers and layups for a few seconds, possibly getting a clue as to who is loose and who is tight. I often observe a misery-loves-company scenario at half-court between a couple of our bench players and a couple of theirs. "Yeah, I'm getting fucked, too," the minutes-deprived stars say to each other as the warm-up winds down. They hug or touch hands and go back to their teams. Two minutes.

A blanket of focus comes over me. If an assistant tells me, "Durant is limping a little bit," or whatever, the information registers, but just barely. Occasionally I wave to the opposing coach—Dwane Casey at Toronto, for example, who was an assistant for me—but it's far more natural for me to stay within the team and within myself. There are a few coaches I never say hello to. They're not my enemies, exactly, but I don't have to know or like everyone. Besides, we're rivals, and they are obstacles to my goal. There's a little insincerity in that wave to the other coach when you're really thinking, *You motherfucker!* One minute.

Sometimes someone from the other team will come by for a hug, for example, Devin Harris, who plays for Dallas, and who graduated from a kids' basketball program I started in Milwaukee.

The horn sounds. In the few seconds before they play the national anthem, I touch or tap every player, a habit I got from Coach Smith. It communicates, hopefully, that I care about them and that we're all in this together. We line up and stand at attention and everyone shifts their weight from one foot to the other while some music star or barbershop quartet goes from "Oh say can you see" to "and the home of the brave." "Rockets' red glare" cues a blast of fire in Houston. Their fans love it.

My heart rate spikes.

The road team is introduced first. Then the lights go down,

music comes up, the cheerleaders run out, and there's some sort of highlight video of the home team. Maybe some smoke and fireworks. I don't know the names of all the songs but I know I'm in Chicago when I hear "Sirius" by the Alan Parsons Project. In Dallas, it's "Eminence Front" by the Who, then "Welcome to the Jungle" by Guns N' Roses.

In the huddle before the tip, my last message is always simple. "Play hard, play smart, play together" is a favorite. So is "Hit first." Sometimes it's a little more inspirational, such as "We can beat these pussies!" Our hands—most of them—meet together in the middle. Thirty seconds.

I sit. I close my eyes and put my palms together in front of my face. I think I took this from Roberto Clemente. My thoughts during this quiet moment have changed over the years. Back in the day, I was mentally narrowing down my focus, concentrating on the battle to come. "We can't allow offensive rebounds. We can't foul their three-point shooters"—something like that. But nowadays my silent moment is more a meditation. I feel thankful—for basketball, for being a coach, for life. And I try to receive whatever message the building is sending. Sounds crazy, I know. But Staples in L.A. and Madison Square Garden in New York in particular give off a vibe and an energy I can feel. I like it.

I open my eyes, the game begins, and I realize for about the three thousandth time that the damn thing is mostly out of my hands. I can influence the outcome, of course, but I can't get a rebound or run down a loose ball.

The adrenaline in me goes away very quickly as soon as the game starts, giving way to a tingling intensity in my brain. My heartbeat slows; surveying and critiquing a basketball game is my expertise and my comfort zone. The players feel their kind of comfort, too, because our rotation is set. The first sub goes in with about five minutes left in the quarter, the second with about three minutes, and so on. Unless there's foul trouble or unusually good or bad individual results, the five starters and first three or four subs know what to expect.

While the ball is in play, only the head coach may stroll, pace, or lean against the scorers' table. Assistants can stand briefly to yell something to a player—"Harden's going left every time!"— but the strong tradition in basketball is that only the captain of the ship can walk on the deck.

I often lean against the padded scorers' table early in the game. I know I look impassive but I feel storms inside. I don't react to bad calls, missed shots, anything, because I don't want to make the first six minutes matter. I don't like the fool's gold of a big early lead. We try not to panic if they're making and we're missing as the game begins. I hate an early timeout, and I don't ever call one unless some motherfucker is playing really bad.

In fact, I don't like timeouts, period, but they come anyway. Besides the ones the coaches call, two mandatory TV timeouts each quarter stop the game in its tracks. As the players walk to the bench, we guys in ties walk out onto the floor without a word. If we've got someone who is screwing up badly, I send an assistant to talk to him.

We're not a chatty bunch out there. I look around, trying to decide what to say to the team and how to say it. An assistant might observe that we're settling for too many jump shots, and back up his assertion with statistics. But I don't care about stats during the game unless the data jibes perfectly with what I'm sensing. If my head and my heart match the analysis, then I'm in. Otherwise, it's not a road I will go down. Metrics, analytics—the new, impressive-sounding words for stats—are for slow games, like baseball and football. I coach instinctively and I don't want anything to interfere with that.

Full timeouts last a minute forty. Some coaches fill the entire time with helpful advice, but I'm not gonna talk that long, because players can't listen that long. I want to deliver a short, meaningful message—"Defend the three, even in transition"—and I want what I say to be the last thing they hear before they go back out on the floor. That way, there's no time for someone to disagree, to say, "Hey, that's bullshit. We need to focus on how we rotate off Robin Lopez."

If it's our ball, we call a play coming out of a timeout, something I think has a good chance of working but is a little unpredictable, because I know damn well that the other coach knows our tendencies. We'll run a screen they haven't seen, or post up a guard, or get the ball to someone who hasn't had enough shots. Players consider plays in which they shoot as "their" play, and they love to have their numbers called.

The game goes back and forth: ten players running and bumping, three refs trotting on the perimeter, and two coaches pacing. I sit more than I used to—bad knees and hips—and I mutter less. I search the game for clues. Among other things, I'm looking for rules violations. Our rules.

Our rules on offense:

Don't hold the ball—drive it, shoot it, or pass it, and do it NOW. No pump fakes: slow, elaborate fakes violate rule one.

Attack. Attack before the defense sets up, if possible.

Prioritize the shots. Option one is always the rim. Attacking the basket gets us a dunk, a layup, or a free throw. Shot option two is the wide-open three. The three from the corner is best, since it's closest (22 feet from the rim) but an open three from the farthest point on the arc (23 feet 9 inches) is preferable to option three, a two-point jump shot. I hate a contested two-point shot. Jumpers are for bailout, when nothing else is open and the shot clock is about to expire.

But lots of players and teams rely on jumpers or step-backs from inside the arc, and there are jump shooters in the NBA who can make 'em all night. LaMarcus Aldridge at San Antonio shoots from midrange better than anyone. Dirk Nowitzki of Dallas is another guy who has made his living inside the three-point line, but not close to the basket. LaMarcus and Dirk are great players and winners but a closely guarded two-point fadeaway is the last shot I want; the shooter doesn't get fouled much and you can't get a rebound because your body is going away from the hoop. I don't like offensive basketball that shies away from contact.

I was onto this five or six years ago. Shot selection is more important than ever, and players who select poorly are coming out of the game.

When we can't play fast, our offense is a combination of freedom, spacing, ball movement, and matchups. I've found that if you try to orchestrate everything, you freeze your players. They become reactive and lose their creativity. When I'm talking to high school or college coaches, my basic advice is always the same: let 'em play!

Our half-court offense is based on "sets" rather than plays. A set is a starting point, like a dribble handoff leading to a guard setting a screen—and that can lead to anything, from a layup to a three. I dislike the isolation play—four players on one side of the court, and one guy with the ball on the other. I don't like to watch it or coach it. It's stagnant, ugly, and four-fifths of the team isn't involved. Sometimes, like at the end of games, the iso is a necessary evil. And, sometimes, the iso was the only play that made Melo happy. That was a conflict.

Since we posted some fancy numbers during my years with Denver, I've been known as an offensive coach. But my heart is always with the defensive side. In fact, since I allow so much offensive freedom, I feel as if I've made a deal with the players: they can score the ball however they want to within our system, as long as they play their asses off when the other team has the ball.

"Laker Red!" I shout.

That's code for one of our defenses.

I love defense. I feel it's my end of the court, and the players have the other end. The most intimidating thing in basketball is not being able to score. I've had that only with one team: the Sonics.

How we defend depends on the types of players we have. I'd trap and switch everything with Gary Payton, who was quick and strong, but not with Andre Miller, who relies on anticipation. Mentioning Gary reminds me of our nasty, mad-dog D in Seattle in the nineties. Someone wrote that that team defended like dogs who'd marked their territory and abused anyone who came inside. Maybe we were like angry bees protecting the queen.

Defense is the insider's game, the part of the NBA aficionados talk about. When to switch and how to switch, who guards whom, man, zone, doubles, traps—defending from behind! (Coach Smith showed me that one, which can really mess with the ball handler's head)—every aspect of defensive basketball turns me on. That's another—probably boring—book.

Just as on offense, we've got a few rules, such as always pushing their pick-and-rolls away from the center of the floor, giving the other team less room to operate in. But more than anything, defense is emotional, and I'm an emotional coach. If you can defend, you can probably play for me.

Halftimes are similar to timeouts. They're for the players to rest and rehydrate, not for a long speech by me. I get my assistants' opinions about the game so far—what are they trying against us? What should we try against them? How are we going to take out their best player? Only after gathering this feedback do I have time to consider stats.

I look at pieces of paper with the basic stuff like rebounds and steals and assists and shooting percentage. Although I don't want to hear about synergy rankings or offensive efficiency rating, sometimes some subtle stuff can be interesting: maybe five out of LeBron James's seven baskets came when he dribbled left three times then pulled up for a jump shot.

For years before it became a tool everyone uses, I looked hard at plus-minus, which is simply how the team did while each individual was on the floor. All the numbers are food for thought, but I usually spit 'em out. As I said, no stat is more important than what I feel. Intangibles like emotion are more important than the nerd game of metrics. It's why the statistically better team often doesn't win.

Halftime gives me a chance to refer to our goals for the game, which we've written on a dry-erase board. "Win" is not a goal. But achieving each game's goals should put us in a position to win.

Our goals are almost always defensive. For example: 20 touches. Defenders don't always have to steal the ball or block it; just getting a hand on it—a touch—disrupts their offense. I borrowed the idea of written objectives, by the way, from Don Bassett, a legendary New York high school coach who was my assistant at my second CBA job (more on that later) in Albany.

"We're behind because of our shot selection," I might say. "Too many hard twos.

"Unless you want to run your goddamn asses off tomorrow at ten, you'd better make better passing decisions, and work a lot harder to get open."

A comment like that refers to my get-out-of-practice bribe. If at the end of the game we've got 30 assists, 30 free throws, and 30 layups or dunks, we get a little reprieve. If we get 30-30-30, we're attacking and we're passing. We still practice if we hit that mark, but it's not "taped." That is, we don't run or hit so ankles don't need to be reinforced.

I might make one more major point before we leave the locker room, but that's it. You can't present a massive amount of information. I follow Bill Belichick on this: the New England Patriots coach never gives his team more than three things to think about on either side of the ball.

We walk back into the arena. No punching.

"Foul! That's a foul, goddammit!"

My psychological warfare with referees ratchets up a couple of notches in the second half. I'm trying to get in their heads, trying to make them think twice about whistles against my team. I can intimidate and dominate some people in certain situations, so I try to use that skill—if that's what it is. Sometimes I look so furious people think I'm out of control but I'm not. I pick my spots. I know each ref's personality and what I can get away with. I've found that I don't usually get a technical if I frame my comment in the form of a question, like I'm on *Jeopardy!* "Why can't you call it both ways? How can we play if you're so inconsistent?" If they've just missed a big call, and they know it, I can get away with a little more.

Of course, all the fines and techs I've gotten prove that I don't always know where the line is. Bennett Salvatore threw me out of a game in which we were ahead by 30 and it was my four hundredth win.

One ref referred to me as "a virtuoso of verbal intimidation" and named two point guards who played for me, and took cues from me—Gary Payton and Chauncey Billups—as two of his five least favorite players in the league.

That ref was Tim Donaghy, who resigned in 2007 after being caught betting on NBA games. He did fifteen months in prison, then he wrote a book—*Personal Foul*—that everyone in the league read. Donaghy confirmed what I think we all knew: refs are human. They're supposed to look and act like impartial judges in the bright arena and on TV, but they make calls based on emotion and they hold grudges (just look up Tim Duncan versus Joey Crawford and Allen Iverson versus Steve Javie).

I don't want a grudge held against me, but the coach has to hold the refs responsible; who else will do it? So when I perceive that a ref is being intimidated by their coach or their superstar, I try to add my own intimidation. Sometimes you'll get an official with a creative personality, someone who wants to be the lead actor in the drama on the floor. I can't do much with those guys except ask them if they took acting lessons.

Maybe I shouldn't talk. Sometimes I have to act, too. When one of my players bitches about a call very angrily, I have to get up and yell and rant, too, whether I saw the play or not. I'm both supporting my guy and distracting the ref enough so that he doesn't give my player a technical foul. A few times I've exaggerated my outrage in order to get a tech that will stop the game, or two techs, which automatically gets me thrown out. The purpose of this showboating, of course, is to inspire the team—I know if I simultaneously violate NBA Rule #12, Section V, parts d (1)—disrespectfully addressing an official, (3)—overt actions indicating resentment to a call, and (4)—use of profanity—I can usually get tossed. But if I ever believed in getting purposely thrown out, I don't now. I don't think it works.

One thing that's always chapped my ass is the superstar call— which is the ref looking at who before what. Fame and reputations get (or got) certain players sweetheart treatment from the refs. As my daughter says, no duh.

The classic example is Michael Jordan pushing off against Bryon Russell to hit the game winner in Game Six of the 1998 NBA Finals. I mean—just look at the tape. If it had been Russell throwing out his left arm at Jordan, it's an offensive foul. Masters of defense probably get away with the most shit; I'm thinking about Bruce Bowen, the human flypaper for the Spurs a few years ago.

Losing combined with superstar calls brings out the conspiracy theorist in everyone, including me.

At times I've felt as if the refs were tilting the game away from me. I've left the floor saying, "What the hell just happened?"

In the 1992–93 Western Conference Finals, it was the Sonics (my team) versus the Suns, with the winner going to the finals against Jordan and the Bulls. We were a great defensive team, but they had a great actor in their point guard Kevin Johnson. Academy Award winner for flopping. We're friends now but . . . throughout the series, KJ exaggerated contact so much and so well that I referred to him in my interviews as "the Princess." In Game Seven, the refs got out of hand. I've asked a lot of knowledgeable people what they think would be an outrageous number of foul shots. The average per team in an NBA game is 20 to 25, so the most any owner, coach, or GM has ever guessed is 50. But in that game, *the Suns shot 64 free throws.* Charles Barkley shot 22. Twenty-two! I called bullshit on that, loudly and repeatedly. We lost the game by 13 because they beat us by 30 points on free throws. It seemed that some cosmic force wanted a Barkley versus Jordan final.

Back to the game:

I don't obsess about the refs like I used to, and I don't taunt them like I used to. I'm busy noticing that our opponent is playing more zone in the second half or they're playing smaller or they're not switching on the high pick-and-roll—or whatever. I study their adjustments to us and analyze our adjustments to them.

When Nellie used to go small against me—with three guards in the game, or four—I'd always go even smaller.

I watch my team closely for mental mistakes and for defenders who are suddenly a step too slow. I break our rotation if someone looks tired or if his body language isn't positive. And if someone is going really well, he stays in longer than usual.

Someone has compared NBA coaching to a chess game but it's more like two or three chess games at the same time, and with ten pieces that never stop moving and almost no time to think about the next move.

From watching hours of video of every team, and from amazingly thorough scouting reports, I know—or I think I know—each team's strategies, strengths and weaknesses, the plays their coach calls out of timeouts, their inbounds plays, where all ten players like to shoot from and if they can create their own shot, whom to foul if we need a missed free throw, and which of their players will take a big shot and which will always avoid it. Meanwhile, the music is loud and the fans are raising hell. I was never fearful as a player but as a coach, I've felt all kinds of weird emotions near the end of a game. There's a lot of pressure and the stakes are high.

But I cope. When fear and paranoia visit me, I don't treat them like they are real. I just put 'em in a little mental box and store them away. I can compartmentalize. I think well when there's chaos and confrontation.

If I feel indecisive, that's my signal to simplify our plan, and to sell it diligently to the team. When we're in crisis mode, there are never not some f-bombs in the huddle.

"Nene!"

I substitute by simply looking down the bench and yelling the player's name. There's no need to tell the sub who he is going in for; he knows. And I'm not whispering advice—"get a rebound!"— because he knows what I want. The player coming out rarely gets a word or even a glance. If you need an attaboy all the time for doing your job, you're playing for the wrong coach.

"Sam!"

Most of my in-game coaching—during a dead ball or a free throw—involves our quarterback, our point guard. Usually I remind him of what's working and what's not. As I said, I'm not that big on plays—we follow principles of ball movement and spacing to generate our offense, not a lot of programmed and rehearsed patterns, like a football team—but when Ty Lawson or Chauncey Billups or Gary Payton or Sam Cassell or Andre Miller or Rajon Rondo turned toward the bench with a "What the hell should we do?" look, I was always ready with a hand signal. For example, three fingers pointed to the floor means "three down," a play for our three (small forward) to get the ball close to the basket.

John Wooden said he coached as if the score didn't matter. I doubt that he really did, but I get his point: that good basketball is good basketball. But I'd never coach that way and I want the players to know the score. The scoreboard can be a powerful motivator.

Another coach I watched was Chuck Daly with his Bad Boy Detroit Pistons teams. He did an excellent job. The NBA was a physical game in the late 1980s. Their big guys did all the banging, all the dirty work, and their guards did all the scoring. He had great guards: Joe Dumars, Isiah Thomas, and Vinnie Johnson. Their offense wasn't perfect but they figured out how to beat you with a balance between offense and defense. Chuck used his personnel intelligently and got the most out of them.

———

H i, Doris."
Since 2007–08, in nationally broadcast games, NBA coaches are required to answer two questions on live TV. The coach of the visiting team talks at the end of the first quarter, and the home coach does it before the start of the fourth quarter. Most of us don't want to have our concentration broken. I don't mind talking with Doris Burke or David Aldridge or whoever, but Pop—Gregg Popovich—hates the interview so much he often gives one-word answers. Sideline reporters dread talking with him.

I remember when the league was negotiating a new TV deal, and ESPN and TNT wanted more access to the locker room and the huddle, and that in-game interview. We—the coaches and the suits—had a thirty-minute discussion about it at the league office in New York. We all said, no way, we're not doing it, it's too disruptive, and the players will feel that they're onstage. Pop and Phil were particularly adamant. "The locker room is sacred ground," said Phil, but our commissioner didn't want to hear it.

"Not another fucking word," said David Stern. "ESPN and TNT are going to give us one billion dollars a year. You're doing the goddamn interviews." By the way, our new TV deal is worth about $2.6 billion a year; each of our thirty teams get one-thirtieth, or about $88 million.

Sometimes I coach against the other coach. It's action/reaction against Pop and the Spurs. He plays a card, and I try to trump it. Some coaches are very close to the vest, and never open up and do anything crazy, but I like to wheel and deal. Play with two point guards? *Three?* I'll try anything. In fact, three point guards is pretty cool. That's three decision makers when you can't afford a mistake with the ball.

Lub-dub, lub-dub. As a close game goes deep into the fourth quarter, my heartbeat is hard in my chest, back to its pregame peak level. I'm coaching my ass off—stopping the clock with fouls if we're behind, substituting, responding to their subs, and calling plays and defenses. Near the end of close games, when it's almost as hard to complete a pass as to make a basket, I've sometimes told our best one-on-one player that he might have to be selfish. In other words, shoot the ball.

Suppose for a moment you're the coach, and you're up three games to two in a best-of-seven playoff. You're up by three points with a couple of seconds left and the ball is in their best player's hands—quick, what do you do? You foul the shooter before he can shoot, you idiot!

I failed this exact test in the 1983 CBA Finals against the Detroit Spirits. We didn't foul Tico Brown, a skinny guard from Kokomo, Indiana, who'd been burning us all night, and he made the three to tie. We lost the game, and then the next game, and the series, because I didn't think clearly enough under pressure.

Not that fouling the three is that easy. Players are clever at throwing up their hands as if they're shooting even when they're not and refs are often fooled. The timing of the foul has to be precise. Foul too late, and their guy gets three free throws, or a chance at a four-point play if he made the shot. Foul too early—before the ball has been inbounded—and it's a dead ball foul. They get two foul shots *and the ball*, so now they're throwing in with the same time on the clock, and they're probably shooting a two or a three to win, not tie.

There are scores of situations like this that require the coach to make a decision. But the bounce of the ball is just as important as tactics and strategy. I'm amazed at the knowledge many fans have but I'm more amazed that they don't respect the luck in games.

For example: In the first round of the playoffs in 1997, we—the Sonics again—were down two games to one to the Suns, at their arena. They had a side out of bounds forty feet from the basket with 4.9 seconds left; we had a three-point lead. Obviously, they were going to shoot a three, but I felt good about having Gary Payton and Hersey Hawkins defending their best shooters, Wesley Person and Rex Chapman. We guessed correctly that they wanted to try a corner three with Person off a pick and we shut that down. They barely got the ball inbounds in time, to Chapman, who was running toward the opposite side of the court with Hawk all over him. Chapman turned and threw up a prayer from thirty feet, a rainbow shot you might try if you were ahead in a game of H-O-R-S-E. He made it. It was a great shot and it was very lucky. Should we have fouled? We went on to win the game, and the series, so I haven't asked that question very much.

And what about Game Six in the NBA Finals in 2012? With a couple of seconds left and a three-point lead, the Spurs were about to win the championship. Miami inbounded. Should Pop have fouled? He didn't. I think he should have. After LeBron missed a three, the ball bounced just right for Chris Bosh to rebound and throw in one motion to Ray Allen in the corner. Allen shot, time expired, the ball went in. The Heat won in OT, and then won Game Seven. It was a great clutch shot by a great shooter.

But it was also luck beyond the reach of the coach or the players. San Antonio was the better team, but Miami got the ring. It's a round ball hitting a round rim. But the damn thing bounces so randomly. And referees can't be predicted.

When I get beat by a lucky shot or a bad call, I walk off the floor just trying not to punch anyone.

Money

SALARY	YEAR	JOB
$35,000 to $50,000	1973—78	player, San Antonio Spurs
$25,000 signing bonus		
$12,000	1979—80	scout, Spurs
$18,000	1981—83	coach, Great Falls Golden Nuggets (only about $5,000 was actually paid in year one)
$45,000	1983	player personnel director, Cleveland Cavaliers
$85,000	1984—86	head coach, Cavs
$225,000	1986—88	head coach, Golden State
$60,000	1988—89	head coach, Albany Patroons
$200,000	1989—90	head coach, Real Madrid (plus rent on condo, a car, and taxes)
$90,000	1990—91	head coach, Albany
$250,000	1991—92	head coach, Real Madrid
$300,000—?	1992—98	head coach, Seattle SuperSonics
$5 to $7 million	1998—2003	head coach, Milwaukee Bucks
$3 to $4.5 million	2005—13	head coach, Denver Nuggets
$4 million	2015—	head coach, Sacramento Kings

Weight

AGE		POUNDS
17	high school	175
20	college	185
25	NBA player	195
30	scout	205
32	coach, Great Falls	220
34	coach, Cleveland	240
42	coach, Seattle	260
48	coach, Milwaukee	280
55	coach, Denver	295
60	coach, Denver	230
64	coach, Sacramento	245

The All North Carolina NBA Team

Sam Perkins

Michael Jordan

Bob McAdoo

Bobby Jones

Brad Daugherty

Five Best Players I Coached Against

Michael Jordan

Larry Bird

Magic Johnson

LeBron James

John Stockton

Five Best Players I Coached

Gary Payton

Shawn Kemp

Ray Allen

Detlef Schrempf

(Do I have to?) Carmelo Anthony

Five Best NBA Coaches I Battled

Gregg Popovich

Jerry Sloan

Larry Brown

Jack Ramsay

(Do I have to?) Phil Jackson

CHAPTER 5

SWITCH EVERYTHING

The cautious seldom err.

—CONFUCIUS

In 1993–94, *the* season Michael Jordan temporarily retired from the Bulls to try his hand at baseball, we—the Seattle SuperSonics—were without doubt the best team in the NBA. We had a mad-dog defense, swagger speed, and the hardest dunker in history. We had a little discord on our team but still we won 63 of our 82 games and the first seed in the playoffs. Denver, our first-round opponent, won about as many as they lost, and crawled in as the number eight seed.

A guy named Brian Williams was their backup center. Naturally, we studied his game.

Their starting center, Dikembe Mutombo, a 7'2" Congolese, was a fantastic defender, but he couldn't do anything with the ball except dunk it, so he wasn't hard to prepare for. Block his ass out, I told our bigs during practice; make him catch it at least six feet from the hoop. But his backup, Williams, had a lot of offense: a nice jump hook with either hand, and a left-handed jumper that he shot from way over his head, making it hard to get a hand on it. Good defender. He could block a shot, too.

Williams got traded a lot, playing in five cities in his eight years in the NBA, a high number for a good player. I was dimly aware that in 1992, after his rookie year with Orlando, he'd tried to kill himself with sleeping pills. A few years later, he changed his name to Bison Dele. A friend described him as angry and frustrated. That sounds right: we competed against him a couple of times a year and I never saw him smile. He had a tragic end, as you may know: confirmation is difficult because his body was never found but authorities believe his brother murdered him on a boat sailing near Tahiti.

What was wrong with Bison Dele/Brian Williams? I had a player on my team with the same unhappy face, and I couldn't figure him out, either. Kendall Gill's joyless approach to basketball drove me crazy. His darkness affected everyone, and he didn't seem to like anyone—especially me. We argued about minutes, we argued about attitude. I taunted him a little, called him Pretty Boy, just trying to get anything out of him other than that scowl. I thought he was a bad apple; he thought I was a fool, and that I was picking on him because of his $3.8 million salary. A couple of years after we traded him, Kendall spoke with the *New York Times* about how miserable he'd been with the Sonics: "I felt that the next time I saw George I was going to do something to him. That's how furious I was. He's the only person in the world I have a serious dislike for."

When Kendall said he felt so bad mentally he couldn't play, I was incredulous. He can't play because he's in a bad mood? The team lied and announced that he suffered from migraine headaches. The doctors told us he had clinical depression. What the hell is that? Unfortunately, I was as uninformed about mental illness as I had been about cocaine back at Golden State. Winston Churchill, Abraham Lincoln, Mark Twain, and Ernest Hemingway were depressives, but I didn't know that then. Kendall got no sympathy or understanding from me.

But it wasn't just me. Despite being the most racially inclusive and tolerant sports league in the world, the NBA had blind spots. In our macho game played and coached by macho men, homosexuality and mental illness were two things no one discussed. Even now, a clinical depression diagnosis is treated as a slightly shameful thing, when it should be no more embarrassing than a groin pull or plantar fasciitis.

Lately, some people in sports have been brave enough to admit that they've been treated for mood disorders—announcer and former Steelers quarterback Terry Bradshaw, for example, and NBA players Delonte West and Ron Artest (aka Metta World Peace). And in 2013, near the end of his thirteen-year NBA career, Jason Collins became the first openly gay player in any of the four big American sports. Support was widespread throughout the league, including from me. I think Jason Collins opened some doors and opened some minds. Maybe we've evolved a little bit.

But the only thing on my mind in April 1994 was the playoffs. We were going to win the championship, but we had to get past Denver first. Best of five.

———

I'd had to overcome some prejudice and bias myself. I don't want to put my struggle on par with Brian Williams/Bison Dele or Jason Collins, but I had a four-year period when my NBA reputation was lower than whale shit.

People took unfair shots at me, writing and saying that I could inspire a team for one year, but then my gung ho style wore thin, and the players tuned me out. I read that I had a drinking problem, which was news to me. Damn right I liked to have a beer and a laugh, or a few beers and a few laughs—but a problem? A friend even asked if I was going into rehab.

Even though certain parts of that take on me were reasonable, the whole of it simply wasn't true. In Cleveland, I inherited a team so bad its own fans called it the Cadavers, but I coached it into the playoffs, and almost beat the defending NBA champions in the first round. Then, in my second year with the Cavs . . .

Golden State hired me almost the moment I became available. The Warriors had done nothing but lose since Rick Barry retired in 1978, but suddenly we won, and even won a playoff series against a team with the home court advantage. Then, in my second year with the Warriors . . .

That season began strangely. In the summer of 1987, Nellie re-signed at Milwaukee and came to Golden State to be my boss and mentor and to improve our personnel. The media wondered why the best coach in the NBA—Nelson—would move into adminis-tration. Sometimes I wondered, too.

There was this cloud of uneasiness hanging over the team. It wasn't just the very unusual situation with Nellie seemingly on deck, waiting for me to fail. I'm talking about Joe Barry Carroll, our biggest asset and best player. I think we all acknowledged that he and I could not coexist. To top off the weirdness: guess who was the best player on the court in the preseason? Yep: Chris Washburn. Not that he'd become dependable.

So Nellie began the tricky work of rebuilding our team. But our judgment was bad and our luck was worse. We traded Pur-vis Short, our leading scorer from the previous year, for a non-scorer named Dave Feitl. We'd exchanged 19 points a game for 6 and a few rebounds—bad idea. Terry Teagle, a shooting guard who'd played in every game the year before, missed almost half our games with injuries. We released Greg Ballard, a bench player I trusted. Larry Smith, our best rebounder, popped a hamstring that wouldn't fully heal. He bounced back and forth between injured reserve and playing and then he was out for the season. With those hits to scoring, rebounding, and the bench, it was a miserable feeling but no surprise to be slogging along at 3-15 in mid-December. We'd just gone down the tubes.

Switch Everything

Then a very big trade became available that was going to solve all our problems. The Rockets would take Sleepy Floyd and Joe Barry Carroll for Ralph Sampson and Steve Harris. I voted yes—bye, JB!—and we did the deal.

Remember Sampson? He'd torn up college ball at the University of Virginia and had been the college player of the year three times, the only time that's happened. In 1983–84, he'd been the NBA's Rookie of the Year by unanimous vote. Sampson had been on the Rockets team that made the NBA Finals for the 1985–86 season. And in Game Five he'd taken a swing at Celtics guard Jerry Sichting. Which I kind of liked. He was a unique player, a 7'4" guy with handles, but he was fragile. Maybe we should have kicked the tires a little more.

"This is your team," I told Ralph when he arrived. "We will build around you."

But he got hurt right away. Knees, back.

So: no Sampson, or not much of him. Harris was okay but he averaged less than half of Sleepy's 20 points a game. It got worse. The day after we made the deal for Ralph, one of our starters missed practice for the second time in a month. I loved Chris Mullin, his game and his dedication to the gym, but no one can blow off practice like that. That was a Thursday. Nellie suspended Chris for the game on Friday. On Saturday, Chris came forward, told us he had a drinking problem, and that he'd be entering rehab. Shit, not again . . .

Without Sleepy or JB or Sampson or Purvis or Smith or Mullin (for 22 games), or Teagle (for 35 games), our talent level sank low. We'd lost four of our top five scorers from the year before. We couldn't defend, either. We were giving up 115 points a game, making us about the worst defensive team in the league. As you know, I always want the *best* defensive team in the league. Injuries and bad trades were killing us; I hadn't forgotten how to coach. To say I was frustrated and angry is an understatement.

A writer saw Nellie run out onto our practice court one day to give Washburn hell about something, and speculated that he'd intruded into my territory, but I took no offense. I had no problem with Nellie as my boss, until the very end.

But the losing . . . that was a big problem. Just like I'd done in Cleveland, I'd stick my foot in my mouth, say the wrong thing at the wrong time. "Why can't you get me some players?" or "Why can't *they* get me some players?"—that sort of thing. I could imagine our front office people saying to themselves, *Why do we have to put up with this shit?*

I just wish someone had managed me, like a coach or GM does with a talented player. A young NBA coach needs weekly, maybe even daily, help from an experienced guy. Dean Smith couldn't do it with a few letters and phone calls a year. McMahon was on the road all the time. Our owners, Dan Finnane and Jim Fitzgerald, also could have helped my attitude and my approach a lot, but they didn't.

Fitzgerald said to me once, "You're the only guy I know in the league who is not here to make money." I took it as a compliment, but now I realize it was an insult. He meant that I didn't understand Rule One: the NBA is a business. Money, PR, and getting along with people matters. The NBA is not all basketball, although I wish it was.

In March, I was reminded of the importance and the depth of owner involvement. Fans and the media think the background owner is ideal, the fossil who just signs the checks and lets the GM and the coach run his team. I don't know what's ideal, but I do know that's not the way it works.

Back in the day, groups bought NBA franchises to have a team their community could rally around. Now the owners are billionaires, and as someone said to me, millionaires listen but billionaires don't have to. Today's billionaire owners know *everything* about their investment, and they make every big decision and a lot of smaller ones. It's not hard to see why.

Switch Everything

They pay their key performers millions of dollars each to win games. Wins cause money to flow—tickets, parking, concessions, T-shirt sales—and increase the value of the investment. Based on recent history, an NBA franchise is worth as much as $2 billion (which is what former Microsoft CEO Steve Ballmer paid Donald Sterling for the Clippers). No matter how big an owner's yacht is and how many companies he owns, he's keeping track of $2 billion. The stakes are too high for him to sit back. None of them do, as far as I know.

So it wasn't unusual when I took a meeting in San Francisco with Finnane and Fitzgerald. We talked at a conference table in some small boutique hotel across the street from the Hyatt. As usual, Dan was the formal one, covering all the bases, while Jim was relaxed and friendly. For an hour or so we sat around and discussed the Golden State Warriors Basketball Club Inc.

Then the conversation took a turn I didn't expect and wasn't ready for: my future with the team. It didn't go well for me; I had no allies in the room. A young coach of a losing team is going to be looking over his shoulder, but what made things worse for me, I told our owners, was the feeling that everyone—including them—wanted Nellie to coach. No, that's not true, they said.

True or not, I was asked to resign, but it was a firing. Ed Gregory, one of my assistants, was going to coach the final eighteen games of the season. I signed off on a face-saving press release, which said, in part, "the pressures of losing combined with personal frustrations led to my decision." Which was not my decision at all.

Fitzgerald rode the elevator down to the lobby with me. He told a reporter that I looked like I was relieved that I could wash my hands of a miserable season. Wrong; that wasn't relief, it was amazement turning to anger.

It wasn't like I'd lost control of the team or that we'd lost our direction. We just didn't have any players. Whose fault was that?

Fire *that* guy—Nelson or Al Attles or Jack McMahon (or Chris Washburn). The rumor everywhere was that I'd been eased out so that Nellie could coach the Warriors.

Nellie acted innocent. He told the press that I'd asked for a contract extension during my meeting with the owners. Which is crap. I just wanted any sort of gesture from them that they weren't about to replace me with my mentor. The team announced that Nellie would be in charge of the search for my replacement. Ten days later, Nellie had his man: himself. Maybe he established a precedent.

In 1996, when the Spurs told their GM, Gregg Popovich, to find someone to replace Bob Hill, the coach he found was Gregg Popovich. I think Dick Cheney did the same thing when George W. Bush asked him to head the search committee for a vice president.

I felt shocked and empty at being fired again, being steamrolled again by politics, and by the lack of support from a friend and ally. *This is a hard way to make a living,* I thought. Great money, but no security, and no stability, and long, frequent absences from the wife and kids. And when I picked up the paper or turned on the radio or TV, my ego got bruises on top of the "you're fired" bruise.

After months of moping and taking hits, I called Coby Dietrick, my former Spurs teammate and my best friend, who'd returned to his home in Southern California when his career as a player ended. We agreed to meet at his parents' beach house in Oxnard, just south of Santa Barbara. We played a little golf, drank a lot of beer, sat in the sand, and watched the sunset on the Pacific Ocean.

"What the hell do I do now?" I asked.

"You're a coach," Coby said. "So coach. What else are you going to do?"

"The CBA again?"

"I don't know, George. Just coach. It's who you are."

Knowing who you are is an important principle to me. Too many people and too many teams waste time attempting to be something or someone they're not. So, yes, I was a coach, I knew that. But in the previous seven years I'd proved to myself that I was a *head* coach of a *professional* team. Therefore, I knew I didn't want the options open to me—assistant for another NBA team or a college job. Even though the Warriors owed me $300,000 for the final year of my contract, not working was not an option. I gotta work.

Finally, I got my balance back and lost that defeated feeling. I was going to take Coby's advice: I would go coach—somewhere. I would win games and educate myself and get better. I made some phone calls.

In the next couple of days, Phil Jackson and I intersected, not for the last time. As I was leaving the NBA, Phil would be re-entering it. After five years of coaching the Albany Patroons of the CBA, Phil had been hired as an assistant to Doug Collins at Chicago. The owner of the Patroons called to see whom I could recommend to replace Jackson.

I said, "What about me?"

"What?!"

Gary Holley had a little trouble believing I'd do it.

I'd be reuniting with Albany GM Gerald Oliver, a great guy I knew from our days together at Cleveland. Ollie was a round-faced guy from Knoxville with so much Tennessee in his voice that he sounded a little rural. But he was no rube. He had a master's in math from the University of Tennessee and he knew basketball so deeply he might have been a genius.

Ollie got a little emotional when I told him I might coach his team. "Oh my, my," he said. "George. Goddamn! Would you really?"

I would, even though it made no financial sense and there was no precedent for it. Fired NBA coaches get back on the merry-go-round, making several times as much as a CBA head coach while waiting for another shot. A very few of us go into television. But *no one* goes down to the minors.

Why did I do exactly that? I could get away with it, for one thing: as usual, Cathy supported the move. And this was me being aware of who I really was, and being bold enough to act on it. I know it's become cliché to quote Rudyard Kipling's "If," but I've always loved that poem. In part, it's about taking risks:

If you can make one heap of all your winnings
And risk it all on one turn of pitch-and-toss
And lose, and start again at your beginnings
And never breathe a word about your loss . . .

For someone who'd been feeling second-guessed, as I was, the Patroons and the CBA were just about perfect. My NBA credentials plus my assertive style made me as powerful as a coach can be. There was no whining, no entitlement, no laziness. If I didn't like someone or his game, I told Ollie to find me someone else. And the players saw me as the conduit to what they wanted, so they worked hard.

We played our home games in the Washington Avenue Armory, built in 1890, capacity 3,600. It was red bricks and a copper-covered steeple outside, and dark and dingy and jammed with people inside. That was another building that spoke to me. I loved it.

But it was the CBA, not the NBA. Toy basketball night shows the difference.

We were in a college gym in Wichita Falls, Texas, to play a late-season game against the Texans. The home team gave away orange, grapefruit-sized mini-basketballs to the first few thousand fans. It was a big game and a full house. When we pulled out to a good lead in the fourth quarter, the inevitable happened. The ref called a foul on them and the angry crowd booed. When we lined up for the free throw, someone threw a ball onto the floor. A few more joined the first, and then there were a hundred balls in the air, and then thousands. "Let's go!" I said, and ran to the locker room with the team close behind. It was like being inside a snow globe. It didn't hurt, but we all got pelted.

Follow the bouncing ball: after a year in Albany (we went 36-18) we went to Madrid. You'll remember what happened there early in that year, when the sudden death of Spanish basketball's folk hero, Fernando Martin Espina, threw us all for a loop. Our point guard, Antonio Martin Espina, Fernando's brother—who'd insisted we play a game while there were still tears in our eyes—lost thirty pounds but kept playing hard. They were dedicating gyms to Fernando wherever we played. After that crazy but ultimately successful year of *baloncesto* in the Palacio, our GM, Ramon Mendoza, was fired—along with everyone he had ever hired, which included me.

They'd kept the door open for me at Albany, so for the 1990–91 season I was back in upstate New York. We went 50-6—the best record ever in pro basketball, unless you want to count the Globetrotters. Our .893 winning percentage beat the .841 of the 1971–72 Lakers (Wilt) *and* the .878 the Bulls (Michael) would have in 1995–96.

50-6.

I'd like to pause for a moment here and just say that number again: 50-6. How do you go 50 and 6? With great coaching—of course!—and with Gerald Oliver.

We weren't very good in training camp but Ollie worked the system and found three very good players whom the NBA would be a little slow in calling up: Mario Elie, Vince Askew, and Albert King. Terry Stotts started as my assistant but wound up as a player and a starter. And we clicked. We won our first 16 games, and our last 16 games. We were undefeated on our home court—the new Knickerbocker Arena, a modern building with luxury suites and 15,000 seats.

We celebrated *a lot* of home wins at our off-campus headquarters. I can't remember its name; some dark place with beer and wings. New York bars are open until 4 a.m. Not good for me.

At the end of our season, Nellie called to ask if I'd come out to Golden State to be their advance scout. No hard feelings? Well . . . I thanked him but declined. It would take me a few more years to get over what had happened with the Warriors.

Real Madrid called again. I was aware that they'd had a miserable time after my season with them. The RM GM, Señor Mendoza (give it the Castilian pronunciation: *Then yore Men doe tha*) was back in power, but I wasn't that keen to work with him again. He didn't exactly have my back in my first year in Madrid. I kept hearing whispers that he wanted to replace me with Wayne Brabender, a naturalized American who'd played for the club. I confronted Mendoza and he confirmed that he was behind the rumor. I told him how fucked up that was. His answer was to ask me to hire Brabender as an assistant.

"No," I said in Spanish.

And we kept winning, so El Señor couldn't fire me.

Cups—we'd call them tournaments—are the big deal in European basketball. We won two of the biggest, the Spanish Cup and the European Cup.

After I left for the 50-6 year in Albany, they hired Brabender, but he didn't win and they fired him quickly. A few months later, Brabender's replacement, Ignacio Pinedo, had an *infarto miocardio* (heart attack) during a game. He fell into a coma and died. They wanted me back, and Cathy and the kids wanted to go, so we went.

But something had changed. The fact that my name was still mud in the NBA had put me in a bad mood, and I didn't trust *Men doe tha*. And I got into a very adverse, angry relationship with the media. In Europe, if you're not winning every game, newspapers and TV talk about getting rid of the coach—that was annoying. And the writers' extreme homerism and anti-American tone only added to our conflict. The tension got very high and I got a little paranoid. I thought there might be a fight or two but that never happened.

Maybe going back to Spain had been just one move too many. San Antonio, Great Falls, Cleveland, Oakland, Albany, Madrid, Albany again, Madrid again . . . eight addresses in eleven years. Following me around took a toll on my family.

I can see better now how my ambition ruled our world. Although both my kids look back fondly on the piece of their childhood they spent in Spain, we'd been uprooted too much, and we were not growing together so much as just surviving. My idea of a vacation was taking everyone to a basketball camp. I'm sure I had mixed-up priorities at times and hurt my family with my absences and preoccupation. I think I was beginning to see that back then.

On New Year's Eve 1991, we went out to dinner at a Chinese restaurant near the Edificio España, a giant hotel. I told Cathy, our nine-year-old daughter, Kelci, and our son, Coby, five, that when the season was over, I would resign and we'd move back to the States. I'd try to get some stability in our lives by taking a college job. I'd learn how to recruit, how to coach twenty-year-olds, and how to run a study hall.

A few days later, Jerry Krause, the Bulls' GM, came to get my opinions about Toni Kukoc and Arvydas Sabonis, two Euro players he was scouting. That was about the only contact I had had with the NBA. Why hadn't I heard from the friends I'd thought I'd made in the league? Why wasn't I at least rumored to be someone's new head coach? What else did they need to see to let me back in? My combined record in Spain at that moment was 47-20. My combined record for my four years in exile: 133-44. Pretty good, but the phone didn't ring. Then it did.

Two weeks after that dinner and the decision to go back home, Bob Whitsitt called. I'm pretty sure Krause *had* endorsed me. The Seattle GM asked if I'd be interested in being an assistant to their coach, K. C. Jones, for $100,000. I might be interested, I said, but first I'd like to know if K.C. wants *me*. Whitsitt called back a day later with K.C.'s answer: no. The Sonics were a good, young team whose record defined mediocrity: they'd won exactly as many games as they'd lost in a year and a half under K.C. Whitsitt probably wanted me to bring a little spark. End of story, I thought.

Ten days later, Seattle fired K.C., and now Whitsitt was on the phone asking if I'd like to talk about a much bigger, better job. I'd be very interested, I said. I flew from Madrid to New York to Dallas, where I paused for a few hours for barbecue and beer with Dan Strimple, the golf pro. "George, this is your last chance at the NBA," Strimple said as he dropped me off for the flight to Seattle. "Don't fuck this up."

I didn't. I nailed the interview. Whitsitt called around to other coaches and GMs to find out what they thought of his potential new hire. "Not much" was the answer; I found out later only one of my peers endorsed me. Maybe the others really thought I was poison or maybe they didn't want to coach against me. But Whitsitt wanted my fire after K.C.'s low-key approach and I wanted the job so badly that I took a pay cut and a laughably short deal, only a year and a half. I also agreed not to drink in public. I never drank to the point of being impaired, especially not in public, but I wasn't insulted. If this was what Whitsitt wanted, fine.

I told Madrid: adios.

I told Seattle: we're gonna win by being the hardest-working, most intense team possible.

Suddenly I had the most talented players I'd ever coached. Eddie Johnson and Ricky Pierce were great offensive players who really understood the game. Nate McMillan and Derrick McKey defended like crazy. Gary Payton and Shawn Kemp were potential

All-Stars and I knew I could coach them up. And then there was Benoit.

Stop me if you've heard this before: I had a problem with our big man. In another line of work—casino greeter, maybe, or Buddha impersonator—Benoit Benjamin's laid-back look might have been an asset. But playing professional basketball for a supercompetitive coach for whom body language is Truth, his chilled-out style was a problem. During a game he looked unfocused, unenthusiastic, and a little bit *happy*. But good bigs are valuable: his $3.175 million salary was the highest on the team by a full million. Benoit rebounded, scored, and defended well most of the time. He also missed a shootaround or two, so he got his share of fines. He was kinda casual about basketball and he drove me nuts.

We went 27-15 after I joined the Sonics, a pleasant shock for our fans, and good enough to make the playoffs as the sixth seed. The third seed, our opponent in the best of five first round, would be Golden State, now coached by Nellie, the Coach of the Year. For a few years we were estranged, but I'm not a grudge holder and I'd had four years to heal. Nellie and I still didn't socialize but our relationship was certainly respectful. But what really brought us back to our strong friendship was the revenge I was about to get.

The Warriors had two all-NBA players in Mullin and Tim Hardaway, but we trumped them with Kemp.

Shawn dominated that series with 22 points and 16 rebounds per game. And he got our crowd into it with the most ferocious dunks I've ever seen. In Game Four, he threw one down so hard I thought the ball might embed in the floor, like a golf ball in soft turf. You can see it on YouTube.

We lost the next series to Utah, but everyone judged my half a season a big success. I got the best vote of confidence, a new contract, although the money was well below average at $300,000. For the third time in my NBA coaching career, I'd brought about huge improvement in an underperforming team. As you may remember, things had crashed in my second years at Cleveland and Golden State. Not this time.

Just as bad trades can kill you, good ones energize you. "I know you and Benoit aren't going to work," Whitsitt told me. "By the trade deadline, I'll have him out of here." It was nice having a GM working with me, kind of adjusting to me, not fighting with me.

By the middle of the season I'd parked Benoit's ass on the bench, so I was ecstatic when Whitsitt traded him to the Lakers for Sam Perkins, a fellow UNC alum whose game I loved. We also traded with Golden State for Vince Askew, part of that 50-6—50 *and 6!*—team at Albany. And in what you might think was the most minor of roster moves, we got a player you've never heard of from the Quad City Thunder of the CBA. Steve Scheffler didn't play much, but it was all-out war when he did.

His jump shot could break a backboard, yet he was very valuable.

A lot of NBA coaching is keeping negative energy away from your team. I want winners who act like winners, not moaners and groaners. That's why a really positive bench and practice player like Schef is worth more than a more talented guy who bitches all the time that he's not getting enough minutes. And that's why I think the coach should be able to pick the twelfth or thirteenth man. GMs often want you to rebuild a fallen superstar or rehab the mood of a malcontent, but if they hurt your chemistry and camaraderie, they're not worth the effort. Schef, David Wingate, Michael Redd, Eric Snow, Kosta Koufos, and Timofey Mozgov are guys I've had over the years who made us better with their amazingly positive attitudes.

I don't see discord as some kind of motivation. There is nothing wrong with everybody generally getting along. A lot of it has to do with winning. My happiest teams were the ones that won the most games. The Sonics team that went to the finals and the 57-win team in Denver stand out as content groups.

Switch Everything

We went 55-27 in 1992–93. A real team was building. I bitched about the lack of recognition then, but now I'm a little proud we didn't have a single name on the All-NBA first, second, or third teams; no one on the two All-Rookie teams; no Players of the Month, no Rookie of the Month, no Coach of the Month, and, of course, no Coach of the Year. Our starless team beat John Stockton and Karl Malone and Utah in five in the first round of the playoffs, then took down Hakeem Olajuwon and Clyde Drexler and the Rockets in seven in the second round. I've already mentioned what happened in Game Seven of the Western Conference Finals against KJ and Barkley and the refs in Phoenix. Charles says that was the best game he ever had, but 64 free throws? Ridiculous.

Being one win from the NBA Finals motivated us in 1993–94 to 63-19, one of the league's best years ever. Now it was our turn, as Payton and Kemp were becoming the best (or second-best) guard-forward combination in the NBA while Michael Jordan was swinging and missing at minor-league curveballs. We were relaxed and confident as the playoffs began. We studied tape of our first-round opponent, Denver. After the Nuggets, we'd probably get Utah, then Houston or San Antonio. We had the Knicks pegged to be our finals opponent.

━━━━

e were good, but we weren't the most stable bunch. I'd describe the 1993–94 Sonics as "chaortic," a blend of chaos and order.

Our point guard was Gary Payton. He and I got so mad at each other so often that we had to have an assistant coach—Tim Grgurich, the former Pitt coach who'd recruited me—act as our permanent mediator.

"Tell Gary if he's going to be that careless with the ball I'm going to sit his ass on the bench."

"Tell George to quit yelling shit at me and sit *his ass* on the bench."—that sort of thing.

In a game day shootaround, you could barely get him to move. He'd keep his sweats on and sort of sleepwalk through it. I'd yell at him. He'd yell back.

"You want me in the shootaround or at seven o'clock tonight?"

Gary defended like crazy, dove for the ball, stole it, and played at all times with a major attitude. He was just like his coach—only much more talented, as he often pointed out—and I guess that was why we screamed at each other so much. For about a year and a half, Gary didn't like me or understand me. But at least I was making basketball fun for him again. He'd hated playing at K.C.'s slow pace so much that he'd thought about quitting.

Our power forward was Shawn Kemp. He arrived late for things—we called it Shawn Time—and, as you know by now, lateness drives me crazy. But Shawn loved the gym, loved to practice, a big positive. I've never had a more popular player. Grunge music had recently emerged in Seattle. Shawn was into it and grunge fans were into him. With his running commentary, there was never a question about what Gary was thinking, but Shawn was more withdrawn, quiet, deep. Most important, there was never a doubt about his effort; Shawn went full throttle every minute of every game. He was a remarkable athlete and a dominating physical presence; his blocks and ferocious dunks demoralized the other team. Our fans yelled "Oh!" in unison when Shawn threw one down.

But it wasn't all sunshine in Seattle. Gary, Shawn, and I had different ideas about the right way to play. Sometimes they decided that a simple fast-break layup or dunk was just too boring. Gary would pass up his easy shot in favor of an alley-oop, or bounce the ball off the backboard for Shawn to swoop in and jam it. The crowd would go nuts. Or I would. I could hardly think of a better example of disrespecting the game and the opponent.

"You're not my dad!" Gary said one time after I yelled at him.

"I don't want to be your dad!" I replied.

Switch Everything

We were both using MFs and GDs. I don't have to repeat because you can easily imagine it. What might be hard to imagine was how much anger we truly felt. I give a lot of credit to Nate and Gurg for intervening and keeping the body count at zero. Gary was a match for all of us.

The rest of our team: Ricky Pierce was twice the Sixth Man of the Year, most recently in 1990. Eleventh year in the league. A hard worker, a great shooter, a poor defender, and he didn't get along with Gary. At all.

Kendall Gill and I stayed pissed off at each other. He said I embarrassed him by putting him back in for the last few seconds of blowouts (when we were way ahead or way behind). He embarrassed me with his attitude. A good teammate, I thought, isn't so into himself. He expected to be the star of our team but he was only our fourth- or fifth-best player. He was low on peer acceptance, too. His teammates didn't like him.

Our glue was Nate McMillan. His basketball intelligence quotient was through the roof, and no one who knows him was surprised when he became an NBA head coach. Sam Perkins was a total pro. Detlef Schrempf was a smart, responsible player who helped smooth our rough edges. Our center, Michael Cage, rebounded and defended pretty well, but I didn't think he set a good pick and he couldn't make a jump shot. His backup, Ervin Johnson, blocked shots and defended the perimeter amazingly well for a big guy, but he had no offense to speak of. At his best, Vince Askew did our dirty work. From his seat near the end of the bench, and off the court, Steve Scheffler improved us with his positivity.

My lead assistants were Stotts, who was on his way to becoming an offensive guru and an NBA head coach; Bob Kloppenburg, our defensive expert; and Tim Grgurich, my old friend from Pittsburgh. Gurg had an intensity that was so bright it was like looking into the sun. And he *hated* taking a day off.

Switch everything.

Our mantra was the obvious but rarely tried counter to offensive basketball's basic play, the pick-and-roll. We had the athletes to do it. Switch everything meant that Gary and Kendall would have to switch on to power forwards and centers, and that Shawn, Detlef, and Sam had to bend their knees and check fast, little guys out on the perimeter. Our risky tactic confused a lot of teams. Sam and Gary were so good at guarding different positions that I thought we had the advantage most of the time.

Switch everything and steal everything.

Gary and Nate were masters at taking the ball away. We led the league in my favorite stat; I think a steal is more exciting and valuable than a dunk or a long three. In January 1997, we would set the NBA record for most steals in a quarter—11—and in a game—27. Poor Toronto.

As for the coach, I had been forced by success and failure to evolve from cocky and overconfident to a more secure guy who knew he didn't know everything. I was still stubborn but I was learning. My relationships with my players deepened. I think they respected how I'd persevered to get back in the NBA, and how much I wanted to win. I liked coaching them; they liked playing for me.

I made a point of having a private meeting with each player at least three times a year. They could say anything to me and I could say anything to them. How's your girlfriend? How's your life? You have any problems with your teammates and your coaches? They usually asked the classic NBA player question: *What about my minutes?* When the GM and I talked about the team, and he asked about the last time I'd talked with a particular player, I could usually say "last week."

We started 26-3 and reached the All-Star break at 35-10. For having the best record at the season's annual pause, I would have the honor of coaching the Western Conference team at the All-Star Game in Minneapolis. Where I felt like a fish out of water.

Switch Everything

It wasn't just that I'd recently been a pariah in the NBA, and now I was in the league's spotlight, although that was part of what made me uncomfortable. Sponsors were beyond involved; they ran this show. Money first, as usual. There were corporate tie-ins to everything, from the Baby Ruth Shootaround to the Gatorade Slam Dunk Contest to the Payless Personal Foul (I made that one up).

But I guess the main thing that put me on edge was being in the center of a circus of celebrities and parties and advertising and dunks when all I wanted to do was organize the Sonics' next practice and analyze our next opponent. Instead, I was doing media.

BOB COSTAS: You were fired in Cleveland and you were fired at Golden State. Who do you blame?
ME: Myself.

(*Why are we talking about failure?* I thought but didn't say. The Sonics were 117-52 since I'd joined them. We had the best team in the league.)

DOUG COLLINS: You have such a deep team. From night to night you must have two or three guys who aren't happy [because they didn't play, or play much]. How do you handle that?
ME: Ninety percent of the time, they sacrifice. But if you're asking for the perfect attitude in the NBA, you're not gonna get it. Individuality has become part of our game. As a coach, you must accept that. But day in and day out our team cares about winning the championship.

So why didn't we? What fatal flaw ruined the 1993–94 Sonics?
We three All-Stars—Shawn and Gary and me—flew back to Seattle, and we continued to play great ball, finishing an unbelievable 63-19, the best record in the league. We got ready for Denver.

As usual, I went a little crazy waiting for the first game. I bumped into a friend who'd come to visit. Bumped into him so hard he flew into a wall. He bumped back and soon we were wrestling. Laughing, grunting, and knocking over chairs. Everyone in the office came out of their cubicles to watch.

"It's the playoffs, man! It's the playoffs!" I said as I got up off the floor, twitching my head and neck for effect. I then noticed that I had ripped the seat of my green corduroy pants. Normally no big deal but I had media to do.

Fans feel it, too, of course.

The emotion in Seattle Center Coliseum spiked extremely high when we hit the floor because we all felt this was the beginning of a championship run for a franchise that had not won it all since 1979.

The Nuggets came out fast, led by their point guard, Mahmoud Abdul-Rauf, whose head jerked around from Tourette syndrome, especially after he made a three. But then our defense and running kicked in. We won by 26.

I remember stopping for gas on my way home that night. A little guy in a hat stepped out from behind my Jeep and told me, in a thick Indian accent, why the Sonics had to play "the up-tempo." He got down in a defensive stance and jumped up and down with his hands up, like he was guarding me while I held the hose. That kind of thing happened all the time. The Seahawks had gone 2-14 and 6-10 in their previous two seasons; we were It in Seattle.

The Nuggets played better in the second game and it made us nervous. I didn't see it then, but in hindsight maybe we were beginning to crumble. Gary and Ricky screamed at each other in the halftime locker room, something about Ricky taking a shot when there should have been another pass. I'm pretty sure they swung fists at each other. And I'm pretty sure one or both of them said something about getting a gun. Someone—Schef, probably—had

I can't look at myself in a North Carolina uniform without thinking about Coach Smith.

Courtesy of Kim Van Deraa

I could make a jumper. That's Bob McAdoo in the background, coming up to get the offensive rebound, just in case.

Courtesy of Kim Van Deraa

Spurs rookie. Note the red, white, and blue ABA ball.

Courtesy of Kim Van Deraa

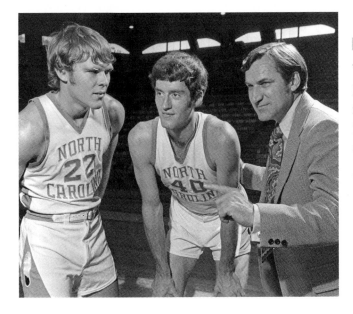

With Donn Johnston, a forward from Jamestown, New York, and Coach Smith.

Courtesy of the University of North Carolina

I coached at Golden State from '86 to '88—about ten thousand follicles ago.

Courtesy of Kim Van Deraa

I take Coby *(left)* and Kelci to the hoop. They couldn't stop me!

Courtesy of Kim Van Deraa

I loved coaching in Spain—until I didn't. *Courtesy of Kim Van Deraa*

Gary Payton and me trying to figure out Michael Jordan and the Bulls in Game One of the '96 Finals. Gary and I had trouble getting on the same page, but once we did . . .

Getty Images/Andrew D. Bernstein

ABOVE RIGHT: Whispering advice to Shawn Kemp, the best power forward I ever coached. *Getty Images/Andy Hayt*

ABOVE: What's the answer, AI? We had Allen Iverson in Denver for two years, but his best basketball was behind him. *Getty Images/Garrett Ellwood*

RIGHT: Andre Iguodala and I tried— and failed—to get past the Warriors in Round One in 2013. They had these two guards who looked like they'd be pretty good. *AP Images/Ben Margot*

Melo and me, the odd couple, during Game Two of the 2009 Western Conference Finals.

Getty Images/Noah Graham

Coby, who overcame thyroid cancer to make it into the NBA. I can't tell you how proud I am.

Courtesy of Kim Van Deraa

"Defense first!" I'm telling the 2010 Western Conference all-stars. About to laugh are Kevin Durant, to my right, and Steve Nash, to my left.

Courtesy of Kim Van Deraa

DeMarcus Cousins and I battle for position. He won, I guess.

Getty Images/Thearon W. Henderson

My main helpers with the Nuggets—and later with the Kings—were Chad Iske (in the gray suit) and John Welch (with the clipboard). *Courtesy of Kim Van Deraa*

"I saw the foul—why didn't you?"

Courtesy of Kim Van Deraa

My year and a half with the Kings was . . . interesting. With Ben McLemore and one of my favorite players, Andre Miller.

AP Images/Nell Redmond

The Nuggets gave me a trophy for my 1,000th NBA win.

Courtesy of Kim Van Deraa

With my youngest daughter, Kaci Grace. *Courtesy of Kim Van Deraa*

to step between them. But Sam made a late three, and Gary threw in a runner. We won by ten but the game was closer than that. We got on our plane and flew to Denver for Game Three.

Where they blew us out. As I was to appreciate more deeply when I coached there twelve years later, it's really hard for sea-level teams to suddenly play at 5,280 feet. Gary yelled at everyone in the locker room after the game. I appreciated his passion but he could alienate teammates sometimes.

We flew home; we probably should've stayed to adjust to the altitude. Barry Ackerley, our owner, was with us. Like a lot of people, he thought we'd win in three games. No one wanted to tell him that the team plane would stay put and he'd have to fly commercial back to Sea-Tac.

I was guilty of assuming, too: I'd only packed one suit. I found out later that our return to Seattle provided Denver coach Dan Issel with a motivational talking point. *See how overconfident they are? They were so sure of a sweep, nobody even brought an extra pair of socks. They don't respect you!* I'd have said the same thing. I learned nothing from Frank Layden, apparently.

Game Four in Denver was close and dirty and went to overtime. It was decided, in the end, by our missed free throws and their sudden ability to make threes. They'd averaged two a game in the regular season; now they were making six. And Mutombo; Shawn went at him time after time. It was strength on strength, the strongest dunker in the league against the best shot blocker. The blocker was winning. He had 31 blocks, a record for a five-game series. A lot of it was my fault. I'd told Shawn to challenge Dikembe, and get him into foul trouble. I wish now I'd had Shawn shoot more jump shots.

Game Five: Before the series, the Sonics had so much confidence we could have sold it in jars. Now we looked shaky against a team that barely qualified for the playoffs. Our arena was humid and overheated, filled to the brim with seriously edgy people. Including me. Someone wrote that I looked like the defendant in a murder trial just before the jury foreman reads the verdict.

A final, bizarre detail: Win or lose, wrecking balls and dynamite were going to demolish our building in June, right after the draft. A new one was going up in its place.

I've talked about the importance of luck in basketball. They had it, we didn't. In the first half, the Nuggets shot *four* air balls that teammates caught. They made shots thrown up while falling down, and guys who'd barely made a long ball all year (especially Robert Pack) were making closely guarded threes. Maybe that's the short answer to what happened. Random luck landed on them like a bird.

There are other ways to look at Game Five. They played really well, first of all, while we got tight. Ricky and Gary both played hurt. We missed free throws. As in Games Three and Four, they had someone play the best game of his life. But we thought we could overcome all the bad omens and reverse the momentum when Mutombo went to the bench with three fouls in the second quarter. In came Brian Williams. A jumper, a slam, a block, and he seemed to get every rebound. Just when we saw a ray of light, he killed us.

Someone had asked him about his suicide attempt a few years earlier.

"You know when you pass an accident in the road, and you look in the rearview mirror and say you're glad that's behind you? That's how I feel," Williams said.

And that's how I feel about the biggest upset in NBA history. Number one seed Seattle lost Game 5 (Kendall Gill made a last-second layup to force overtime but we lost 98–94) and the series, to the eight seed, Denver.

I had the most miserable summer.

CHAPTER 6

HOW TO BEAT MICHAEL JORDAN

A lot of coaches act like they're getting a root canal without Novocaine. . . . George is one of the few who really seem to enjoy the give-and-take.

—CHUCK COOPERSTEIN, ESPN RADIO, DALLAS

I called *Michael Jordan* after the Biggest Upset in NBA History.
"Should we do this?" I asked.

I'd recovered in the six weeks since our loss to Denver, in that I didn't constantly feel like crying or punching someone. But while the playoffs played off without us, chaos hit the Sonics.

In mid-May, our GM, Bob Whitsitt, was named NBA Executive of the Year. Two weeks later, our owner fired his ass. The torches and pitchforks came out: fans mostly liked Whitsitt, and they mostly didn't like our owner. They hated that he'd cut down trees that blocked the view of his billboards—that didn't play too well in eco-conscious Seattle. And while a new arena was being built on the same ground as the old one, the boss had decided to play next year's home games in Tacoma. Which was inconvenient. And with higher ticket prices. Which pissed people off after the upset loss to Denver. I thought Ackerley was a good guy but my business and personal closeness was with Whitsitt.

After getting a few earfuls of anger from call-ins to KJR, the Seattle sports talk radio station he owned, Ackerley had second thoughts. He rescinded Whitsitt's firing—sort of. Was he in or was he out? It was confusing for about a week. Nerve-racking, too. The draft was about to start. Janitors removed everything from Whitsitt's office but a desk and a chair and the dust bunnies. Whitsitt was advised to report to work anyway. Lawyers were involved.

My lawyer got involved after Ackerley told me to be ready to run the draft myself. Warren LeGarie advised it would be a bad idea. He also reminded me that job was not in my contract and that I was already underpaid. I'd met (and liked) LeGarie in Spain, where he represented a few American players. "It's not something George is comfortable doing," Warren told a reporter. "It's not his expertise. Do you know his drafting history?" Referring, of course, to the part I'd had in selecting Turpin, Washburn, and Keith Lee.

Ackerley finally let Whitsitt go, so we went into the draft with no GM. I tried and failed to get them to hire my UNC teammate Mitch Kupchak, or Rick Sund, both very creative and experienced basketball men.

Then out of the blue came Walter "Wally" Walker, a former Sonic who'd been the color man for the team's radio and TV broadcasts for two years. Ackerley assigned him to be our "basketball consultant," in part because he was smart and in part because he was already on the payroll. Right away, Wally and I didn't see eye to eye. We were an unsettled bunch. Would someone try to take advantage of us?

The Bulls saw an opportunity. Four days before the draft, Jerry Krause called. The Chicago GM, who'd visited me in Spain, had a proposal: Kemp, Pierce, and our number one for Scottie

Pippen. Pippen was the best small forward, or 3, in the league. Nothing he wasn't good at. During one of Michael's retirements, Scottie led his team in all five of the main categories—rebounds, scoring, blocks, steals, and assists—so rare that it had only happened once before in NBA history (Dave Cowens, for the Celtics, in 1977–78). But with his running buddy MJ now a baseball player, maybe Pippen was a little disconnected. When I tried to imagine the Sonics without Shawn I knew I'd miss him, but I got pretty excited picturing Gary and Scottie teaming up on a trap; they'd smother opposing guards. But every trade prompts a debate. I was in favor of this one but I wasn't sure.

So I called Michael. We talked about minor-league baseball, North Carolina basketball, and golf. Then we talked about the big deal on the table. Should we do this?

"Do it," he said. "Scottie can make your other players better. Kemp can't."

So, the day before the draft, we said yes. News of the trade immediately leaked out and onto the KJR airwaves. More anger from the callers, a lot more; our fans loved Shawn. Again, Ackerley listened. That afternoon, he called our draft headquarters in the Sonics locker room. It doesn't *feel* right, he told Wally. Better wait. I had the unpleasant job of calling Krause, who was not happy.

While we dragged our feet on draft day, Krause got desperate. He called to tell me the Bulls would drop the demand for our number one pick. He offered a big chunk of money in the next call. Then he called back to double it. Literally minutes before the draft started, Ackerley backed us out of the deal. When I delivered the bad news, Krause dropped f-bombs and called me names. We'd keep Kemp, they'd keep Pippen.

We'd see Scottie again two years later.

The season after the Denver disaster felt disrupted and weird because, as I mentioned, we played our home games on the road in the Tacoma Dome. In the playoffs, we drew the Lakers for the first round best of five. We blew them out in Game One, then lost three close games and the series. L.A.'s Nick Van Exel scored 25 a game. For the second season in a row, our fans felt betrayed, the writers and talking heads called us chokers, and we weren't too happy with ourselves.

Our big trade that summer was an exchange of 2's with Charlotte. It was Kendall Gill—who hated me—for Hersey Hawkins, who thought I was pretty cool. We also replaced a couple of guys who couldn't remember our plays with good, adaptable teammates in Eric Snow, David Wingate, and Frank Brickowski.

So what did we have? Was this a team that could win a championship? In light of our playoff results the previous two years, and in the interest of everybody keeping their jobs, I decided to have a coaches' retreat to talk about everything. So in late September 1995, a week before training camp, the basketball staff drove to a resort in the center of the state. Lake Chelan: mountains, vineyards, and a big, blue glacier lake at the bottom of a valley. A beautiful place to get lost in thought, I hoped, and to evaluate our team honestly. We sat in a conference room with a scenic view. Some very smart people pitched in with their opinions.

First there was Gurg. Imagine a taller, more intense Yoda: brief, wise observations delivered in a hoarse voice. But he sure as hell didn't want to be at any retreat. The workaholic Gurg always preferred to be working out a player or working out himself. His intensity made players trust him and they confided in him, too. A great assistant coach.

As their de facto doctor, our trainer Frank Furtado knew our players on a different level than the coaches. He'd been with the Sonics since 1974. Terry Stotts, the son of a coach, was prepared as usual. Bob Kloppenburg had been coaching basketball for thirty-something years, and he'd invented our switching, trapping defense. Chad Forcier, our video guy, had only been alive for twenty-something years. He took notes.

I wondered aloud about our leadership. Gary didn't want the job; that was obvious. Leaders emerge in practice and Gary acted like he'd rather be anywhere else. Sam was too quiet, Detlef too arrogant. Nate led sometimes, but he hid from the responsibility too often. Shawn? No. He wasn't quite a loner, but he was independent; Coach on the Floor was just not in his DNA. Schef would do it, but it's hard to lead from the bench. He was only playing five minutes a game.

We decided to have Gurg try to fire up Gary early in every practice. Since the one thing a leader's got to have is followers, maybe the other guys would follow Gary if he showed a hint of enthusiasm.

What about discipline? I never crack the whip for the hell of it, but a team has to have rules and everyone's got to obey them. If not, people get unhappy and our performance suffers.

We settled on a few key thoughts:

No sitting in practice.

No rehab during practice.

No talking while a coach is talking.

We would post an "emphasis of the day"—echoes of Dean Smith—like "boxing out" or "spacing," but not an inspirational quote.

And since showing up on time seemed like the most basic part of keeping order, we decided to remove any excuse for lateness on practice days. We synched the digital clocks in the gym, the training room, the locker room, and the weight room. When it was 2 p.m., it was 2 p.m. everywhere a player might be. Everybody would have to be by his locker thirty minutes before practice, and Frank would stop taping ankles fifteen minutes before. We all knew who this policy was aimed at: Shawn and Gary.

Speaking of Shawn and Gary, how could we make our All-Stars even better?

Shawn was a simple fix: improve his fitness and his free throws.

Gary was more complicated. We had a lot to address: gets really agitated in the personal challenge game within the game . . . dribbles left too often, becoming predictable . . . great shooter off the glass . . . thinks he's a three-point shooter, but he's not . . . a legitimate All-Star but will not get better unless we fix his poor practice habits, poor off-court habits, his body language, and attitude. Other than that . . .

We discussed each of our players.

Nate McMillan: bad ankle? Body deteriorating? Doesn't get to the line enough, doesn't finish well. Thinks he's a three-point shooter but he doesn't make them . . . Needs to work on his shot.

Vince Askew: not making as many blue-collar plays as he used to . . . Needs to play better in the flow . . . Harder to coach now that he knows how good he is . . . Like Gary, too often caught up in the personal challenge game.

Ervin Johnson: big heart, good character . . . but is he talented enough to be the center on a championship team?

Sam Perkins: excellent execution . . . asked to do a lot of things because he's so good . . . won't turn it over . . . how is his health?

I found out that Detlef Schrempf had offended the coaching staff. After the best year of his career, he hadn't given his coaches any credit for his improvement, and they'd worked with him a lot . . . Hates Gary and Gary hates him . . . Shawn doesn't respect Det, for some reason . . . Should we bring the three of them together to discuss their importance to the team?

Of the new guy, Hersey Hawkins, we only had some impressions from playing against him: moves well without the ball, can hit any open jumper or three. And we had some questions. Is he soft? Will he buy into our defensive program?

By the time we retreated from our retreat, we also had new policies and directions for conditioning, nutrition (no beer after games, no soda or potato chips on the plane), weight lifting (guys who'd played fewer than fifteen minutes would have to lift after the game), and how we'd run our training camp.

As you'd expect, we also dissected how we played basketball. On offense, we decided to make a point of scoring in the first six seconds of the twenty-four-second shot clock, or the last six seconds. I didn't—and don't—like what we called "secondary action," a slow and inefficient buildup to a shot. We still wanted a lot of our offense to come from our strength, our defense.

We talked for an hour about White, Go, Laker Red, and PR 5—our basic defenses—and how to increase our intensity and energy. Gurg got fired up on this subject. "It all starts on the ball," he croaked. Which meant: Gary.

We settled on two priorities.

Attack penetration meant we wouldn't hang back or give space to an opposing player taking the ball to the rim.

Deny ball reversal would frustrate a basic part of the other team's offense. Here's what I mean: we'd try to keep opposing 2 guards from catching the ball in their favorite spot—they all like to start their moves around the three-point line opposite the foul line, aka the wing. But when other teams did get the ball out there, we'd take away the pass back to the top. In other words, we'd cut the court in half; they'd have to run their offense from one side or the other, not both.

Michael Jordan, we all agreed, was the best in the league at both those techniques—offense from the wing, and, on defense, denying ball reversal. He'd be our model.

———

We hadn't analyzed me at the retreat. If we had, Chad's notes might have read: in eighth season as an NBA head coach, a happier guy than before, more settled . . . weight increasing, must reduce intake of Miller Lite and butterscotch sundaes . . . still open to new basketball ideas . . . team plays hard for him . . . needs more caution with media . . . horrible relationship with GM . . . good delegator . . . bad loser.

Bad loser? Yeah. I can't explain why the pleasant feeling from winning melts away while losses stay with me like a bad haircut. Maybe it's just the coach's life; on the other hand, Doug Moe.

I've read that the human mind naturally seeks out negativity and threats, a not very useful souvenir from caveman days when survival required being alert for saber-toothed tigers or human enemies. Nowadays, with little real danger except for what we do to ourselves, a lot of people get their highs and lows from how the Steelers or the Cowboys or the Knicks or the Kings did in the game today. Life seems worth living for fans of the NBA champion, and a cheap, hollow thing if you lose in five to goddamn Denver.

Butterscotch sundaes? Yes. A lousy diet and decreasing mobility from bad hips and knees was making me fat.

GM problem? True: I had no chemistry with Wally Walker. He kept us coaches in the dark about trades and roster decisions and we didn't like it.

On the other hand, I felt far more settled personally than ever before. After years of hopscotching between the CBA, the NBA, and Europe, it was nice to have a little rhythm and predictability in our lives. Summers consisted of fun at our house on a lake in McCall, Idaho, near Boise; the draft; the annual UNC reunion in Chapel Hill; and Gurg's Camp in Las Vegas (more on that later). October meant squeaking sneakers and thumping basketballs in practice. Then the intensity of eighty-two games plus the playoffs and the sudden letdown after each game, like coming off a sugar high.

I was happier, too, definitely. For the first time in my career, I had real friendships on my team. Turnover had been too great, and my time with the teams too brief, for me to get as close with my guys in the CBA, Madrid, Cleveland, and Golden State. I also might have been too insecure about my job to be much of a friend.

That wasn't an issue in Seattle. The consistently excellent

basketball the Sonics played made the bonding possible, because we wouldn't have had that much fun, and we wouldn't have stayed together, if we lost. And we had a team personality that I liked, a blend of loud (Gary), proud (Detlef), quiet (Sam), intuitive (Nate), and funny (Brick). My son, Coby, hung around practice and was the home game ball boy; he was part of the mix, too.

My key relationship on the team was the one with Gary. A point guard is to a basketball coach exactly what a quarterback is to a football coach. We two alpha dogs had to get on the same page. Not easy. Gary had learned to stand up for himself on the playground in Oakland and his f-you attitude never left. I'm not exactly the silent type either, but Gary could trash talk *all day*. "He makes you just want to go find a library or something," said Michael Cage, a Sonics teammate. "Someplace totally quiet." Sometimes Gary would even talk smack to the guy guarding him while *he*—Gary—brought the ball up the court! And for a while he walked the insubordination line with me.

After about a year and a half of this bumpy ride, we had a conversation at the Pro Sports Club in Bellevue, near where we both lived. I played a little tennis there. "I just can't coach this way," I said. I talked about how we'd both fail if we didn't work together. Gary listened, nodded, said, "Okay, I'm in." We shook hands. Now he says that Gurg and I became like second and third fathers to him. Today I consider Gary to be one of my best friends.

Those Sonics teams played hard for me. Even Gary liked my toughness and we all liked winning. I'd give them unexpected days off, and have the bus driver detour to a movie theater instead of to our shootaround. One day after practice in Seattle, we went as a team to play paintball. Brickowski seemed to be an expert at it, and he got me right between the eyes in the first minute. Red paint. They'd earned plenty of space from me and they had their own culture apart from me. Perfect. Before a big game, our older players felt comfortable enough to give little motivational speeches. Then we'd go out and win, team-style, and with very scary defense.

Another part of that mythical scouting report on me was about dealing with the press.

Win or lose, I've got to be available after a game. I get fined by the league if I don't. My media relations were pretty good but my GMs and owners did not always see it that way.

Ten minutes after the game, the locker room doors open, and the media troops in. TV guys bull their way to me or to a player in front of his locker. One guy holds a boom mike, another a light, another a camera. The reporter asks a question, while the print guys stick out handheld recorders and try to hold their ground. The bright light makes me squint.

Sometimes it's that stupid "how much" question reporters are addicted to. "How much did you miss Chauncey's defense tonight?" or "How much did you want to steal a game on the road?" Shit, I don't know: seven? Seventy? What are the degrees of these things? I can't always tell you "how much." And I might not agree with the premise. Maybe I didn't miss Chauncey's defense.

I've been known as a good quote for a long time because I try to avoid clichés. Stock answers are no fun for me and useless for the reporter. But even though I'm cooperative, there's always tension. In the 1980s and '90s, every writer had a deadline, so he needed to hear your best thoughts on the game and then run off somewhere and write his story.

Now three-quarters of the writers in the room are just bloggers. They're headhunters. They try to trick you into a mistake, so they can make their column or story as spicy as possible. That's the problem with some of the digital media; there's no barrier to entry. Anyone can do it. All you need is a smartphone to post to the Web. Most bloggers don't have editors or training or ethics. It doesn't pay very much, so it doesn't attract the best people. Sorry, bloggers: have at me.

How to Beat Michael Jordan

Talking about the game with people who have roasted me is not easy. Some clown writes this on Tuesday: *Don't be surprised if Karl mails in another season as he continues to dare management to fire him for keeping players on the roster he's either incapable of coaching or has no desire to coach.*

On Wednesday, the same guy wants my thoughts on the fourth quarter. I want to slug him but I have to play nice.

If I say something like "We're pathetic at protecting the ball," my guards will know who's being insulted. It took me a while to learn that blowing up my team in the media is a bad idea. In this digital age, anything you say winds up everywhere immediately. Besides, my first analysis is often wrong. The video may show something I hadn't seen or expected.

Shit I've said after the game:

I just wish someone would grab some of these Lakers fans and choke them.

Isiah is a jackass.

Kenny Smith is a loudmouth.

We have some players who seem to take a certain joy in losing.

I don't know if I've ever been involved in a game that was so unfair.

Somebody asked me recently if I would trade Gary Payton. I said I would keep Gary Payton and fire management.

I don't think I lied yesterday. I did fib a little.

When you have Ruben Patterson and Reggie Evans out there? When you don't know what play to run—just let them play. Let them go into the backyard, lower the fence, and let the dogs do it.

I don't know what I meant by this last quote, but I'm pretty sure it was an insult to Ruben and Reggie. But I praise *much* more often. I said this, too: "Ruben Patterson is the type of basketball player I like playing with and being in battle with."

———

That imaginary scouting report on me was correct in another respect: I hadn't stopped learning basketball. I'd taken the UNC ideal of pace, space, and team first and twisted it a little bit. In the game founded by James Naismith, there were two little guys (guards), two big guys (forwards), and one really big guy, the center. I'd begun to see less and less value in the back-to-the-basket seven-footer. I saw a trend to interchangeability—five players who could handle, rebound, shoot, and defend anyone anywhere on the floor. The "switch everything" strategy didn't work unless all five positions could do it, at least a little bit, but a really mobile big man is rare.

For the Sonics in 1995–96, I started Ervin Johnson, a 6'11" kid who played great D all over the court but couldn't score. I'd replace him pretty quickly with Perkins, an amazing player who could shoot a three, guard a guard, and take care of business close to the basket. Erv would play 13 or 14 minutes a game; Sam averaged more than twice that.

Another thing: although the three-point semicircle had been painted on our floors since 1979, I didn't think we coaches really understood its value. In a three-year experiment in the mid-1990s, the league moved the line in a little closer, to 22 feet all around. Attempts doubled, to about 38,000. Then they moved the line out to the current distance, and attempts fell by half. Then they went up again. What was the right number of long balls to shoot? I decided that I wanted to find more players who could make it from 23 feet, 9 inches. So we could shoot more threes and run more plays to set up the three.

I entered the league with a few ideas that eight years of experience confirmed. My focus on defense was hardly a new concept but it's not the way most players and fans see basketball. The guy who scores 25 a game makes the All-Star team. A great defender who *stops* 25 a game doesn't get the recognition and makes less money. In the sports page, it's always "In New Orleans, DeMarcus Cousins scored 28 points to lead Sacramento to its eighth straight win. Peter Piper's 24 points paced the Pelicans."

The summary you don't see is "DeMarcus Cousins guarded three positions, deflected the ball eight times, and stole it twice as the Kings rolled over Golden State for their tenth straight win." I know, deflections; that'll be the day.

I'd also decided that I like to win without an offensive star. If we've got four or five guys in double figures, we're harder to defend, and harder to prepare for. In huddles in the last two minutes of games, I've told great players that they might have to be selfish and take care of scoring by themselves. But I know we're a happier, better team if there's no big ego to handle and we play offense by committee.

Of course, most teams have one big scorer, one guy who is almost impossible to stop—Michael Jordan being the best example. We tried to conquer the impossible when we played the Bulls and MJ in the 1996 NBA Finals.

We'd see how much I'd really learned.

We *were* 64-18 in 1995–96, only the tenth NBA team ever to win that many games and the most wins I've ever had in a season. We would have been the talk of professional basketball—if the Bulls hadn't gone 72-10 for the best regular season record in league history. In the playoffs, they beat Miami, New York, and Orlando to reach the finals. Actually, they *killed* Miami, New York, and Orlando, winning the three series 3–0, 4–1, and 4–0. We took out Sacramento and Houston without much drama, but then, Utah. Wow. While we sweated out the Jazz in the Western Conference Finals, the Bulls rested up and watched to see who they'd play for the championship.

We went up 3–1 and looked strong doing it. The idea that Gary and Shawn were the new Stockton and Malone seemed reasonable. But then we lost something and the actual Stockton and Malone found something. They scraped by us at our place and then blew us out in Game Six in Salt Lake City. Aside from the game, we also lost Nate—herniated disc in his lumbar spine. Bad, bad timing.

A newspaper headline showed that we had not been forgiven for Denver, or for the first-round loss to the Lakers the next year. "Sonics leave guts home as gut-check time looms."

But we showed plenty of guts in Game Seven.

Before the game I made two points: Malone will try to win it himself and we've got to play dirty. We shot up Nate and he made it through twelve minutes. Payton-Kemp outplayed Stockton-Malone. We won 90–86. We were Western Conference champions. We sprayed, spilled, and drank champagne in the locker room, a first for all of us.

As usual, after practice the next morning, the players formed a circle around me at center court. I looked at every face and saw several hangovers, some leftover jubilation, and lots of fatigue. They were like a dozen runners at the end of a marathon, all of them dressed in sweaty gray and green. I knew their legs felt dead from playing 99 games—82 regular, 17 playoff. They were mentally worn down, too. They carried a deep exhaustion from concentrating and competing so hard for so long. But the finish line was in sight: the finals.

As usual, I'd prepared my talk to the team. My speech would not dwell on disadvantages. I like to think and talk about how we can win, not why we can't. Besides, no one really needed to be reminded that the Bulls had *three* guys on the five-man All-Defensive team (Jordan, Pippen, and Dennis Rodman) or that they were being called the greatest basketball team ever or that

Bob Costas said that a Sonics win would be one of the greatest upsets in sports history. Or that they'd been resting for eight days while we'd been working our asses off to beat Utah. Or that Nate might not play.

"We're *not* just happy to be here. We're here to win," I said. "This needs to be a physical, boring series. If they're able to pressure you and make you passive on offense, their pressure will only grow and kill you. But if you attack their pressure, it will shrink and wilt and they'll go away from it.

"They got the ball out of Penny Hardaway's hands [in the Orlando series] and he just stopped playing. They'll do the same thing to Gary, and try to make Hawk and Det handle the ball. Gary, you've got to keep working to beat them, get the ball back, hurt them.

"Gary, Nate, get up on Pippen. He doesn't like it physical. He really likes the walk-up three—most of his threes come in transition. Hard fouls. Don't give him any easy baskets or lay-ins. Kukoc is soft. Hit him. Hit all of them.

"Schef, you're gonna knock someone on his ass and set solid screens. You're gonna frustrate Rodman.

"They give [Steve] Kerr the second most offensive opportunities on their team. He shot fifty-one percent on threes this year. Respect him, be aware of him.

"Gary, Hawk, Nate, David, Det, Vince—we're gonna mix it up on Michael. Give him different looks all night long. When he gets the ball, make him see a crowd, and double him from the top. When he doesn't have the ball, push him out. The farther away from the basket he catches it, the better for us. He's mostly a jump shooter now. He doesn't want the rim like he used to.

"We can't give him layups. We can't foul him. I don't want him to shoot more than five free throws in any game. We've got to make him take as many hard shots as possible.

"While we're on Michael . . . he's a trickster. He's competing against you all the time, even off the court. Even if your kids are asking you to get his autograph, I don't want anyone hanging with him, buying him a cup of coffee or going out to dinner. You'll think he's your friend but he's softening you up."

We went over their triangle offense ("It all starts with a pass to the post") and the other theories about slowing down Michael. During its championship years, Detroit had some success with its "Jordan rules," which basically consisted of pushing him left, double teams, and hard fouls. We'd hit him, for sure, but we weren't going to completely rely on double teams. Part of that thinking came from the threat of three-ball. Pippen, Kukoc, and Kerr could make a three, and MJ had become a pretty good passer. Besides, we had some excellent one-on-one defenders.

I also talked briefly about this thing Michael did when he got the ball out on the perimeter. It was such an ingrained habit, it reminded me of the waggles a golfer takes before he hits a full shot. I must have seen it on tape a thousand times.

You've seen it, too, if you were watching basketball back then. Pippen or Harper throws it to Jordan on the wing. He catches and immediately tucks it, both hands on the ball, head up, elbows out. Not unusual: this is the "triple threat" position you learn in junior high. You can shoot, pass, or dribble from this semi-crouch. Then Michael "wipes" the ball, swinging it low and back and forth in response to the defender's digs at it. Again, everyone does this. Then, *almost* every time, Michael jab-steps with his left foot. That little fake was his golfer's waggle, the thing he had to do before he could shoot or attack the rim.

Before his year and a half as a Birmingham Baron and a Scottsdale Scorpion, no one was quick enough and strong enough to get in his grille and disrupt this routine. But even though he'd scored 30 a game and led the league in scoring, it was plain to us that he'd lost a little of his speed.

What if we took away his jab step?

began the psychological warfare while I still had champagne in my hair (I still had hair). When I talked to Tom Friend of the *New York Times* in my office a few minutes after we beat Utah, I gave every indication that Gary, who would be named Defensive Player of the Year, would be guarding Michael.

"When I came here four years ago, Gary Payton was the only guy who had the guts to play him," I said. "He always challenged him. Never backed off him. Gary was not afraid."

But Gary had a torn calf muscle we weren't talking about. I needed to save him a little bit, have him focus on running the offense, and stay out of foul trouble. He'd be part-time on MJ, at most.

Friend asked if other players were in awe of Michael. Yes. No question.

"Jordan abuses the younger guys," I said. "They're 'Ah, you're my idol.' But you've got to kick his ass. Michael Jordan's biggest talent is not his skills, it's his heart. It's his complete attitude."

I didn't think these were fighting words, or even bulletin board material, but Michael read this and told everyone that he felt disrespected. What was I supposed to say, when we were about to go against the greatest player in the world in the NBA Finals—"no comment"?

The writer asked about the colorful Rodman. Dennis had an incredible knack for rebounding and for being so annoying that opponents wanted to slug him. Sound like anybody you know? But Rodman never fought, as far as I know. An instigator, he just *started* fights and let the other guy get thrown out.

"My old Spurs teammate Coby Dietrick says I was Dennis Rodman before Dennis Rodman," I said to the reporter. "I mean, I was the only one who ever fought Pete Maravich. . . . I told Dennis when he was in San Antonio, I said, 'Dennis, I don't know about my team, but I'm not afraid to fight you.' He looked at me and said, 'I think you're telling the truth.'"

Dennis didn't like what I told the *Times*. He felt disrespected, too. I'd annoyed the annoyer. Not a bad thing.

The Bulls also fired some shots in the pre-finals war of words. Both Pippen and Phil Jackson tried to put the refs on notice by accusing us of playing a zone. Back then that was like saying we corked our bats or deflated our footballs. Zone defenses were illegal in the NBA until the 2001–02 season. A zone, for you newbies, means defending an area instead of a man. Although I would never have admitted it then, hell yes we played a zone. A lot of teams played man-to-man on the strong side (the side of the court with the ball) and zone on the weak side. The rules allowed double teams—which we used all the time—but both players had to "commit" to the double, and were not allowed to hedge. But man, did we hedge. It was part of our defensive philosophy and part of the reason we stole the ball so often. We knew that commitment and hedging were really hard judgment calls for the refs, so we took advantage. We got by far the most illegal defense calls in the NBA but they only caught us a fraction of the time.

"George has to work the officials in a lot of different ways," Phil told the media before the first game. "I applaud him for doing it."

Phil—you applaud me? Yeah, right.

GAME 1—WEDNESDAY, JUNE 5, 1996—UNITED CENTER, CHICAGO

After a slow start, Michael made jump shot after jump shot. He was too strong for Hawk, and too quick for Detlef. When he dribbled once or twice toward the basket and then shot a fadeaway, there were no defensive hands within three feet of the ball. He went to the rim a few times, too, and shot 10 free throws.

Rodman's hair looked like graffiti—blue, purple, and red swirls on a blond background. One of the swirls spelled the letter W, for his nickname, Worm. He could irritate you just standing there, in other words, but he didn't just stand there. Within two minutes after I put him in to give Sam a rest, the Worm's bumps and pulls and conversation got to Brick, who pushed back when the refs were looking. They threw him out. Rodman looked triumphant, and their crowd loved it.

Gary seemed tired. Nate could hardly move in the six minutes he played. But the Bulls couldn't handle Shawn's post-ups, and the score was 75-all late in the third quarter. And then we stopped getting the ball inside, and they challenged Gary's passing and penetration—his entire game, in fact, including his desire. Shawn had some trouble passing out of their double teams. We should have pressed when they started to pull ahead. Their guards, Harper and Kerr, tended to go east and west under pressure and we might have forced some turnovers. Bulls 107–90. They'd lost only two home games all year. Maybe we could make it three on Friday.

GAME 2—FRIDAY, JUNE 7—CHICAGO

O*n Thursday, I* considered blowing off some steam by playing nine holes at Chicago Golf Club. A couple of my golf pro friends from Texas had come up for the games and they saved me a spot. But I just couldn't do it. After our coaches' meeting in the Fairmont hotel and a light practice, I stayed wrapped up in figuring out how to beat the best team in NBA history.

We worked out a plan. We'd go away from whoever Michael was guarding, and attack Ron Harper's matchup (if Harper guarded Gary, Gary would look for his shot more). We'd push their center, Luc Longley, away from the rim, and make him turn toward the baseline if he started an offensive move. We'd post up early, which meant that even after their made baskets, each of our guys would sprint down court, find a body, seal him off, and call for the ball. When that wasn't there, we'd play draw and kick. We'd take the ball hard to the rim, draw the defense, then pass it out to our shooters because Phil had all five Bulls collapsing on the ball when we took it in close. We stole a double screen play from Utah to get Hawk free from MJ.

For Rodman: our bigs would go face-to-face and chest-to-chest to keep the league's leading rebounder off the glass. This was unusual and a little bit risky. Unusual because in the standard defensive rebounding position you keep your opponent behind you and face the basket. Risky because if you're looking at Dennis, you obviously can't see the ball come off the rim—so you just hope a teammate can get it.

For Michael: double teams, then more double teams. He didn't like them.

We had a plan, and we had questions. Should we rest Gary when they take Michael out of the game? With Nate probably lost for the rest of the series, should we give his minutes to Eric Snow? Could Eric handle the pressure, or would he try to do too much?

Our plan worked.

Everyone in the arena noticed when Rodman came up to me just before the game to say he didn't appreciate what I'd said about him in the paper. Gary stole the ball from Michael in the first quarter, took it down the court, and dunked it. Then he gave MJ shit while he ran back, like we were on a playground in Oakland. Psychological warfare.

We got a lead—our post-ups with Shawn and Det were really working—but lost it in a bad stretch at the end of the third quarter.

Even though Phil's aggressive bitching got us four illegal defense calls (and four technicals), we clawed back.

The Bulls led 90–86 with 26 seconds left and the shot clock about to run out. Every fan, player, and coach was on his feet. Kerr tried a long three. It was way off but the long shot led to a long rebound—to Rodman. Total luck. His 11th offensive rebound tied a playoff record and it cost us the game. They won 92–88.

D*o I have* to recall this game? It's *my* book. I'd rather talk about golf.

At halftime, we walked through loud silence to our locker room. The Bulls had succeeded in taking our crowd out of it. They led 62–39. I drank a glass of water and glanced at the stats, including their 21 points off our 13 turnovers versus our scoring only 4 points off only 4 turnovers. "You're not defending," I said. "You're not playing together on offense."

It didn't take a genius to see that what we were doing with Michael wasn't working; he had 26 points already. I told Gary and Hawk to switch men (Gary on MJ, Hawk on Pippen) for the first couple of possessions in the third quarter.

We played a good third and made up 10 points and our fans came alive but we had too far to go. Rodman's antics got Brick thrown out again. We didn't get loose balls or long rebounds and we didn't play hard for the entire forty-eight minutes.

I was one pissed-off motherfucker afterward. The shit luck of losing Nate meant a huge part of our puzzle was missing. I wondered if Shawn and Gary were jealous of each other as each tried to be the Man. Gary wasn't making his teammates better and Shawn took only 7 shots in 42 minutes. Vince Askew infuriated me with his poor play and selfish attitude; he was about to find his ass on the bench. I made a list of free agents we'd let go when the time came. Four names: Vince, Brick, Ervin, and Gary.

Then Gary came into my office. "Nothin' to lose now," he said. "Let me take him."

GAME 4—WEDNESDAY, JUNE 12—SEATTLE

eing down in the series 3-0 to the Bulls gave us a helpless feeling. All year long we'd hidden our weaknesses, and now they were being exposed: we weren't a good passing team, and although we kicked ass with our offense in transition—when the game was played fast—our half-court offense was mediocre.

We felt despair, but we didn't give up. The coaches discussed the three things we needed: more passing, more rebounding, and fewer turnovers. It was much harder to answer our basic question: what could we do to restore our confidence?

Ignore Rodman, I told the team before the game. Bust your ass every single minute. Go after every rebound. Play with your heart and your pride. Get angry and pissed off at them—not at each other or at the refs.

And: Gary, play MJ straight up on the perimeter. We're only going to double him on the low block.

It worked. The refs were letting us play, as they say, so Gary's NFL cornerback defense threw Michael off balance a little bit. Gary even took away his jab step, getting up on Michael so tight he had no room to jab. MJ scored 23 but he had to take a lot of shots and work his ass off. He made only 3 of 9 in the second half. He was tired, frustrated, and losing trust in his teammates—even in Pippen and Kukoc. He tried to win the game by himself, but couldn't.

Nate, who hadn't played a minute in Games Two and Three, said he'd give it a try, so we shot him up again. The crowd went nuts when I put him in with five minutes left in the first quarter. This was Nate's Willis Reed moment.

The fourth quarter was huge. We fought them and played with big balls. We didn't get tight; instead we turned up the pressure and intensity on D and made *them* get tight.

After winning 107–86 we were still down 3 games to 1, but we had hope.

efore this game, I reminded the team about the success Detroit and New York had had against the Bulls in years past. Remember the intensity and pressure of those games? We haven't had a game yet where there are hostile face-to-face confrontations or there's hate for each other in the air. We haven't seen enough frustration or anger on Michael's face. Michael is leading a band of pussies that will back down and not put up a fight. We need to get this series to the boiling point!

If we get Rodman pissed off enough, he may even go into head-butt mode. (In March, while arguing a call in a game against the Nets, Dennis had lowered his *cabeza* hard onto a ref's head. Six-game suspension, $20,000 fine.)

And I repeated our new rallying cry: Forty-eight minutes!

Again, Gary stayed up on Michael without getting beat left or right and without fouling him. How many basketball players in the world could do that? I loved Gary again. MJ shot only 5 free throws. In the previous four games, he'd shot 10, 16, 11, and 13. We rebounded at both ends and we bothered them into 3 for 26 from three-point land.

"We should have come with this a little earlier," Gary said. We'd won, 89–78. The Bulls still led 3 games to 2, but the momentum obviously belonged to us.

We all met at Boeing Field at nine the next morning for the flight to Chicago. In the sky over Idaho or Iowa (or somewhere), I wondered what Phil would do to neutralize Gary's glovelike D on Michael. And I wondered if I should have had Payton on Jordan all along.

've got to decide how to remember this day and this game. It was Father's Day, I know that.

The emotion of the moments before the tip felt like someone sitting on my chest. We popped each other hard in the mosh pit at 3:59. For one last time we listened to "The Star-Spangled Banner" and to "Sirius" and to Ray Clay on the PA. "From *North* . . . Carolina . . . a guard . . . six foot six . . . *Michael* Jordan!" We touched hands in our huddle.

Forty-eight minutes. Forty-eight damn minutes!

If Phil did anything to get MJ free—more or different screens or new plays or post-ups—I couldn't see it. Gary stayed in Michael's shirt and bothered him into 5-of-19 shooting and 5 turnovers. Our team defense was great, too: as good as Chicago was offensively, we held them in the low 20s for all four quarters.

But we couldn't make a basket; I guess they played defense, too.

Our two best shooters—Sam and Hawk—were 5 of 20 combined and 0 for 11 from three. Rodman tied his playoff record with 11 offensive rebounds. We shot only 12 free throws—the same as Michael by himself—which shows we weren't aggressive enough. They won the game 87–75, and the series, 4 games to 2. After the game, for the first time in the series, Michael Jordan and I recognized each other, and shook hands.

I've just spent a few hours and several hundred words recalling the 1996 NBA Finals and our comeback that came up short. If we'd only been down 2–1, not 3–0, we might have won it. But in one of his books, Phil dismissed our effort in four words: "Seattle had its moment." The winners write the history, I guess.

I'd get some more shots at Michael and Phil, but not soon, and not with the Sonics.

CHAPTER 7

FIRED, HIRED, FIRED

uring the unusually hot summer of 1998, I discovered that they butter the burgers and butter the buns in Milwaukee. "Medium rare, Swiss, fries," I'd tell the waitress at Elsa's, Jake's, or Dr. Dawg. "Let's have some onion rings while we're waiting. And I'll have two Miller Lites. Yeah, two!"

Sharing this rich delicious diet with me from time to time would be Rick Majerus, the basketball coach at the University of Utah. Rick was like a brother to me and he had a Santa Claus body that made me look almost thin—and I was well on my way to 295. Coach M usually had the bratwurst.

"Mequon's nice," Rick said.

From having coached at Marquette for a long time, Rick knew the best places in Milwaukee to live and the best places to eat. He also knew someone at the Harley-Davidson factory who could give me a great deal on a Softail or a Road King. Hell, Rick thought they'd probably give me one. Nellie got one when he coached the Bucks.

Rick and I also talked about our teams. Rick's Utes had almost won it all a few months before, losing to Kentucky in the NCAA final (and beating North Carolina in the semis, dammit). Rick really liked his point guard, Andre Miller, and predicted he could run an NBA team. Which led to a review of the thirty or so Marquette players who'd played in the NBA over the years.

Dean Meminger was one, for example, and Jim Chones, Maurice Lucas, and Glenn "Doc" Rivers (Rick had given him that nickname; little Glenn had shown up at a basketball camp wearing a Dr. J T-shirt). In 1996, the Sonics had signed a Marquette baller named Jim McIlvaine. He'd set the school's career blocked shots record.

"I got this," I usually said when the check came. I could afford it. It amused me that my new monthly paycheck was more than I made in my entire first year as a head coach in the NBA. Which was nice, and a little weird, because in another set of circumstances, I would have coached for free.

In a couple of years, I'd get a bump from $5 million a year to $7 million, making me the highest-paid coach in the NBA and probably the best-paid coach in the world. Being identified with a giant salary bothered me a little. It puts a target on your back. You're much better off to have the *second*-highest salary. And, to be frank, we coaches and players do not deserve $500,000 per month. Or whatever the number is.

"This is stupid money," I always say to players. "You're not worth it, and neither am I."

Many people in my position have claimed that it's not about the money for them. But I really have made lots of decisions based on what I thought was best for my development as a coach instead of only thinking about the pay. We've been really broke a couple of times as a result and I don't mean Hillary Clinton broke. I coached in Great Falls, Montana, when I could have made a *lot* more money in college or as an assistant in the pros. But I think my time in the CBA made me better. I know it did. So what if I depended on the pregame media buffet for a few years. It was worth it.

On the other hand, I want to get paid what my job is worth in the NBA. If I'm worth *this*, don't try to pay me *that*. It's score-keeping. I do it as much as anyone else. The market decides what we get paid. So, yes, it is stupid money. But you'd have to be stupid to not get your fair share of it.

But wealth without health isn't worth much, and Rick and I were crazy to be eating like that.

Remember Rick? If you watched college basketball, you saw Coach Majerus on TV at least once a year. His teams regularly qualified for the NCAA tournament. Everyone in basketball knew how brilliant he was. But he had a fatal flaw. You saw it in the white Utah sweater with the red stripe stretched around his gut as tightly as the bark on a tree.

Rick didn't drink, so he gave himself permission to eat a lot. He'd order every appetizer on the menu, then an entrée and then more appetizers. If you hadn't cleaned your plate by then, he'd eat your food, too. As a result, my friend became obese. Everyone who knew him worried about his health.

What that food was doing to us wasn't good. I'm not asking for warning labels on menus, because I'm responsible for what I eat. The data about my dangerous diet was out there; I just wasn't paying attention to it. I guess the athlete's bulletproof attitude persisted in me for a long time. I just wish I'd grasped this basic fact: cancer is a disease of abnormal cell growth. The more weight in your body, the more cells you have, and the greater the statistical risk of something going wrong in the cell division. Having too many fat cells is particularly dangerous. Too much alcohol definitely increases the odds of getting cancer. Those rings and burgers and fries and beers were little time bombs.

So what was I doing with buttered buns and Wisconsin cheese and Rick Majerus in September 1998? That's a little sad, too.

In a way, my unexpected trip to Milwaukee had taken years. In

1996–97, the year after we took the Bulls to six games in the NBA Finals, the Sonics went 57-25, another great season.

But as I know better than anyone, in the NBA it's all about the playoffs, baby! We beat the Suns in five, then lost in seven to the Rockets and Hakeem. Unhappiness swirled around the Seattle SuperSonics, and not winning a championship after coming so close was not the only problem.

Money was a big part of our dysfunction. It may seem crazy that anyone could be less than ecstatic with his NBA paycheck. And it seems unfair that teachers and firefighters get so little compared to successful actors, athletes, and singers. Obviously, our society places a high value on entertainment. But I'd point out that NBA-level skill is a very rare thing—there are only about four hundred players in the league at any time, with ten times that many who want in.

These desirable jobs are extremely physical and punishing to the body. Yes, a laborer with a shovel or a trowel works his ass off, but nobody jabs an elbow into the neck of a concrete finisher, and a ditch digger doesn't have to run 2.5 miles of wind sprints (the average distance run in an NBA game) a hundred times a year. Plus there are the sprints in practice—I make 'em run *a lot*.

Although concussions aren't a big problem for us, the NBA player gives up his body as surely as the athletes in the NFL do. Just have a look at the wobbly walk of Kevin McHale and at how hard it is for him and other former players on NBA benches to get up when there's a timeout. Limps and bad backs and chronic pain are almost a given for us. We get our hips, shoulders, and knees replaced so often we should get volume discounts. The pay is fantastic but careers are short. According to forbes.com, the average career is 4.8 years.

In other words: NBA players really care about their paychecks, and their number relative to everyone else. This is probably not news to you.

Fired, Hired, Fired

We'd signed the 7'1" McIlvaine to be our Shaq-stopper, but the guy he stopped instead was his new teammate. Shawn Kemp resented Mac's seven-year, $33.6 million deal, and I didn't blame him. After all, Shawn had helped take us to the finals—he was the best player in that series, not Michael—and he'd made the All-Star team six times. Mac obviously was being paid for mere potential. Our new center had come off the bench for the Bullets in his first two years in the league, as a backup to the 7'7" Romanian giant, Gheorghe Muresan. Mac's career averages were about 2 points, 3 rebounds, and 2 blocks. While playing a lot more minutes, of course, Shawn averaged about 20, 11, and 1.6. But Shawn would be making about a million a year less than the unproven new guy.

Like a lot of players, Shawn could recite the money and the length of everyone else's NBA paycheck. Michael was in his own special category; he got $30 million a year from the Bulls. Gary Payton made $10 million annually, and Rodman, $9 million. Orlando was paying Horace Grant about $15 million. Even middle-of-the-road guys like Dino Radja and Tom Gugliotta were getting $5 million or so per year. But Shawn had signed a contract extension in 1994 that paid him $3.6 million per year until 1997. He wanted a new deal but the team reminded him it was against NBA rules. He wanted a trade to a team that could pay him more.

His attitude cratered at this point. My underpaid power forward sat out the first three weeks of training camp. When he finally joined the team, his chronic lateness got worse. As you know, I take lateness as an insult to me and the team. I took Shawn out of the starting lineup for four games, punishment for missing a flight and a practice. As you can imagine, our relationship suffered.

"You're not acting like a professional. You're setting a bad example," I'd say. He'd just shrug.

In February, Shawn went out the night before a home afternoon game with the Bulls. When his waiter was disappointed with the tip, he counted up Shawn's seven 7-and-7's and called the newspaper. He'd had more than a few. The incident got a lot of press, to say the least. After that loss to Houston in seven games in the second round of the 1997 playoffs, Shawn said he never wanted to play for the Sonics again.

The Kemp drama highlighted the problem I had with our GM, Wally Walker. You could say it was a communication issue but, less politely, Wally and I just didn't like each other. He'd gone to Virginia, and you know my automatic and unreasonable mistrust of anyone from any ACC school not North Carolina. Wally had the superior attitude the Virginia Cavaliers are known for and he didn't think I could keep a secret. So he didn't tell me anything more than he absolutely had to. When Cleveland got interested in trading for Shawn in September 1997, their coach, Mike Fratello, kept us in the loop about the negotiations and Wally didn't. Hard to like a guy like that.

In a three-way deal, we got Vin Baker from the Bucks, the Cavs got Shawn, and Milwaukee got Terrell Brandon and Tyrone Hill. Wally called a meeting with the coaches to announce the trade— which was laughable because we'd known about it for two days.

"I'm sad. I won't coach many better or more talented players than Shawn," I told the media. "But our focus and mental health might be better."

As the Kemp mess came to an end, my battle with the Sonics got more attention. Everyone knew my contract hadn't been renewed beyond the end of the season. But instead of tuning me out, which usually happens with lame-duck coaches, the players and I developed a bunker mentality. We dug in; it was us against management and *the world*. As a result, our focus really *was* better.

We went 61-21 in 1997–98, winning our third division championship in a row and our fourth in five years. We got a lot out of a couple of older guys we'd picked up—Jerome Kersey and Dale Ellis—and Vinnie played great, making the All-Star team. We were a different team with Vin; less powerful, but a little more sophisticated offensively. Because of Gary, we still defended pretty well.

That was a fun coaching year. Stotts and I grew playoff beards to try to change our luck. I wore my decreasing inventory of hair a little bit long. I looked like a country singer. Or a fishing guide.

We squeaked by Minnesota in five games in the first-round best of five. In the semis, we shot great to beat the Lakers at home in the first game. We wondered: were the whiskers working? But that was the last game I ever won as the Sonics coach. We lost four in a row to end the series and our season. Shaquille O'Neal outplayed Mac by a wide margin. Shaq was in his prime then and Mac had a sore back.

The post-playoff blues hit hard. My five Sonics teams had averaged 59 wins a year—one of the best streaks ever; only the Bulls had a better record over the same time frame—but the fans and media were mad at me because we hadn't won a championship. A labor dispute looked like it might interrupt or even shut down the next season. My favorite player, Nate McMillan, announced his retirement. I still hated Wally. Bad vibes all around.

Which made that summer an interesting time for me to negotiate a new contract. The Sonics made an offer I'd call frugal, but not insultingly cheap. We countered. They didn't find our numbers reasonable.

So we didn't make a deal. I wasn't fired and I didn't quit.

"The Sonics allow Karl to walk away," the papers wrote, which was about right. I was bummed. I had the feeling of not quite finishing the job in Seattle. I still thought we had the players and the attitude to win big.

What a summer. In July, the owners declared a lockout, which is management going on strike. Their argument with the players' union was over money, of course. The players wanted more, while the owners wanted to put a ceiling on salaries, and to test the players for PEDs and marijuana. The owners said that 15 of the 29 teams in the NBA had lost money the previous season; the players said it was only 4. But I think both sides missed the point in the boring and stupid accounting and revenue-sharing arguments. The real money was in the teams themselves.

For examples: U.S. senator Herb Kohl (Kohl's department stores) paid $18 million for the Bucks in 1985. He sold the team in 2014 for $550 million. Dingbat real estate investor Donald Sterling bought the Clippers for $12.5 million in 1981 and sold the team in 2014 for $2 billion, about 160 times what he paid for it.

Were the players entitled to some of that windfall? It never came up, as far as I know. They might want to look into that.

Anyway, in previous years there'd been two NBA lockouts/ strikes that hadn't caused us to miss games but this one looked bad, and it was. Both sides dug in.

There were no training camps. No trades were allowed. There were no games in November. Or December. Shawn Kemp put on thirty pounds, which would surprise his new team. Our money fight disgusted fans and the media. "A dispute between rival gangs of millionaires," wrote *Newsweek* (and when the strike finally ended, TV ratings and ticket sales were off by quite a bit).

After Commissioner Stern set a deadline for a deal in January, the players' union started to cave. A supposedly impartial arbitrator had ruled that the owners didn't have to pay players with guaranteed contracts during the lockout. Meanwhile, the owners' cash was still flowing; they got TV money whether we had games or not. I got paid, too.

The owners got another show of support, this one from USA Basketball—the group that organizes our Olympics and World Championship teams—when it announced it would disinvite locked-out NBA players. This meant something because they played the International Basketball Association (aka FIBA) World Championship tournament only every four years, including in

Fired, Hired, Fired

1998. We sent a team of college, CBA, and Euro league players, only one of whom, Brad Miller, would go on to have a good NBA career. Our guys won the bronze, a hell of an accomplishment under the circumstances.

I got a call from Bret Adams, another lawyer/agent I worked with. "Milwaukee," he said. "Four years. Twenty million." The Bucks had just fired their head coach, Chris Ford.

This was Rick Majerus at work, at least in part. Rick and the Bucks' owner, Senator Kohl, went way back. "If George becomes available, you've got to go get him. He makes bad teams better," Rick had told the senator—which I know because Rick told me.

Rick had introduced us that summer when he and the senator came out to my summer place in McCall, Idaho. At breakfast, Rick quickly worked his way through some bacon and eggs at the Shore Lodge. He then excused himself. While Senator Kohl and I talked, we watched Rick swim back and forth from the shore to a dock out on Payette Lake. Rick was down a bit from his peak of 370 pounds. From time to time, Rick would look up at us, his big pink and white body shiny from the water and a question on his face. When he saw that we were still talking, he'd do another lap. Despite heart and weight problems, Rick swam a mile every day. He said the extra fat made him buoyant.

The senator and I talked for about two hours. I immediately liked his intelligence and his dedication to Brew City and the Badger State. I even liked his politics; I'd have voted along with him if I was in the Senate. Anyway, the senator was resisting offers to sell the team for a big profit for fear the new owner would take it to Oklahoma City or somewhere. Like me, Kohl loved history and he loved basketball and he wanted very badly to win.

But he wasn't winning. The Bucks endured some awful years on their way to seven straight losing seasons. They had two guys you could build around, however, in Ray Allen and Glenn Robinson, the number one draft pick of 1994. The rest of the team was a strange Milwaukee brew: 6'8", 300-pound Robert "Tractor" Traylor was the bad half of one of the worst draft day trades in NBA history (Dallas got Dirk Nowitzki). Scott Williams was the center; he played the right way—with a lot of passion—and he'd gone to UNC. We had two Currys, Michael and Dell (Dell had a little dribbler at home named Stephen); and a 5'11" point guard in Terrell Brandon, who was part of the Shawn Kemp trade. Two Bucks I knew well from the Sonics were Ervin Johnson and Ricky Pierce. Ricky was on his last legs as an NBA player and I knew I didn't want him.

In a general way, the Bucks had what I was looking for. They were at least mediocre—they'd finished ten games under .500 the previous year, which was an improvement from the seasons before—and they had a decent bench. I could coach them up, I thought. I'd done that before.

In the lockout's toxic atmosphere, on August 30, 1999, I was introduced as the Bucks' new coach. And that was why I was in Milwaukee, eating butter burgers and trying to act like I really was worth Gugliotta-Radja money.

In the weeks and months to come, nothing would have made me happier than to put down the onion rings and get to work. I wanted to be in the gym, showing Terrell Brandon how and when I like to trap, discussing pick-and-roll defense with Glenn Robinson, and teaching everyone our plays and nomenclature. But the lockout prevented any contact with players.

Milwaukee. Just saying the word brings back some crazy memories. While in Milwaukee, I received my greatest honor that was simultaneously my worst experience as a coach. I endured my most embarrassing PR fiasco. We kicked some ass, moving past teams that thought they owned the East. Another NBA conspiracy theory erupted. My father died, my wife divorced me, my team collapsed, and I lost my job. I turned fifty. My son and I tried to repair our damaged relationship. I started dating for the first time in twenty-six years, and cancer smoldered inside me.

In other words, life got in the way of basketball.

———

The strike ended and a new agreement was ratified on January 20. Games began on February 5, so we didn't have much time to get to know each other. In order to play the most games possible, the owners and the players agreed to cancel the All-Star Game and to play 50 games in a little over 100 days, a brutal pace for all of us. We had many back-to-back games, and long stretches when we played every other night. We would have to learn about each other on the fly.

The first thing I learned was that our perimeter guys were offensive machines. We took any good shot whenever it came, especially early in the clock before the defense set up. We played a lot of zone defense, which was of course technically illegal back then.

The first thing *they* learned was that their coach was running their asses off. My style of basketball requires excellent conditioning. I made them lift, too. Strength is so important in our game. One thing about me they may have liked was that we weren't going to have a thick playbook; on offense, they just had to master certain principles about spacing, ball movement, and shot selection. I'd teach defense—the more complicated side of the ball—during our short season.

I explained how we would play: with force, every day. You make the decisions on the floor, not me. Just don't hold the ball. Drive it, shoot it, or pass it BUT DO NOT HOLD THE BALL.

By keeping it simple, we hit the ground running. We would not be going for perfect. In high school, college, or pro ball, all of us had played for teams searching for perfect execution, which to me is so dull. Some coaches rehearse, rehearse, rehearse; mine hit and run. There's nothing wrong with perfection as your focus, but I think basketball is too fluid to get very strict about doing things just right. It's also about half as much fun to play or watch. Remember how the controlled game made me cry when I was a rookie with the Spurs?

Too soon for comfort, the season began. We won some games, and Milwaukee got all giddy at having a competitive team again.

An interesting part of coaching the Bucks was my efficient assistant, a superfit blonde named Kimberly Van Deraa. Kim had played four years of basketball at Wisconsin–Parkside and had coached D-1 volleyball. A jock. She knew hoops and she wasn't afraid to tell me when our rebounding or defense or whatever disappointed her. After a couple of years, Kim and I began to see each other socially.

Mentioning Kim makes me think of another behind-the-scenes person in Milwaukee: Toody. Someone once described Tom J. "Toody" Cirincione as "the World's Most Devoted Basketball Junkie." A little guy with thick glasses resting on a big nose, Toody was a hanger-on, a friend of a friend who was happy to do anything to make a buck and be near a team. *"He's the greatest player ever, baby!"* Toody's proclamations about basketball could make Dick Vitale seem listless. He fascinated Herb Kohl, who gave him a scouting job for a while.

Coaches and players are only the tip of the NBA iceberg. There are hundreds of hardworking people with every team, from HR to marketing to Toody.

In March, at the trade deadline, we swapped for a new quarterback, a brave (or foolish) move for a team fighting to get into the playoffs for the first time in seven years. I liked Terrell Brandon as a player and as a person—he was quiet, humble, good-natured—but he could not give us the kind of leadership I thought we needed. We already had too much nice and not enough fire.

Glenn Robinson barely spoke and Ray Allen smiled as if he was *amused* when he made a mistake on the court.

I also want my point guard to be my man, to know that I chose him. It can be hard to get that feeling with someone you inherited. And Terrell's contract was expiring. He had a Shawn Kemp situation, in that he'd signed a long extension for not that much money—about a million a year—and then he made a couple of All-Star teams. He expected to make about $7 million a year in his new deal.

So we traded with the Nets and Timberwolves for Sam Cassell. While Sam couldn't defend like Gary Payton, he was a good passer, and a very good shooter. And, man, did he bring the noise. Sam talked constantly, like Gary. A happy, likable guy; I'd have preferred he become meaner, more of an asshole to the other team—like Gary.

I'd describe the Bucks as a little soft on both sides of the ball, with me constantly asking for more toughness. Scoring from defensive pressure—forcing turnovers—didn't happen, not like at Seattle.

We went 28-22 and squeaked into the playoffs as the eight seed. Bucks fans were *very* happy at being in the postseason for the first time in eight years. However, we'd have a hard time getting past the first seed, Indiana. They were good. They had Rik Smits, Reggie Miller, Chris Mullin, Mark Jackson, and a smart coach in Larry Bird. They were obviously better than us, so I talked up my belief that superior teams can trump superior talent.

Didn't work. We took them to overtime in Game Two but they won the series 3-0.

After one season, I thought I knew why the Western Conference routinely kicked (and still kicks) Eastern Conference ass. For one thing, it was the luck of the draw that there are great coaches in the West. Then there are two other things working in combination. The most influential teachers in the East, Howard Garfinkel and Hubie Brown, were defensive masters. Brown coached the Knicks and Garfinkel ran a famous basketball camp.

In the West, the most influential coaches were Jerry Tarkanian, John Wooden, Stu Inman, Buzz Pressley, Don Nelson, Bob Kloppenburg, and Doug Moe. They were offensive innovators. When the NBA made rule changes in the 1990s to increase scoring, Western Conference coaches were more than ready. They welcomed a game with no hand checks or defensive forearms, no grabbing screeners, and the defensive three-second rule.

For example, when Pete Carril came west to teach his back-cutting offense to the Sacramento Kings teams that had Vlade Divac, Chris Webber, Doug Christie, and Mike Bibby, he made them very hard to beat.

We went 42-40 in 1999–2000 and got into the playoffs again. The Bucks weren't making anyone forget Wisconsin's Team, but even Packer Backers were ecstatic that the Bucks were in the playoffs for the second year in a row. We were the eight seed again, playing Indiana again in the first-round best of five. Once more the team heard my underdog speeches, how superior teamwork and selflessness often beats better talent. I grew another playoff beard, the gray whiskers reminding me that I was about to turn forty-eight.

I don't think anyone but us saw it coming when we took Indy to the last second of the decisive fifth game. We had the ball, side out of bounds, down one with nine-tenths of a second on the clock, plenty of time for a catch, a fake, a dribble, and a shot to win the game and the series. I called a play for Ray but they slid the picks and pressured him into shooting the ball over the backboard from 28 feet. They won the game 96–95 and the series 3-2. Reggie Miller had killed us. He had 18 in the fourth quarter.

"We were very lucky," Reggie said to his sister Cheryl, who came onto the court to interview him for NBC. "They were the better team. George Karl really had them prepared."

Fired, Hired, Fired

But I don't believe in moral victories, nor do I find satisfaction in being a close second. Between our defense allowing 41 points from Reggie, having every important call go against us, and losing in the first round again, I was furious.

And I was distracted. Something big had come up: the North Carolina job. Coach Smith had retired unexpectedly in 1997, and his longtime assistant Bill Guthridge took over. Guth took the Heels to the Final Four twice in three years, but then he'd had enough of the stress. He announced his retirement in the spring of 2000. Coach Smith and Guth wanted Larry Brown or me.

Did I want the job? Hell yes! By now you know the depth of my love for Carolina basketball. But I didn't have a way to get out of my contract with Milwaukee—and a call from Coach Smith to Senator Kohl didn't change anything. With the opportunity out of reach, I suggested Coach Majerus.

And then I wondered: do I *really* want this job? UNC couldn't pay me anything close to the bucks I got from the Bucks, but that wasn't it. The more I thought about it, the more I began to doubt I could coach college ball. The recruiting, the NCAA rules and regulations. I'm just not a rules and regulations guy, if the rules and regulations get in the way of winning. With Larry, me, and Roy Williams backing away, the job went to another alum, Matt Doherty.

A visit from Charles Barkley distracted me that summer. We drank a few beers and played some golf. Charles is not a good golfer, as you may have heard or seen. Which is a shame. Because he wants to be good so bad. His swing is painful to watch. He may need to find a genie in a bottle, because lessons are not helping. Of course, we had some bets going. Just as in basketball, Sir Charles was a very unhappy loser. He would storm off the eighteenth green. I think he still owes me some money.

I was still mad at my team when we had our coaches' retreat in upstate Wisconsin in September. The one big thing we decided had to do with Allen, Cassell, and Robinson, whom the Milwaukee newspapers called the Big Three. What I had to say to them, well, I knew it could get ugly psychologically. But a coach has to know when it's time to rock the boat. Enough with compromise and communication, I told my assistants. I'm going after their asses.

What I liked about the Bucks at that moment was our offense—we were an outstanding jump-shooting and three-point team, probably the best in the East.

We had an offensive flow going that I loved. Our defense most nights was at least adequate. Our new guy, forward Tim Thomas, was going to be really good.

What I hated about my 2000–2001 team was its happiness. A couple of guys had the snarly attitude I like—Scott Williams, Jason Caffey, Darvin Ham—but a couple of others could laugh during a game, and you rarely see a great player crack a smile. For what was at stake, and for what they were being paid—Ray made $9 million a year, Glenn $7.2 million, and Sam $3.5 million—I wanted a lot more focus and passion. I wanted losses to hurt.

I laid it out for Ray, Sam, and Glenn in training camp. You three are selfish, individualistic, and obsessed with your own numbers. You're always thinking about your next contract. You don't work hard enough and I don't see enough professionalism or accountability.

I guess they didn't take it well. We started the season 3-9.

Then I upped the ante and went after them publicly, which I have noted is almost always a mistake. But it worked. We went 49-21 the rest of the way, the best in the league over the last 70 games. "George motivates differently," Sam told the *Chicago Tribune*. I think I'd scared him.

During those optimistic days the senator offered me an extension that not only would make me the highest-paid coach in sports—although $1 million of my $7 million A YEAR would be deferred for ten years—I would also become a 1 percent owner of the team. Crazy! The contract sat for months on a table in my living room while I tried to understand this insane amount of money. I didn't sign it for a while. It was also an insane amount of responsibility and it would ratchet up the expectation that I would bring an NBA championship to Milwaukee. But so many pieces have to fall into place for a team to win it all, and a lot of them—injuries, trades, luck, the other teams—are not in the coach's control.

"What should I do?" I asked my father. Joseph Karl was ninety-four, very ill, and living in a nursing home near Seattle. But he still had his marbles. Go ahead and sign it, he said. "If you don't like it, you can quit." I signed.

Our 52-30 record in 2000–2001 got us the Bucks' first division championship in sixteen years and the second seed in the first round. Orlando had Tracy McGrady scoring and Doc Rivers coaching; we beat them in four, for the Bucks' first win in a playoff series since 1989.

Charlotte nearly beat us in round two. It was a totally odd series but remains one of my favorites. We won two, lost three. Now we're facing an elimination game in their arena. Sam had 33 to help us win that game, and Glenn and Ray came up big in Game Seven at our place. We were a young team that no one expected to do much, but Ray, Glenn, and Sam really grew up. We'd made the Eastern Conference Finals.

If we beat NBA MVP Allen Iverson and Philly, we would surely face the Lakers in the finals. We'd gone 4-0 against L.A. in the regular season. Their coach: Phil. Oh, how I wanted another shot at him. How I wanted to be NBA champ.

I guess there are a lot of ways to tell you about that series with the Sixers. Before it was over, reporters, fans—even mild-mannered Ray Allen—were saying some pretty shocking things.

We were going to hear from the league for "disparaging comments made about the officiating in the Milwaukee-Philadelphia series."

Want to hear what $85,000 worth of fines sounds like?

"The league [is] a marketing machine," Ray said after Game Five. "The bottom line is about making money . . . the league knows that Philadelphia is going to make more money [in a playoff series against] Los Angeles than it would with Milwaukee."

And: "Nine times out of ten, you know the ref has no biases. But in the back of everybody's mind it's like Philadelphia and the MVP need to play in the finals."

That will be $10,000, Mr. Allen.

I agreed with Ray, but I didn't want us to obsess about it. I dismissed the idea of a rigged series as what I call "summer talk," the worthless rehashing and could've-beens a losing team wails about in the off-season. But when the conspiracy questions continued in the postgame presser, I referred to that infuriating day eight years before. I think I've mentioned this about ten times: Game Seven of the 1993 Western Conference Finals, when Phoenix shot three times the normal number of free throws, three Sonics fouled out but no Suns did, and I bitched loud and long about the refs.

"Here was the scenario," I told the writers, implying that we were seeing a replay. "The league wanted a Barkley-Jordan final. Charles even did a finals commercial for NBC three weeks before. He told me about it. And then they shoot sixty-four free throws."

That will be $25,000, Mr. Karl.

And Senator Kohl, please send a check for $50,000 for not controlling your player and your coach. Our owner was not pleased.

I coach against other teams, for the most part, not other

coaches. But I look back at that series with the opposing coach in mind. Larry Brown had been a great friend for years. In 1974, after my rookie year with the Spurs, Larry recruited me to help him with a team of college All-Stars on a thirty-day summer tour of the Soviet Union. I remember bad food, KGB agents lurking around, and getting stranded after a party in Leningrad because the drawbridges were up. Who knew Leningrad was the Venice of Russia? I spent the rest of that night on a bench.

So. I'll always be grateful to Larry, another UNC alum, for giving me my first taste of coaching. But now I was coaching against him without a thought of the good old days in Moscow and Kiev.

We'd defended our asses off and held Philly to 78 and 74 in Games Two and Three, and won them both to go up 2-1. Our anger and frustration began to build during Game Four. At a crucial point late in the fourth quarter, Glenn Robinson plainly got smacked on the elbow as he shot a jumper—you could hear it!—and the Sixers got a breakaway layup. We lost, at home, 89–83, and the series was tied. In Game Five, Glenn and Ervin Johnson got called for touch fouls, then, when Iverson hit Sam on the arm as he shot, right in front of referee Ronnie Nunn: no call. Thanks to a couple of techs on us, the Sixers had a five-point possession and two fouls.

Commissioner Stern watched the game in person in Philly's arena, and forgot himself for a moment and acted like a Philly fan. I didn't see it but a lot of people noticed when he stood up and seemed outraged when AI got fouled and it wasn't called. We lost 89–88, and Ray and I did the bitching that cost us and the senator some money. I'll always remember that Game Five and I'll always hate it.

Emotions were the highest I've ever seen in the playoffs. It felt like someone—possibly me—was going to snap. It was entertaining to watch, I suppose. I remember a line from the *Los*

Angeles Times: "Raise your hand if you don't want this series to end," wrote Diane Pucin. "It's been fun—nasty, astounding, mean-spirited, high-spirited, pushing, shoving, elbowing, body-slamming fun."

Elbows and nasty came together in the first quarter of Game Six at our arena, the Bradley Center. AI drove the lane—guarding him was like trying to hold a handful of water—and Scott Williams, unfortunately, put an elbow in his neck. It was Scottie's third flagrant foul of the playoffs, not that many in 17 games for a guy whose job was to protect the rim.

But this was the Ray game, when he saved our ass by scoring 41, an incredible shooting performance. And to give credit where it is due, Iverson had 46. But it was the MVP's first big game in the series. Simply by never letting him go right, we'd bothered him into a horrible shooting percentage, something in the 20s. We survived their 26–6 run and won 110–100. On to Game Seven.

I don't remember much of what happened on June 3, 2001, at the First Union Center in Philly. Maybe I've blotted it out. But I can't forget that a couple of hours before the tip, I was informed that our starting center was suspended because of his elbow on Iverson. What?! The suspension seemed totally unfair, and so did the late notification.

Hours later, with my tie off and my dress shirt wrinkled and sweaty, I slumped on a chair in the locker and read the final stat sheet. In the part of the game decided by the refs, we got absolutely killed. For the series, we committed 12 technical fouls, they had 3; we had 5 flagrant fouls, they had none; they shot 186 free throws, we shot 120.

Maybe the refs don't like me, I thought, and not for the first time.

We didn't go to L.A. I didn't get another shot at Phil, and another shot at a championship. Too bad; we could have beaten the Lakers.

Fired, Hired, Fired

Maybe *I should* have known better.

Eight years earlier, some nonsports magazines did big stories about the Sonics. We were flattered by the attention from *Newsweek* and we liked what they wrote.

But a month before our playoff loss to goddamn Denver, *Esquire* embarrassed us. Their story made us look undisciplined and a little bit stupid, more like a tall motorcycle gang than a basketball team. Gary Payton's motor mouth fascinated the *Esquire* writer, who quoted him exactly as he spoke when among friends, double negatives and wrong tenses and all. Gary said he never saw their writer take a note, and he wondered if the guy had worn a wire.

Partly because of the great honor I mentioned—I'll tell you about that next—*Esquire* came calling again. Okay, I'll talk, I said; as you know by now, I like to talk.

But before I relive the quote that got me in trouble, a little background: The first thing a coach does in a new job is assemble a staff. For me—in Great Falls, Albany, Golden State, Seattle, and Milwaukee, that meant, first of all, Terry Stotts. As good a coach as he was—and he was and is damn good—Terry was an even better guy. He'd played basketball professionally in Italy, France, Spain, and the CBA; he was the son of a coach; and in a timeout huddle he was almost clairvoyant about the other team's next play. He'd been my assistant for twelve years. We'd won a shit ton of games and almost an NBA championship together but not once had he been considered for a head coaching job.

And a little more background: except for, possibly, the military, there's no place in American society with more black and white cooperation and friendship than in the NBA. There's really no room for a bigot in our league; we've got problems, but racism isn't one of them.

The *Esquire* guy asked me about Doc Rivers. Doc's career path had been NBA player, TV commentator, NBA head coach. In the back of my mind, I was thinking about the dues I'd paid before I was put in charge of an NBA team. And the dues Terry was still paying but couldn't even get a look. While Doc immediately proved he could handle the job—he was Coach of the Year in his first season in his first job with Orlando—he had never been a scout or an assistant or coached at a lower level anywhere. So I said . . .

"Doc's been anointed and that's okay. I understand that that happens but it's not necessarily right. Doc does a great job. Now there's gonna be four of five more anointments of the young Afro-American coach. Which is fine, because I think they *have* been screwed. But I have a great young assistant who can't even get an interview."

Before I could apologize for "Afro-American"—once an okay term for black that had fallen out of favor—and before the February 2002 issue of *Esquire* even came out, there was hell to pay. Doc took some shots that hurt a little bit.

"George never complained about Larry Bird when he got the job [as head coach of the Pacers]. I don't think George has an opinion anyone should listen to on this subject. . . . He thinks he's more than he really is. We call him Naismith. George gets old. He has problems with players. We also call him player hater."

Mark Jackson took the stand. "Disrespectful," said the Knicks point guard. "Doc Rivers and Byron Scott are some of the best coaches in the game. . . . A lot of times players know more than assistant coaches."

Doc and I had dueled before, and had coached against each other in the playoffs, so his name-calling probably had a personal edge. I would have told Jackson that I hadn't mentioned Byron Scott. But neither Doc nor Mark really responded to my point that some former players get fast-tracked to head coaching jobs, while guys who'd paid their dues and learned their craft have to step aside. Steve Kerr, Jason Kidd, and Rivers have made the transition extremely well. Not doing as well were Magic, Brian Shaw, Derek Fisher, and quite a few others, from George Mikan to Wilt Chamberlain. So I stood by my point: that an apprenticeship is a very good idea for an NBA head coach. Having played the game well doesn't mean you can coach it well. The same is true in golf and tennis and every other sport.

But many people took what I said the wrong way, inferring that I thought some kind of affirmative action was getting African-American former players head coaching jobs—when all I was doing was standing up for my assistant. Under a headline that read "George Karl's Alternate Reality," Harvey Araton of the *New York Times* made fun of me as a "self-important watchdog" of pro coaching, a job that he said coaches like me "liken to brain surgery."

I apologized. "I should have been smarter," I said. "You hang out with a writer for two or three days and you think he's your friend." And you think he understands you, even when you make a point as awkwardly as I made that one. I didn't say I'd been misquoted and I didn't deny my main point. Still, it felt funny having to convince anyone I'm not a racist. After all, my professional life has depended on extremely close mutual cooperation with black men. As I mentioned, Gary Payton is one of my five best friends. My daughter married a black man, Jackie Robinson, a high school basketball coach in Olympia, Washington. I love Jackie and their two children, my first two grandchildren.

I considered some of the differences between black and white when I vacationed with Kelci, Jackie, and his family at Dauphin Island, Alabama, last summer. Jackie is from nearby Mobile. Are Jackie's parents like mine? Is his mom's cooking like my mom's? Are his attitudes and points of view the same ones I have? Hell no. How could they be? But I focus on what we've got in common. Life is a lot more fun that way.

Everyone tiptoes around this subject, but I'm comfortable with it. I know that observing the cultural differences between black and white doesn't make me a bigot.

That moment of controversy died down and other ones took its place. The usual: Milwaukee fans and media wondered if I had coached the right way in the conference finals. Was I smart enough to make the adjustments to get us one step further? Was I inspiring or alienating our star players? As usual, my problems seemed a little more manageable when I gathered friends around a table filled with delicious Milwaukee fried food and beer.

CHAPTER 8

WE'RE NUMBER 6

Disengaged? Dogging it on defense? Yeah, that's about right.

—KELVIN SAMPSON, ASSISTANT COACH, 2002 USA WORLD CHAMPIONSHIP TEAM

Oh hell, I thought, *what have I done now?*

I reread the fax: "The Commissioner would like to see you in his office on October 7 at 10:00 am. Please let us know immediately if this presents a problem for you." I called, but no one would tell me why I was being sent to the principal.

Maybe they wanted more money from me. I usually get fined about $100,000 a year—mostly for technical fouls from standing up for my players. Maybe David Stern wanted to deliver more punishment for the *Esquire* thing. Maybe they wanted to increase my fine or even suspend me for my loud bitching about the refs in the previous Eastern Conference Finals and for giving credibility to the conspiracy theorists saying that the league preferred the spectacular Allen Iverson and the Sixers in the finals over the bland Glenn Robinson and Ray Allen and the Bucks.

I flew to New York. Ate dinner at the hotel. Put on a suit the next morning. Took a cab to the NBA office at 645 Fifth Avenue in midtown Manhattan. It was sunny but chilly, about 40 degrees. Took the elevator to the fifteenth floor.

Right this way, Mr. Karl. Would you like some coffee?

Stern rose from his desk, but not very far. The commish had the forceful personality and confidence you often see in little guys. He was a micromanager with a bad temper and he swore like a sailor but he was also very smart. He and I had tangled before, and I always lost. We had a pattern: I'd say something the suits hated—angry criticism of the refs, usually. They'd announce my fine. I'd call Executive Vice President of Basketball Operations Stu Jackson to complain and get no satisfaction from the Lord of Discipline. Then I'd call Stern. "That's the way it's gonna be, Jawge," he'd say in his New York accent. "You undermine the entire league when you tawk like that."

So I was totally surprised when, instead of another fine or reprimand, Stern told me that he and the USA Basketball Senior National Committee—which was mostly NBA GMs—had decided to offer me the job as head coach of our national team for the World Championships in 2002.

"We're very impressed with what you've done with the Bucks, and what you did with the Sonics. We think you can motivate our guys, get them playing as a team, and win a gold medal," Stern said, approximately. "The games are the first week of September next year. I know you'll be getting ready for a new season then but you won't have to go to Africa or South America or Russia. It's a home game. Indianapolis."

I looked out the window in Stern's corner office. I could see a bridge and a river and hundreds of buildings, and taxis and people on the streets, but I couldn't see the World Trade Center. Violent cowards had just blown it up. New York City and the rest of the country were still stunned and grieving from 9/11, and basketball didn't seem all that important.

"As you know, we've never lost a game in international competition with NBA players on our team," Stern said. "Forty-eight games in a row—that includes the '92 Olympics in Barcelona, the '94 Worlds in Toronto, the '96 Olympics in Atlanta. The '98 Worlds you know about. Because of the lockout, we had no NBA players there. And you know with our players back, we won the gold in Sydney last year, still without losing a game."

I didn't really need to be sold on international ball. I'd played in Spain and China, and coached in the Soviet Union and Spain, and my hero and mentor had coached in the 1976 Olympics in Montreal. Coach Smith's team hadn't lost a game, either. Back then, and until 1992, we always used amateur players.

I asked about the where and when of training camp (San Francisco, early August). We discussed who I'd want as assistants (we wound up with Gregg Popovich, the Spurs coach, Kelvin Sampson of the University of Oklahoma, and Stanford coach Mike Montgomery). Stern said he expected a lot of interest in the United States, and sellout crowds, partly because Reggie Miller of the Indianapolis Pacers would be on the team. Reggie was an All-Star, a dead-eye from three, and they loved him in Indy. Remember how he killed the Knicks in the playoffs?

After the eight- or nine-month grind of an NBA season, no one wants to give up a big chunk of his summer. But the pull of patriotism and the pride of being recognized as one of the best from the country that invented the game often got players to change their plans. I would, too. I told Stern yes. This was an honor even greater than coaching in the NBA All-Star Game, which I'd done three times.

We talked for a while about who might be on the team, the all-stars of the NBA All-Stars. In November, we announced the first seven of the twelve: Ray Allen, Antonio Davis (also an Indiana Pacer—we were gonna sell out Conseco Fieldhouse!), Michael Finley, Jason Kidd, Shawn Marion, Reggie, and Jermaine O'Neal. We only announced seven because some guys were playing hard-to-get, but we knew they'd come around.

"Versatile. Incredible talent," I told the media. "We can play fast, we can play big, we can put a team of shooters on the floor, or go with a slash-and-penetrate lineup.

"I think all the players understand that it's not just an honor, it's also a commitment to work, to prevail, and to not let anyone beat us on our home soil."

We'd be able to do almost anything defensively. Shaq, Tim Duncan, and Kevin Garnett would protect the rim and give us scoring and power inside. Tracy McGrady could make a basket from anywhere. Jason Kidd would direct the offense, and pass the ball to Ray Allen and Reggie for threes, or to Kobe for drives and dunks. I felt as if I'd been given the keys to a very fast car.

But the car lost a lot of power before we got to the race. Not long after I was announced as coach, Pop, Kelvin, Mike, and I met in Chicago for a long discussion about our team and our strategy, all of it based on Kidd running our show. With him reading the floor and leading the team, the coaches knew we wouldn't have to work that hard during a game. We valued his leadership as much as his other skills.

But one by one, Kidd, Shaq, Kobe, Duncan, Garnett, Iverson, and McGrady announced that they'd prefer not to interrupt their summer vacations with more basketball. Fatigue, they said. I didn't take the news well. Some of these absences smelled like the usual NBA greed to me, players protecting their earning power instead of accepting a challenge and a great honor.

Not having Kidd left us in the lurch. Our other two point guards were great players, but Baron Davis couldn't approach Kidd's genius as a passer, or as a coach on the floor. Baron could score, but he had the instincts of a 2 guard; assists were not his thing. I loved Andre Miller's game (and I still do), but he wasn't Jason Kidd, either.

It was strange—bad strange—that our team didn't have a player that Pop or I was currently coaching. No Bucks, no Spurs.

Practice and exhibition games began. So did trouble. When Andre tried to direct Paul Pierce, the Boston Celtics forward got mad, and they had words. Paul obviously didn't accept Andre as a leader. Then my relationship with Pierce became a problem, too. He looked disengaged, and he was dogging it on defense. He'd miss 19 free throws during the tournament, a sure sign that his mind was elsewhere. He thought I couldn't decide what role I wanted him to play. Listen, goddammit, I said, I want you to score, but you have to play both sides of the ball!

So we had no leader and we had a conflict and we had no time. There's no question we could have used more than three weeks to prepare. And I don't mean to say that Pierce was our only personnel problem. A couple of guys admitted they hadn't picked up a ball in six weeks, and a couple of others came in twenty pounds overweight.

As I was finding out, our competition took the World Championship a lot more seriously than we did. Argentina's national team, for example, had been practicing and playing together for nine months. Other countries kept their teams together for years. But it wasn't just that we didn't have time to blend; the game itself required some getting used to.

As you probably know, the court in international ball has a shorter three-point line and a wider and differently shaped three-second lane than what we use in the States. Goaltending is more or less allowed. There are fewer timeouts. The favored style of play is fast and wide open, with lots of passing, drive and kick, and an emphasis on the three-ball. No one plays a big man-oriented power game. Not every ref understands English. The coaches wear sport shirts or sweats, not suits.

And another thing: our NBA player advantage had been trumped a little bit. In the eight years since we'd won the Worlds, our GMs had been combing the globe for players and they'd found quite a few. For examples: Yugoslavia's national team had five

NBA guys, including two really good ones in Peja Stojakovic and Vlade Divac, both of whom played for Sacramento. Yao Ming of the Houston Rockets and Mengke Bateer of the Denver Nuggets formed the Great Wall of China; Dirk Nowitzki of Germany and the Dallas Mavericks would be named tournament MVP.

We lost an NBA player, maybe our best one, when Reggie Miller rolled an ankle in training camp. With the international three-point arc only 20 feet, 6 inches from the hoop—about three feet closer than what we were used to—there's no telling how many treys Reggie might have made. I remember Reggie lying on the training table after he got hurt and how upset he was. The coaches were, too. He didn't play in the first three games and he couldn't play much in the other six. He would score only 36 points in the tournament. Losing Reggie *really* hurt.

We beat Algeria by 50 in the first game, then Germany (not much help for Nowitzki), China (cracks in the Wall), Russia, and New Zealand. Winning was expected; what we glorious representatives of the United States weren't prepared for was the half-empty arena and the lack of excitement. Except for familiar food and a shorter trip back home when it was over, we had no home court advantage at all. I don't know if the apathy was some failure of marketing or from Reggie getting hurt or from not having our biggest stars on our team. Maybe, in the United States, even in Indiana, basketball in the summer just doesn't sell.

As a result, sometimes it felt like our opponents owned all the emotion in the building. I especially remember all the yellow-shirted Yugoslavians raising hell and chanting something or other in Serbo-Croatian. They had a World Cup soccer energy. We had applause.

Our first really tough game was against Argentina.

During the tournament, Pop, Kelvin, Mike, and I had watched them when we could. They played the international game extremely well: an attacking style with lots of passes resulting in lots of assists. They had no current NBA players, but one of them was about to begin his career with the Spurs. Pop had drafted Emanuel "Manu" Ginobili in 1999. In about ten months, he and the Spurs would be NBA champions. Manu was damn good, in other words. Argentina would have made a pretty good NBA team.

We wouldn't have been as good. What else can I say? Argentina beat us 87–80. It was the first loss ever in international competition for a U.S. team using NBA players—a 58-game winning streak—and I was not happy to be a part of it. That we lost by only seven doesn't really give an accurate picture. The game wasn't that close. We caught up with some meaningless baskets in the last minute or two.

We played Puerto Rico next, and shut down Elias Ayuso and Carlos Arroyo to win by ten. The next day, we got Vlade and Peja and Yugoslavia. Still steamed from losing to Argentina, we coaches got out our best motivational speeches. Pop's and Kelvin's were particularly good. We reminded them that the gold medal was still within reach. We led by ten in the second half but they made five of six from three in the fourth quarter, while we went cold. Someone wrote that I should have used Raef LaFrentz more. Raef could shoot from three pretty well for a center and he might have drawn Vlade away from the basket. We lost to Yugo by three.

Now feeling angry down to my bones, I walked into the locker room the next day before our game against Spain. With a win, we'd at least get a medal. Several players, including Pierce, were watching the U.S. Open tennis women's final on TV. Venus versus Serena. Very interesting, but it shouldn't have been nearly as interesting as getting ready to play for your country. "Turn that damn thing off," I said. The players watching didn't like it. Serena won, by the way.

Two of our guys hadn't played a minute in the tournament. I put in Jay Williams, soon to be a rookie for the Bulls, and Nick

Collison, a senior at Kansas. They did pretty well but we lost 81–76, with Spain winning the fourth quarter 25–10.

Yugoslavia beat Argentina in overtime in the final. With our 6-3 record, we finished sixth. Sixth!

Serena won, by the way.

I felt hollowed out and empty. During the very long walk from the basketball floor to the media center, I tried to gather my thoughts.

Being the coach of the first USA team to lose with NBA players made me doubt myself for an instant. Maybe I was the wrong coach with the wrong players at the wrong time. But then I realized, and Jim Tooley, the CEO of USA Basketball agreed, that we were doing things all wrong. The world had caught up to American basketball. Our second-tier players were not good enough to win the Worlds or the Olympics.

Lesson learned. Under Jerry Colangelo, we no longer treat the Worlds like some meaningless All-Star games. We see it as some really important NBA playoff games. Look at the firepower on our current national team, which includes James Harden, Stephen "Steph" Curry, Russell Westbrook, and Kevin Love. And now we have stability on the coaching side. Mike Krzyzewski has coached our national team since 2005. He's gone 62-1.

I went back home and tried to get ready for another NBA season.

It was a frying pan into the fire deal. The Bucks and I had some problems.

CHAPTER 9

NOTHING TO DO
BUT ME

So much of coaching is cheating your family.

—ME

We *knew there* was a hole in the metal fence at the back of the driving range. We shoved a twelve-pack through the opening, and a couple of clubs, then the four of us wiggled through. It was around midnight but there was moonlight: perfect for golf.

Being back at Pecan Valley in southeast San Antonio on an off night brought back many pleasant memories. It reminded me that golf and friends are a big part of why I love life. It had been twenty-five years since I was an off-duty Spur patrolling Pecan nearly every summer day. I was part of the Game back then, a regular weekday gathering of golf pros, golf addicts, and gamblers. There'd be about a dozen of us, usually. We met at noon.

The first tee was like the trading floor at the New York Stock Exchange: "Hey, Macnak, I want you for ten across, and I want six shots."

"You're nuts. Give you two *a side*."

"Frank and me against Tommy and Mark. Automatic two-downs. I get shots on the par fives. Nassau for twenty."

"You're nuts. George gets one shot, on thirteen. Five-dollar team skins, double on birdies. And *I* get Frank."

"Six and thirteen. Ten-dollar skins." And on and on, with four conversations going at once.

Frank was Frank Conner, one of only two men to have played in the U.S. Open of tennis and of golf. He had amazing hands, and was very hard to beat in either game (I tried). Jim Macnak looked like he'd been left out in the rain but he could shoot something very low, and he played like he needed your money. Mark Abley bounced around between the PGA Tour and professional golf's minor leagues. Tommy Garcia, another pro, often went really low at Pecan. Although the pros had a lot more game than me—I could break 80 on a good day, while they could get below 70—golf's handicapping system allowed us to have a very involving bet.

I also used a needle to even the score. "Is that as far as you can hit it? You're such a pussy. Are you laying up again? Why don't you play like a man?"—that sort of thing. The way I talk to my players now and then. My comments and teasing were good-natured, of course, and etiquette does not allow anyone to mouth off while his opponent is actually playing his shot. Which is too bad. I guess I'm frustrated that you can't play defense in golf.

Speaking of which: The worst anyone ever got in my head happened in the early nineties one afternoon at Ben Hogan's club, Shady Oaks Country Club in Fort Worth, on an off day before we Sonics played the Mavericks. Hogan always sat alone at a table by a window in the second-floor dining room, drinking martinis and smoking cigarettes and watching the play on nine and eighteen.

I killed my drive on nine this day and had only a hundred or so yards left to the green. "Hogan's watching," my son of a bitch of an opponent whispered.

I choked like I had a bone in my throat, and skulled the damn ball so far over the green that I was practically in Hogan's ashtray.

"He *can't help* watching you now," my friend/SOB said. Playing too fast, and trying too hard not to hit into the middle of the ball again—I hit behind it. So far behind it that all I hit was ground. The ball disappeared; the chunk of Fort Worth I'd excavated flopped over my Titleist like a blanket.

The needling can be fierce at the annual Doug Moe Invitational, which Doug organized as a way for some of us former Carolina players to have a reunion with Coach Smith. No one would mess with Coach Smith. Except me, of course. I'd imitate his Kansas accent, which always gave him a nice laugh. Anyone else is fair game. "Hey, Michael," I said one time. "You swing like a girl. Can't you afford lessons?"

We play the DMI around Labor Day, at Pine Needles, or at one of the other courses in or near Pinehurst. It's a collection of some of the most competitive people on earth. Roy Williams, Larry Brown, Eddie Fogler, Doug, and I are or were coaches. Former players Phil Ford and Michael Jordan also get invited to the invitational. It's two-man teams, with $1,000 or $2,000 at stake, enough to hurt if you lose. I've played with or against all of the guys I've mentioned. Roy Williams is the best player. Michael is good, as you've probably heard, but he's not as good as he thinks he is. I think he's got some ego in his handicap. He claims he's a three but he's more like a six.

When I could afford it, I began to take occasional summer golf trips to Scotland. My first time, in 1980, it was just me and Terry Stembridge, the Spurs radio guy, driving for a week on the wrong side of the road and playing some great golf courses. The Old, Carnoustie, Turnberry, Muirfield. I remember the six-hour drive to Royal Dornoch. I remember crashing the rental car in the parking lot at the Rusacks Hotel in St. Andrews.

Another time, in North Berwick—they pronounce it "beddick"— Stotts, Strimple, and I drank with our caddies after we played. That took a few hours. With our accents and our willingness to buy another round, I suppose we Yanks amazed them as much as they amazed us. Our caddies were colorful, very thirsty guys with thick brogues and more fingers than teeth. They wore old ties and weather-beaten, shiny-on-the-right-shoulder sport coats to the bar, a little pub called the Quarterdeck. Which was where the late Deborah Couples, Fred's wife, amazed the locals and ended their marriage during the 1992 British Open when she got up on a table and did a little striptease.

That day on the ancient (circa 1832) North Berwick course, I'd had the hilarious experience of chipping my ball through a gate in a stone wall by a green.

Which brings me back, kind of, to slipping through that fence protecting the driving range at Pecan Valley. We had a lot of laughs that night. I needed them because my thing with Milwaukee had turned to chaos.

———

can think of two ways to remember the two years after the Bucks came within a game of the NBA Finals. I guess this would apply to anything in the past: I can try to re-create all the emotion I felt at the time, or look at the spilled milk with the calmness time can bring. Those two years were a disaster, but I'm not angry anymore. I've forgiven everyone involved, including myself. Especially myself.

My father's death in early December 2001 had nothing to with the basketball stuff, of course, but it put me in the expected somber mood. Joseph Karl was ninety-five. He was not athletic at all but he learned to throw and catch a ball so he could help me and so he could spend time with me. A good man, very steady and supportive. I loved him and knew I'd miss him.

I flew out to Seattle for the funeral, missing my first game in three years with the Bucks. I came back to Milwaukee and faced more unhappiness. My family was falling apart: fed up with my absences and preoccupation, Cathy, my wife of twenty-six years, was divorcing me and had moved to Las Vegas. Kelci, our oldest, had finished college and had started her career. But what about Coby?

Being my son was rough for the same reasons it was miserable to be my wife. I just didn't spend enough time with him or invest enough emotion in our relationship. My team was what I really cared about. Coby and I did some stuff together during the summer but not all that much. I was always preparing for the draft or talking about a trade or going off to a basketball camp. In Seattle, Coby had snatched a couple of hours a week with me as our ball boy, and before school, when the Sonics were at home, I'd take him to McDonald's for breakfast. Before our home games, our ritual had him carrying my suit from the car into the arena. When we swept the Rockets in the second round in 1996, thirteen-year-old Coby jumped into my arms at center court. It's far and away my favorite memory in thirty-something years of coaching.

And one of my least favorite memories: near the end of a game between the Sonics and Minnesota, their J. R. Rider threw a wild pass over a teammate's head and right at Coby, who was sitting near the baseline, head down, folding towels. The ball hit him squarely in the face. It was such a shock, he started to cry. The arena went quiet, and all eyes went to me. Would I rush over to comfort him, maybe lead him to the locker room, and let Stotts finish the game? No. I wanted to go hold him or help him, but I thought that at his age he would prefer me to not make a big deal out of it. After a couple of seconds, I went right back to coaching.

By taking up his father's game and becoming passionate about it, Coby had another set of pressures. I was a coach but I never coached him. When he shot at the hoop in the driveway, Cathy got the rebounds, not me. Everyone wants a dad in his life but I stayed just out of reach. I made Coby cry once when he asked me how he'd done in a game. I told him I didn't like his half-assed effort. He was twelve.

And more than once, Coby came home from school with a grim face and red eyes after the Sonics' first-round playoff losses in 1994 and '95. Teasing from the other kids.

I'd just gotten the Bucks job when Cathy and I split. We both wanted custody. The family court judge asked my somewhat shy and introverted sixteen-year old-son: Mom or Dad? Las Vegas or Milwaukee? I'm so sorry he had to answer that question. Desperate for some time with me, Coby said, "Dad."

At that point, the court ordered a sociologist to check out what the living conditions would be. I knew my likely address—a room at the Hyatt—would not make the grade, so I bought a big house as soon as I could. And to fill it up, to give Coby some company and some structure, I convinced an old friend, Bret Adams, to move into the house with his family. I also enrolled Coby at Marquette University High School in Milwaukee.

The court said okay to my plan but Cathy didn't like the idea of only seeing her boy sometimes, so she moved back to Milwaukee. Coby split time between her place and mine. Which, he says, made his last two years of high school the worst two years of his life.

But it wasn't just the two addresses that made Coby miserable. He didn't like that his new high school was all boys—I don't blame him. He only stayed at Marquette Uni High for one year. He moved to Homestead High in Mequon and it was a better fit.

He also resented the other people in the house and hated that I rarely broke away from the NBA to watch his games.

This was a lockout year, remember, when we had to play forty games in three months, so I was always either gone or preoccupied. The time he expected to get with me wasn't amounting to much.

In the bigger picture, Coby struggled with the very idea of his parents' divorce. He felt like his mom's protector, to some extent, but he was also desperate for time with his father. He had a hard time understanding his anger and frustration.

But at least we got *some* hang time. Man's man stuff: poker games, sports on TV, and grilling steaks. Coby and his friends would loiter in my office in the Bradley Center sometimes, doing their homework, talking about girls, bouncing basketballs, whatever. One day, Ray Allen walked by and made a teasing comment about Coby's friend's plaid pants. "We oughta TP his house," one of them muttered when Ray walked away. I slapped a hundred-dollar bill on the desk. "On me," I said.

I heard they did a hell of a job.

Maybe my whole team needed to be swathed in toilet paper. A year after we came so close to playing for a ring . . . we went nowhere. Eighty-two games plus playoffs can be a miserably long ride when things aren't going well. Can you imagine taking fifty business trips a year with everyone in your office? Do you think some cliques would form? Or that there'd be some annoyance with how Al from accounting slurps his soup? Or with the negative attitude of Marge from Marketing? And in this scenario, the boss/coach—me—could really get on some nerves.

The whole thing is tolerable—even fun—when you're winning. But we were not winning.

Our only personnel change had been losing Scottie Williams, whose hustle and attitude I loved, and adding Anthony Mason, a free agent power forward who had made his bones with the Knicks. In his previous season with Miami, Mase had averaged 16 and 10 and had made the All-Star team. He was expensive—$21 million for four years—but I pushed our GM, Ernie Grunfeld, to get him.

"I like Mason with my three-point shooters and Tim Thomas as a sixth man," I said then. "I think that's a dynamite team. We need some toughness and some leadership." But the late Mase (he succumbed to a heart attack in 2015) didn't add to our team, he subtracted from it. The local press had this one right when they said he upset our chemistry. But I'd have said Anthony Mason *destroyed* our delicate balance of talent and egos. While projecting a moral, Christian persona, he was the guy in the back of the bus or the back of the plane, bitching about minutes, the guards not getting him the ball near the hoop when he wanted it, and turning his teammates against the coaches. Mase was Marge from Marketing.

I'd put my ass on the line to get him. He put on weight. I put him on the bench. He put on his unhappy face, and he didn't take it off.

We started out okay and were ten games over .500 in early March. We were a streaky team, for some reason; we lost 4 in a row, then 5 in a row, then we won 8 in a row. But in the last quarter of the regular season we just fell out of the sky with the worst streak I was ever a part of. Was it me? Having no leaders? Bad luck? All three? What? I still don't know.

During that miserable stretch, we lost six games in OT. I think four of our five starters dealt with a serious injury. We didn't win a road game for *months*. As we lost and lost and lost, our team mood darkened, and we grew testy with each other. I tried everything I could think of, from leaving them alone to getting in their faces.

After losing 15 of our final 21 games, we had to win at Detroit just to get the last spot in the playoffs. Detroit blew us out 123–89. Humiliating. Again, there was hell to pay.

The senator ordered me to shake up my staff, a symbolic gesture meant to let the players know we wouldn't stand for their shit the next season. We wanted to fire the players but their contracts and their money—Ray was at the top, making about $11.2 million—made that impossible.

I didn't want to do it and agonized over it for a couple of days. It was not easy dismissing Mike Thibault, Ron Adams, and Gerald Oliver—you may remember that Ollie and I went way back, to my first NBA head coaching job, with Cleveland.

Hardest of all was cutting ties with Terry Stotts, who'd been my loyal right-hand man and best friend for fifteen years. I could tell him honestly that this detour was for the best because it would be better for his career to get out of my shadow. And that's exactly what happened: in a matter of weeks Terry had a job assisting Lon Kruger at Atlanta. When they fired Lon twenty-seven games into the season, Terry was promoted to head coach. But he felt as if he'd been thrown under the bus to save my ass. Maybe he had. Our friendship suffered, to my deep regret.

I was mad about the way things were playing out and I stayed mad. I could have been comparing my selfless, competent assistants to my players when I told the *Chicago Tribune*. "They always blame me, not themselves. That's how too many of these players are now. They're constantly talking about respect, but they respect no one but themselves. They're reluctant to accept any responsibility for their shortcomings."

Now I had only one year left on my contract. As I've said before, and as everybody in the league knows, the lame-duck coach has less authority, making a hard job even harder. The senator and I met a few times during the year but we beat around the bush about my situation. I didn't blame him; he had a lot on his mind. On top of his job representing Wisconsin in Congress, and his second job as an NBA owner not going great, he'd found someone he might be willing to sell the team to: Michael Jordan. With the Bucks and Michael in negotiations, Senator Kohl told us to cut the payroll, one of the five highest in the league.

So we broke up the Big Three. Not that hard a decision.

In August 2002, we traded Glenn Robinson to Atlanta for Toni Kukoc, Leon Smith, and their number one draft pick in 2003 (which would be T. J. Ford, a guard from Texas). Midway through the season, we were still an unhappy team, losing as often as we won. At the trade deadline in February 2003, we sent Ray Allen to Seattle, for Desmond Mason and . . . Gary Payton.

The media, Bucks fans, and Ray were shocked. Allen was

twenty-seven and one of the best shooters in the league. Gary was thirty-four, had lost a step, and would be a free agent at the end of the season. But Desmond turned out to be pretty good and I really wanted Gary's defense and his attitude to try to save our season.

But most of all it was a relief to see Ray gone. It was like popping a blister. Although Ray and I had a very good relationship for a few years, eventually he inhabited a sort of shadowland with the Bucks; he was too good and too well paid to be under my control and he knew it. And the other players saw it. The coolness of his personality reminded me of Joe Barry Carroll, unfortunately. Ray wasn't a negative guy, but I didn't think his teammates liked him. I knew I didn't. "Ray Allen has been nothing but trouble," I told the press. "We had no choice but to get rid of him."

Payton wanted out of Seattle—not enough veterans, he said, and too many people demanding the ball. He liked being reunited with me but trading for him was basically a Hail Mary. Because unless we had some real success in the playoffs, I knew there was no way Gary would stay. There'd be a market for him at the end of the season. Like me, he wanted a ring badly.

I should have said *if* we made the playoffs; we did, barely, tying for the last spot with Orlando. We got the Nets, who were good, because they had Jason Kidd. They beat us in six games, and a really crappy season was over.

We disintegrated. That summer, our GM, Ernie Grunfeld, left for the Washington Wizards. Gary left to try to bring another championship to the Lakers (he didn't). Sam Cassell got traded to Minnesota, and the last of the Big Three was gone. And me?

The Bucks' new GM was Larry Harris, son of Del, whom I've mentioned as a great guy and an unrecognized basketball genius. Larry had been with the Bucks since 1987, working his way up from video coordinator to scout to player personnel director to assistant GM. He was thirty-nine and in his first couple of days as GM he had to have a very serious talk with his head coach.

We met at our practice facility and spoke for about three hours. Believe me, I felt the weight of the disappointment from our owner, our fans, and myself. We'd had three years that were pretty damn good, but after we'd made the Eastern Conference Finals, what had we done?

It was a grim meeting. We discussed personalities and egos and trades and disappointment and the team's direction. We couldn't agree on a number for an extension that would keep me as the Bucks' coach. I think we both knew that going in. I didn't quit and I wasn't fired but I walked out of the meeting unemployed.

The Bucks would have to pay me for the final year of my contract. I'd get $7 million not to coach the team.

The *Chicago Tribune* was pretty brutal. Under a headline that read "Unrelenting Ego Costs Karl his Job," the story said that I was known for my big salary "and for combative relations with players." It said that I had been the most popular sports figure in the state except for Brett Favre. And it said that I was washed up: "It's sad to see a bright coaching career end like that."

I *mourned all summer.* Went to the lake, played in the Doug Moe Invitational, visited Rick Majerus and Roy Williams and a couple of other coaches for X's and O's conversations. Going through the motions a little bit. If I were in academia, it would have been the perfect time for a sabbatical. My body and my brain were stressed. I was heavy and still eating like an idiot: fried food and beer. I wonder now if I had cancer then, maybe the beginnings of it. I was lost.

I had some sour thoughts. In the NBA, if you're good this season, you've got to be even better the next one. Appreciation is two days of the year and "let's get better" is 363. There's a posse after your ass the moment you get worse.

What had my life become? Was the score of an NBA game

the only important thing in my life? Was I only a coach, so completely defined by my job that I couldn't be anyone else? No: I was also a father. Figuring that out helped me decide what to do next.

Coby had been a pretty good basketball player at Homestead High in Mequon and he wanted to play in college. He was 6'5", an excellent shooter, and, with me as his father and his rare proximity to the NBA game, he had a very good idea of how to play. He rarely made a mistake. But he didn't get any Division 1 interest: too skinny, they said, and he's not exactly a tiger on D. I couldn't even get Rick Majerus to give him a scholarship.

So Coby decided to walk on at Boise State—that is, he went to a big university in Idaho and attempted to make the basketball team as an unrecruited athlete, with no scholarship, which is usually a long-shot strategy. Cathy was from the area, so she moved back there with him.

And then, I did, too. Finally, something good about being between jobs. In fact, I bought a house and lived in it with Coby and one of his teammates. Best decision I ever made. Coby became my team, an overdue change in my thinking if ever there was one. Coby got my focus and my time and we both loved it. I went to his practices, watched game film with him, bought him chocolate cake at Chili's after his home games, and we talked and talked. It was, at long last, quality time.

My teenage son blossomed as a basketball player—he not only made the team, he started for the Broncos for four years. I have never felt more peaceful and proud than when I watched Coby play college basketball. He played very well, too. It was great to see how much he loved the game I loved.

More important, Coby grew dramatically as a person. His increased confidence and happiness amazed me.

"It was his first time not coaching in forever," Coby told a writer years later. "He had nothing to do but me."

Nothing to Do but Me

Not that I hovered—that's not good for the parent or the kid. I spent a week in July in Vegas, as usual, for the annual, all-volunteer, pay-your-own-way workout for NBA players called Gurg's Camp. Tim Grgurich started it in the 1990s and I always help. It's drill after drill, and gallons of sweat, for guys who want to improve. The gym culture: I love it like a fat kid loves pie.

In October, I got offered a part-time job. ESPN thought I might be good at analyzing basketball games.

For years, TV and radio has been a good place to land for ex-coaches. Some guys, such as Jack Ramsay, Dick Vitale, and Hubie Brown, stayed with it forever. Other out-of-a-job coaches—Doc Rivers, Steve Kerr, Mike Fratello, and Jeff Van Gundy, for example—used the platform to stay close to the game, and to make a paycheck until some owner and GM decided they deserved another chance on the bench.

All of these guys were or are really good behind a microphone. I'd had a lot of practice with the media, of course, because an NBA coach gets interviewed so much. But this was going to be different. I really appreciated the difference the first time someone coated my face with makeup and I looked into the camera and opened my mouth. I wasn't just answering questions anymore.

Along with another newbie, Dan Majerle—formerly a player for the Suns, Cavs, and Heat—I would be an NBA game analyst, which meant going to occasional games and commenting on the play. I'd also be a studio analyst for ABC from time to time, which meant I'd yak before and after the game and at halftime (ABC and ESPN are sister companies, as you probably know, both owned by Disney). Majerle and me and former Spur Sean Elliott were being brought in because ratings had been down the previous year. The TV boys don't hesitate to shuffle the deck to get the right mix. At games, I'd be paired with Mike Tirico, the play-by-play guy, and another former player, Tom Tolbert.

To prepare, I rehearsed in front of a camera in Bristol, Connecticut, at ESPN headquarters and got plenty of help from producers. I also watched a lot of tape. NBA coaches are always watching games when they're not coaching one—a lot of times with the sound off—but now I paid closer attention to what the announcers said, and how they said it. My new partners, Mike and Tom, were excellent: they made clear points, they made them briefly, and they didn't rely on too much jargon.

For example: To a casual fan, the phrase "stretch four" might be meaningless. Ex-coaches and players and keen fans know that it's a big guy—a power forward, aka a 4—who can shoot from the outside, stretching the defense outward. Sam Perkins, for example, or Kevin Love, or Dirk. Pocket pass, defensive rotation, length, box and one, triangle and two, run and jump, and pick and pop are perfectly clear concepts to some but need explaining for others. It's tricky: you want to be clear while also not dumbing it down too much for the true fan.

As I learned, verbal tics come and go, but mostly, they should go. For a while, the useless "I'll tell you what" preceded many NBA broadcasters' observations. "I'll tell you what, Bird is really feeling it tonight." Another one was "players like" or "teams like." Announcers and writers still use this one. "Teams like Orlando and New Jersey should be competitive in the East this year." What are the teams that are *like* Orlando and New Jersey? Just leave out the *like*!

Other bits of intentional vagueness I was warned about: don't say "the Sacramentos and the San Antonios of the Western Conference could be competitive this year" when you mean exactly those two teams. And don't say "*a* DeMarcus Cousins or *a* Dwight Howard could have an impact" when you could just drop the damn *a* and be specific and a lot more clear.

As I watched the 2015 finals, I noticed that Mark Jackson and

Jeff Van Gundy began many of their observations with an impossibility. "If you're the Warriors, you like this pace," and "If you're LeBron, you must get other players involved." That's more words and less clear than "LeBron must get others involved." Besides, I'll never be the Warriors. Or LeBron.

I know, I know: I'm on thin ice criticizing any other announcer. If you've heard me, you know I can mangle the language or screw up a sentence. For example, I once discussed a team's mentality, its *psyche*—a two-syllable word that rhymes with Nike—but I pronounced it with one syllable. As in to psyche out an opponent . . . not that big a deal, maybe, but you've got to use the language right when the cameras are on.

Maybe I wasn't Bob Costas, but at least I didn't hide, spin, or try to be controversial just be controversial. I remained positive and tried to serve the game I love. I also became good friends with my main producer, Bruce Bernstein; Bill Polian, a former NFL executive; and Seth Greenberg, a former college hoops coach.

I was okay as a color man, and a little better in the studio. I guess. As I already mentioned, you don't get much feedback in TV. At the end of the night, it's "Nice job everybody" in your earpiece, and that's it. It's two or three in the morning, and you go back to the hotel. It's not like coaching, where you're either up or down according to the result of the game.

ESPN brought me back for the next season, 2004–05, and dropped Majerle and Elliott. I never saw TV as a long-term thing. I didn't like being encouraged to focus on what was wrong with a player or a team and finding the doomsday in every situation. Still, I liked it. Going to games and trudging through the snow in Connecticut didn't bother me. My year and a half as an announcer allowed me to stay in the game and get closer than ever to my son. Not having responsibility for wins and losses felt like a relief, but I still wanted to coach.

———

*T*wo thousand five.

A lifetime of stuff happened in that one year. The broad strokes, in no particular order:

- I didn't expect to start another family, but I was very happy at the news that my girlfriend, Kim, was pregnant, and ecstatic at the birth of our daughter, Kaci Grace, in August.

I should explain about the names. Coby, Kelci, Kaci: Karl is such a plain, one-syllable handle that I think it needs to be preceded by something a little romantic sounding. And I guess Coby agrees. He and his wife named their daughter (my newest grandchild) Kennedy. I like alliteration, the double-*K* sound. I hate the name George.

- In March, in Reno, I watched Coby, then a sophomore at Boise State, play an incredible game in the semifinals of the Western Athletic Conference postseason tournament. He ran his team and controlled the game as if he were Magic Johnson: 7 for 10 from the field including a couple of threes, 5 assists, 4 steals, and smart defense, in a one-point win over Fresno State.

"How was that?" he said when we met at midcourt. "Good enough?" As cheerleaders and fans danced around us, we hugged and laughed and almost cried, a replay of when I held on to a much smaller Coby years before in Houston.

- In January, when another underperforming NBA team got serious about hiring me, Coby and I talked about it. He and I had had a good thing going, and if he'd said, "Don't go," I probably would have kept that life in Boise and with ESPN.

But, as he said later, "I told him to go. He'd showed me as much love as I'd seen in my life. But I could tell he hurt not being around the guys." I took the job—with Denver.

• In May, I watched Coby and some other college kids work out in a gym at Marquette. Big mistake: it was "contact between an NBA team and players not yet eligible for the draft." The league fined the Nuggets $200,000. Sorry, boss!

• In October, I got suspended for two games for some unusually passionate bitching about the refs.

• In my half season, we went 32-8. 32 and 8!—by far the best record in the league over that span, and an NBA record for a midseason replacement coach. We had winning streaks of 6, 8, and 10 games. Oh my God, that was fun.

• I got cancer.

• Coby got cancer.

CHAPTER 10

NOW ENTERING THE GAME FOR THE LAKERS

I just love the dignity of the game being insulted right in front of me.

—ME, REACTING TO A 50-FOOT THREE-POINT SHOT BY J. R. SMITH

oby was right: I wanted to be around the guys, and in the gym. Despite every bitter ending, I still deeply enjoyed the challenge of building and improving a team, of forming a basketball family to go to war with. The possibility of a championship still turned me on.

I already had a business connection with the Nuggets' owner, Stan Kroenke (pronounced "kronky"). We both owned a piece of the Columbus (Ohio) Riverdragons, an NBA D (developmental) league team. If you invested in sports, it was hard *not* to be in business with Kroenke. He built and ran an empire.

It was as if this man from St. Louis had learned the concept of vertical integration when he got an MBA at the University of Missouri, then decided to build a pure example.

Imagine for a moment that you're in Colorado's biggest city, and you want to go to an NBA game. You'd buy a ticket from Kroenke through his company, TicketHorse (now Altitude Tickets).

You'd go to the arena, the Pepsi Center, owned by Kroenke. The tall gentlemen down on the floor in powder blue, gold, and royal blue—that would be the Nuggets. Owned by Kroenke. But say you decided not to pay Stan for parking and a ticket and a hot dog, and you just wanted to watch the game on TV. You'd punch in 681-1 on your remote, the channel for a regional sports network called Altitude Sports & Entertainment. Also owned by you-know-who.

During the game, you could calm yourself with a glass of Cab from Stan's Screaming Eagle winery.

Kroenke Sports Enterprises owned a lot of things besides its NBA team—such as the St. Louis Rams of the NFL (as of 2010); the Colorado Avalanche of the NHL; Arsenal, a Premier League football (soccer) team in England; the Colorado Rapids of the MLS; and a professional lacrosse team, the Colorado Mammoth. He had his own money, from real estate development, and about $6 billion from his wife, Ann Walton, a Wal-Mart heiress.

In January 2005, one of Kroenke's subsidiaries was in crisis. The Nuggets had tanked the 2002–03 season, winning only 17 games, tied for the worst record in the league, in order to get a shot at LeBron James. (Don't believe it when teams say they don't lose on purpose to improve their draft position. It happens every year. I know of a Western Conference owner who called his coach *during games* to remind him to keep an end-of-season losing streak alive.)

Anyway, Cleveland got lucky and got LBJ, then Detroit stupidly took Darko Milicic with the second pick; Darko was a bust. Denver, drafting third, chose Carmelo Anthony. He was really good offensively, very quick and strong and an excellent shooter. In his one-and-done season with Syracuse, Anthony led the Orangemen to a national championship.

Denver improved a lot in Melo's rookie year. They won 43 games and made the playoffs. For 2004–05, the Nuggets traded three future number one draft picks for a good but batshit-crazy power forward, Kenyon Martin. Nene Hilario and Marcus Camby played center, and Andre Miller ran the point—you know I like him. That's a pretty good team, if it could get organized and play together. From the first game of the season, management, media, and the fans expected to see Denver in first place or close to it in the West.

Kroenke lost patience with coach Jeff Bzdelik pretty quickly, and fired him in late December after the Nuggets started the season 13-15. Interim replacement Michael Cooper was 4-10 and was about to be asked to move aside—for me or someone else. Also in the fold as assistant coach—but not a candidate for head coach— was my favorite guy in basketball, Doug Moe.

Things happened pretty fast. I met with Nuggets GM Kiki Vandeweghe in Chicago, settled the usual contract items, and signed. My hiring was announced in Milwaukee because the Nuggets had a game with the Bucks that night, Friday, January 28, 2005.

In my first game back, I'd be coaching against the team that had recently fired me. I had no clue about our offense so I just turned that part of the game over to Andre and we won a close game, 106–100. I won't say that it didn't feel better than your average win.

Still, that game introduced something to my coaching life that wasn't nearly as sweet as beating the Bucks. From the day I took the job and for years to come, the name on my lips and in my ears was Carmelo. In fact, there was a question about him in the first minute of that first press conference when I was announced as Denver's new coach. "I'm going to be demanding certain things he might not be happy with," I said. "I see a great player who has plateaued."

I didn't know Carmelo specifically, but I'd seen him play, and I knew him in a general way. I'd coached a lot of players with his background. I call them AAU babies. Basketball's AAU babies are similar to the spoiled brats you see in junior golf and junior tennis, but with a few important differences. The USGA and the USTA have some control, and prevent the worst abuses, because there's less money floating around, and they're strict about handouts like merchandise and free travel. The best young tennis players rarely bother with college, and great young golfers such as Jordan Spieth give it only a year or two. Besides, golf and tennis are country club sports, with country club parents. Basketball is nothing like that.

For some stupid reason—a double secret agreement with college basketball?—the league doesn't want kids to go from high school straight to the NBA. So a great young player has to play a year of pro ball overseas, or do the one-and-done thing at the University of Kentucky or wherever.

In the years before the teenage hoops stars turn pro, they inevitably become part of the AAU's corrupt system.

The Amateur Athletic Union has been around since 1888, and it does some good, I suppose. Its camps and tournaments and All-Star games for pre-college basketball prodigies are sponsored by Nike, Adidas, Under Armour, and a couple of other big players in jock apparel. From junior high on, these kids get free trips, shoes, and clothes, gifts they can't accept once they get into college and have to toe the line painted by the NCAA. Or pretend to.

Sharks swim around the best teenage hoopsters in the United States—colleges willing to sell their souls to get them, agents who'd like to be hired when the kid turns pro, and "street agents" recruiting for schools. The one-and-done thing means we're robbing college basketball of its players. The coaches are perpetually recruiting, with little time left over for team building and true player development.

But there's a lot of money at stake; sports agents usually get 3 percent of a player's first contract, and 10–15 percent on endorsements. The shoe companies pay the street agents to get a kid to a school where their logo is everywhere.

Now Entering the Game for the Lakers

You need some money, son? You're gonna need a car at school. I can help with that. Have you ever eaten at Morton's? Does your girlfriend need a job? Wink, wink!

In this environment, parenting is a liability.

And coaching is an impossibility. Since the only goal of AAU ball is showcasing kids for college scholarships, there's not much need to learn the team game. In fact, the me-first AAU atmosphere makes teamwork practically a foreign language. Fundamentals usually aren't taught or learned in AAU ball. The kids are so athletically gifted they don't bother to fill out their games. They do what they do but they don't get better. The coaches just let them play, teaching nothing. So, our best young basketball players learn only to keep their hands out. They learn entitlement and greed.

It may sound dumb or hypocritical coming from me, but I feel that money corrupts our game at every level. For these kids, obviously. In the NBA, owning a team used to be a civic good, something a rich guy could do for the community. Now it's all global marketing, branding, and revenue streams. Most or at least many NBA players would rather get paid than win. The game is the servant of the business, and it ought to be just the opposite.

The Nuggets team that I would try to lead and coach had three AAU babies: the starting forwards, Kenyon Martin and Carmelo Anthony. And J. R. Smith.

———

Kenyon snapped first.

In order to create a team that can play well together, I try to figure out my players and their motivations. Which guy is a leader? Who can follow effectively—followers are always dissed, but they're as important as leaders—and who will always rebel against authority? Who is confident and who is covering up? What personalities might work best together?

I knew right away that our power forward was one of the most insecure, immature players I ever coached. Kenyon Martin had grown up poor in South Dallas. Single-parent home; his mother worked two jobs. He was teased unmercifully, for his stutter, and for his skin color. The other kids didn't think he was black enough, so they called him Yellow Boy. That must have been miserable, but he found some refuge in sports, especially in high school and AAU basketball. The University of Cincinnati won the battle for his services. The Nets had first pick in the 2000 draft and they took Kenyon.

Out of anger at the world, poor impulse control, a strange form of showing off, or whatever, Kenyon decided that he was an intimidator, and he got many, many suspensions and fines. His absolutely stupid $345,000 worth of fines in 2001–02 got him a *Sports Illustrated* cover during the 2002 finals. "Bad Boy," the headline read. "Nets Flagrant Flyer Attacks the Playoffs." The Nuggets had traded for him the year before I got there. His deal: seven years, $93 million.

Let's jump ahead a little bit, to the 2006 playoffs. After coaching him for a year and a half, I knew that Kenyon was really good. He could rebound, run, and defend. His straight-ahead offensive style was a nice contrast with Carmelo's flashiness. But his knees were a problem; he missed about thirty games that season. In the locker room at halftime of Game Two of our first-round series with the Clippers, he bitched loudly about only playing seven minutes in the first half.

"I ain't playin' in the second half," he said.

"You're not *playing*?" I said.

"Not fucking playing. You need a hearing aid?"

The second half started—no Kenyon. He came out of the tunnel after a while, put a towel on his head, and sat on the bench like a statue until the game was over.

We lost the game and were about to lose the series. I was pissed at the insubordination. Also incredulous: who'd ever seen such a thing? But if I came back hard, with anger, I knew I'd only make the situation worse. I remembered how Gary Payton and I were at each other's throats until, after more than a year, we found some common ground. I knew I had to work with this guy, keep trying to figure him out.

We suspended Kenyon for the next two games, saying we couldn't tolerate such disrespect to the coach and to the team. But I was calm when I met the media after the game. I gave his ego a little break by taking some of the blame.

"I understand Kenyon's gone through a tough year," I said. "I know he's frustrated at the coaching, his knee, his playing time. I'm part of this failure, part of this relationship. I think I can get better from this, and hopefully he feels the same way. I think Kenyon's a damn good player and he has a competitive heart I love."

Maybe I was getting better at dealing with eccentric players.

But then: Carmelo.

Did I handle him as well? The volume of questions about Carmelo eventually wore me down. Sometimes I got so sick of talking about him that I'd just throw up my hands and say, "I don't know what he is and I don't care."

Carmelo was a true conundrum for me in the six years I had him. He was the best offensive player I ever coached. He was also a user of people, addicted to the spotlight, and very unhappy when he had to share it.

Wait. There's more.

He *really* lit my fuse with his low demand of himself on defense. He had no commitment to the hard, dirty work of stopping the other guy. My ideal—probably every coach's ideal—is when your best player is also your leader. But since Carmelo only played hard on one side of the ball, he made it plain he couldn't lead the Nuggets, even though he said he wanted to. Coaching him meant working around his defense and compensating for his attitude. I'd have to try to figure him out, too. How could I get more from him?

Carmelo grew up poor in West Baltimore. Single-parent home; his father died when he was two. With the drugs and violence in his neighborhood, it must have been like a combat zone. But like Kenyon, he found a safe place under a hoop on the playground. Hard work, skill, talent, and lucky DNA got Carmelo into a private high school and onto an AAU team. He put himself on the map when he averaged 25 a game at the AAU's Adidas Big Time Tournament in Vegas. Syracuse won the competition for his services, and he played one year in college, as mentioned, and won an NCAA championship. His deal with the Nuggets as a nineteen-year-old rookie was for five years and $80 million.

He was such a talented kid. If he'd decided to lead the league in rebounding, or to become the best defender at his position in the NBA, he could have done either one.

But Kenyon and Carmelo carried two big burdens: all that money, and no father to show them how to act like a man. As you've read, I grew up in a safe suburban neighborhood, with both my parents. I had a second father in my college coach, the most moral, decent man I ever knew. And I never made enough money as a player to get confused about who I was. When I compare my background to Kenyon's and Carmelo's, it's no wonder we had a few problems.

J.R. had a slightly different story. He went straight from high school in New Jersey to AAU success to the NBA. His father was on the scene and in his life, which is obviously good. But Earl Smith Jr. urged his son to shoot the ball and keep shooting it from the very moment I put him in a game, which is obviously bad.

In his defense, sometimes J.R. can make it from anywhere and score in bunches. But I wanted defense and commitment to the team. What I got was a player with a huge sense of entitlement, a distracting posse, his eye always on his next contract, and some really unbelievable shot selection.

For example, near the end of a close Game Five in the first round of the 2007 playoffs, I drew up a play that had Melo or Allen Iverson shooting. (We'd traded for AI. More on that later.) But J.R. got the ball first and took a guarded three that missed. "I have no idea what planet that came from," was my reaction after the game.

With eight seconds left, and the game still theoretically winnable, J.R. put it up from half-court, the shot that inspired my sarcastic remark at the beginning of this chapter. It was quite easy for J.R. to play basketball in a way that mocked the very essence of the sport as well as any concept of being on a team, let alone trying to do the smart things that lead to victory. I could not understand him at all.

I kept his ass on the bench a lot, the coach's last resort. The media called him my whipping boy, displaying the fundamental lack of awareness so common in beat reporters. I had no need for a whipping boy. I needed players on the court I could count on.

He had problems off the court, too, which is none of my business. Until off the court affects on the court. J.R. collected cars. He drove them fast, resulting in tickets and license suspensions. He also got some jail time for a 2007 crash that killed his passenger, his friend Andre Bell. He kept getting speeding tickets between the accident and the sentencing, so the NBA suspended him for seven games.

When we traded J.R. in 2011, I was disappointed that I hadn't helped a clearly talented player advance his game more.

Thinking about Kenyon, Melo, and J.R. now reminds me of the player my friends always asked about: the guy with the Woody Woodpecker haircut and the vast acreage of Technicolor tattoos.

People assume that Chris "Birdman" Andersen was crazy but he may have been the sanest guy on those Denver teams. He was no AAU baby. No one in college or pro basketball really wanted him. Despite a broken home and poverty in his childhood, and a two-year suspension from the NBA for drug use, Chris built himself into a really good defensive center and the Nuggets' most popular player.

He may have looked a little unusual—okay, a lot unusual—but more than once he truly calmed me down during game. "You're coaching too much, Coach," the Birdman would say.

Or was that Chris talking?

Some great athletes, Ben Hogan and Ted Williams, for example, had alter egos, imaginary versions of themselves that somehow helped them perform better. Chris was a mild-mannered man who became a flamboyant and pretty good player when he flapped his wings as the Birdman.

We had another player on the Nuggets with an alter ego. JaVale McGee's second identity is "Pierre." Pierre has facial hair on his upper lip so JaVale got a tattoo of a handlebar mustache on the inside of his right index finger. He holds this finger under his nose when he summons Pierre. Maybe he is trying to tell the basketball gods that it's Pierre's fault when JaVale does something stupid on the court. He's a talented player when every switch is on and the plug is in. But he's got a lot of plugs and switches. As noted, I didn't really understand JaVale.

Meanwhile, Carmelo Anthony . . .

Our main problem was that he liked to separate himself from our team. A player can talk back to me, we can argue, but that's between us. One player is a lot less important than how everyone performs together. I don't think Melo cared enough about being a good teammate.

But he got away with some shit over the years because he made All-Star teams and averaged 24-6-3 (points, rebounds, assists). His incidents were spaced out, so listing them here may make them sound worse than they were. If all my screwups were compressed into one paragraph, I'd look pretty bad, too, but Melo had a pattern of bad judgment.

Now Entering the Game for the Lakers

He got a DUI; he got busted at the airport for having a bag of weed in his backpack; he got in a bar fight; he got suspended for fifteen games for punching a Knick during our infamous brawl in 2006. And he did a Kenyon when he refused to go back into the last minute or two in a game on the road against the Pistons. That didn't make his coach too happy.

But his real WTF moment occurred in March 2009 in the third quarter of a game against the Pacers. Carmelo had not scored much all night but then made two in a row. It was time for him to come out for a rest so I sent in his backup, Linas Kleiza, as I usually did. At the next dead ball, LK went in. But Carmelo refused to come out! After long moments of people staring at each other in confusion, but before we got a technical foul for having too many men on the court, Kenyon, to his credit, walked to the bench.

Well, well, well. Here was a new wrinkle in the coach/player power struggle, one I'd never seen before. It was also an incredible F-U to me. We suspended him for the next game.

After the game, which we lost 100–94, I had to talk to the media about it. Should I show my disgust at Melo's childishness and lack of respect? No. I tried to be calm and understanding of behavior I couldn't understand at all. So I swallowed my tongue.

"There's a thin line between passion and emotional immaturity," I said. "It happens all the time, to coaches, too. We snap and act like idiots on the sideline because of the emotional stress of the game."

The positive side of this incident was that it embarrassed Carmelo. He played harder and better for a while. Not coincidentally, we made a deep playoff run.

———

In the spring of 2005, while the Nuggets were going 32-8, I got the call no one wants to get.

"Positive," the voice said.

I was sitting on a blue couch in Room 1540 at the Westin Riverwalk in San Antonio. I stepped to the window and looked down at the dark water in the canal far below.

Totally unfamiliar emotions filled me up. I felt empty, frightened, and preoccupied. Though my father had died, I hadn't yet considered my own mortality. Life keeps telling the same big, ironic joke, I thought. In the midst of happier times in my personal life, and a great winning streak for my team—I had to deal with this. I didn't tell anyone about it. Why bring everybody else down?

I had prostate cancer surgery that summer, and was pronounced clean. And my unmopey personality returned. I joined the fight against the disease, by donating money to this charity and that, and by opening my mouth. To everyone in front of me with a microphone, a camera, or a notebook, I advocated a very big, very organized federal program to research the hell out of cancer to find a cure. My natural fight and optimism returned.

But in an instant six months later, I fell into a bottomless mental pit. Coby had called. He'd been having trouble figuring out his energy level, an important thing for a college athlete. He had a little lump on his neck, just below the Adam's apple. He'd gone for some tests. And then he also heard a doctor say "Positive."

My son had papillary thyroid cancer. When Coby told me the news, I couldn't talk. My silence on the phone scared him.

Once again, dying, surgery, and percentages filled my thoughts and my conversation. But now it was five times worse than when I was the sick one. I'd wake in the middle of the night in a state of anxiety or fright, and I'd stare at the dark or walk the floor. I thought a lot about God. Life seemed more precious than ever, and more insubstantial. Existence could just get turned off, like a light switch, or it could blow away, like a leaf in the fall. I was humbled.

I wondered if I'd done something wrong. Had I contributed

some bad DNA? Had it been his nutrition, or, somehow, mine? I only knew I wanted to snatch away Coby's cancer and take it myself.

When I told my staff about how sick Coby was, I cried like a baby. When I knew I couldn't control myself well enough to give my son an encouraging call, I'd ask Rick Majerus or Larry Brown to do it. Because he'd been a friend for so long, contact from Rick was like hearing from an uncle.

Coach Smith and Jerry West wrote letters to Coby without being asked.

In March 2006, oncology docs injected Coby's thyroid with radioactive iodine. It's usually a very effective treatment, because the thyroid is the only human organ that absorbs iodine. But we all learned that scary word *metastasis*, which is when cancer migrates from one part of the body to another.

Meanwhile, the NBA life continued. There was business to do, and I had to concentrate, or try to.

In December 2006, we traded Andre, Joe Smith, and two number ones to Philadelphia for Allen Iverson and J. R. Smith. Now we had a third wild child in Allen, and a fourth, if you count J.R., which I do. As you may remember from Chapter 2, everyone in the league knew about Allen's crazy drinking/gambling lifestyle. We had to pay him $17 million a year, so trading for him was a measure of how optimistic we were.

"First good shot" was the ideal offensive philosophy for AI and Carmelo, two gifted scorers. We played very fast, especially at home, and forced opponents to try to keep up. We scored 105 a game in Allen's half a season, then 110 a game in 2007–08, his only full year with the Nuggets. That was third-most and second-most points in the league. We gave up a lot of points, too, but we were winning, and we were very entertaining.

With our attitude and a mile of altitude—and fans who were absolutely crazy for the Nuggets—we began a long streak of protecting our court better than any other team in the league (although Utah, only one thousand feet lower than Denver, might argue the point). Other teams couldn't keep up with our pressure and pace. When they had to play Denver in the second game of a back-to-back? Forget it.

From 17 and 27 wins in the sad seasons before I started with Denver, we won 32 in a half season, then 49, 50, 54, 53, 50. Pretty good.

But winning was not enough. I had to answer questions about the playoffs, because we weren't doing nearly as well in the post-season as we were in the regular season. I couldn't deny it.

As you've heard a thousand times, the game slows down in the playoffs. Each team knows the other's offense and its plays intimately, so every pass and every cut is contested. Coaches become conservative and players become cautious. Refs allow rougher play. No way can you score as much. You have to come up with a new strategy. And the emotion we played with all year was suddenly matched by all of the other teams.

Was our track-meet regular season style too far from the bump-and-grind, slow-motion, clog-the-lane playoff game? Could a team be intense for 82 games—and stay as fired up in the tournament? Did our fast pace simply wear us out?

Maybe. But what are a team and a coach supposed to do in the regular season but win games? Resting your best players too much puts the team's rhythm and momentum at risk. Job one in winning in the playoffs is *making* the playoffs.

Most fans regard postseason results as the whole enchilada, and the only yardstick. I don't. I think I have a greater passion for the regular season than for the playoffs. The marathon from Halloween to May Day is a tougher challenge. I think excellence over the long haul is the real measure of an NBA team.

At any rate, our teams in Denver tended to overachieve in the regular season. We made the playoffs every year, a major accomplishment in the Western Conference. But best of seven can be a coin toss: a slump, an injury, or bad luck can put you out in a heartbeat. You can also win lucky, of course, like Dallas in 2011, when some other team beat the teams that could have beat the Mavs.

After we went 32-8 in my first half season with the Nuggets, we lost in the first round of the playoffs. Spurs.

The next season, 2005–06, we got beat in the first round again. Clippers.

In 2006–07, we lost in the first round, to the Spurs again. It was hard to care. Coby had to have more surgery in April, after his final game at Boise State, to remove cancerous tumors on his lymph nodes. He was in the operating room for seven hours, while I paced back and forth in the hospital waiting room. Were we going to lose this kid? I worried about him constantly.

In 2007–08, we won 50, but we got swept in the first round by the Lakers. Misery. Carmelo screamed at me during the last game in L.A.: "Don't just sit there—do something!" Maybe he'll be a coach someday.

But there was something amazing and great about that series, too: the identity of that skinny white kid at the end of the Lakers' bench—Coby Karl!

My boy had worked so hard, and had recovered so thoroughly from his cancer—and his game had come so far—that he'd made a very hard-to-make team. I don't think any of his friends ever thought he'd make it to the NBA. And after having had cancer? I think his journey shows an incredible amount of passion and heart. We were the first-ever father and son to face each other in the NBA playoffs. We held on to each other and smiled for the cameras before the first-game tip-off. Imagine my pride.

But did it have to be the Lakers? Any team but the Lakers! They'd sent me home far too many times.

Coby says he felt it, too. "But when it started, it was just a normal playoff game. But, honestly, it felt like an unfair fight. We had a much better team. I felt bad that we kicked Denver's ass."

Not as bad as I felt about it, Coby.

In November 2008, we ended our two-year experiment with Iverson, trading him to Detroit for a completely different kind of point guard, Chauncey Billups. And finally we went somewhere in the postseason.

Our 54-28 record in 2008–09 was the Nuggets' best in twenty years, but the media kept reminding us of some less happy streaks. Denver had lost seven consecutive postseason series—the last four of them on my watch—and the team hadn't advanced past the first round since 1994. The Nuggets hadn't really contended for the NBA championship since 1985.

But this was a special team playing at a very high level.

We beat New Orleans 4-1 in the first round, Dallas 4-1 in the second, and then we had—it was almost a given—the Lakers and Kobe and Phil in the Western Conference Finals.

Melo and Kobe had become friends on the 2008 Olympic team (the United States won the gold). In Game One, it looked like Kobe's hypercompetitiveness had rubbed off. I never saw Carmelo battle more intensely for rebounds, or play harder D. Those two had an incredible shoot-out, with both scoring about 40. We were down two with less than a minute to play, but we threw away an inbounds pass—or Trevor Ariza made a great play to steal it, depending on your point of view—and we lost.

We won Game Two.

Carmelo's offense cooled way down for the rest of the series (or Phil defended him better). But we were not a one-man team and we had a great chance to win Game Three. We were down two with less than a minute to play, but then we threw away an inbounds pass—or Ariza made a great play to steal it . . . wait, didn't I just write that? Yeah, it happened twice in three games.

It seems almost funny now, but I wasn't laughing then. Because I've always made a big point of inbound passing, and my teams always practice it. It's an assist waiting to happen when you do it right, but it was a turnover and a disaster when Anthony Carter (Game One) and Kenyon (Game Three) didn't give it enough attention.

I hated losing Game Six and the series at home, in a game that wasn't close. There'd be no finals, and the frustration of losing to Phil remained like a burr in my sock. We didn't run and pressure like normal in that game—"Tonight wasn't Nuggets basketball," I said.

But after a period of being depressed, what I felt in the aftermath was hope. Chauncey had been the only player on our team with high-level playoff experience. Now we all did. Given their ages and skills and momentum, this, I knew, was the prime of the Denver Nuggets, and maybe, at last, a championship team.

Personally, too, everything was on an uptick. We loved Denver. My daughter Kaci gave me a happy spark every day. Although Coby hadn't stuck with L.A., he was enjoying life as a pro in the D league with the Idaho Stampede in Boise and then with high-level club teams in Spain and Italy. My oldest daughter, Kelci, had a great job in government in Olympia, Washington, and she and Jackie seemed pretty happy.

I was right to be positive about the Nuggets. We were the same great team at the start of the next season, maybe even a little better. Our 31-16 record at the end of January 2010 made me the coach for the Western Conference All-Star team, the fourth time I had that honor. I'd be coaching two Nuggets—Melo and Chauncey—at the big show in Dallas in February.

Except . . . It seems like there's always an "except."

I had a little lump on my neck.

PLEASE REMIT
$470,000

Love finds its greatest intensity when rooted in the acceptance of mortality.

—AMIT SOOD, *THE MAYO CLINIC GUIDE TO STRESS-FREE LIVING*

He's willing to adapt, to trust his players and staff, to delegate some of the power. That wasn't a strength before he had cancer.

—COBY KARL, CURRENTLY AN ASSISTANT COACH WITH THE WESTCHESTER KNICKS OF

THE NBA D LEAGUE

thought a lot about food because I couldn't eat any.

I'd lie in a bed or sit in a chair and dream about the shrimp Parmesan at Paesanos in San Antonio, the go-to dish at my first go-to restaurant. Cold Coors Light washed it down; I rarely drank wine back then. I could close my eyes and feel the sidewalk and smell the air in Chicago, where we'd walk under the big green awning at Gibson's on North Rush Street. I like steak a little less than most guys, I suppose, but the sides at Gibson's were so ginormous and delicious that the entrée shrank in importance a little bit. Tony's in St. Louis; I'll have the fettuccine with crab and tomatoes, please.

Nene and I had a little ritual in New York City if there was time before we played the Knicks or the Nets. Our Brazilian center and I would take a cab to Churrascaria Plataforma, for Brazilian food, obviously, in Hell's Kitchen. Waiters carrying long metal skewers of roasted meat swirl around you there, and they slide some on your plate, and, wow.

Decades as an NBA coach had allowed me to eat the best food at the best restaurants, as if I had a show on the Food Network. That part of my life now seemed over, but the area in my brain that remembered tastes and smells stayed fired up, even though I could no longer taste or smell. Like feeling an amputated leg, I guess. I particularly felt my last meal at ChoLon in downtown Denver: potstickers with ginger mustard, bacon fried rice. Lobster crepes. Braised lamb shank. And the chef, Lon Symensma, coming to the table to ask if everything was all right.

I thought about great food and the great places I'd eaten and the people I ate with as I watched mud-brown liquid gurgling down a clear plastic tube inserted into an incision above and a little to the right of my belly button. Mealtimes in the winter and spring of 2010 were discouraging and dehumanizing. I felt like a robot getting injected with whatever robots run on. But regular eating was impossible. My throat was literally burned, as if there'd been a fire in there.

―――――

They held the 2010 NBA All-Star Game in February at Cowboys Stadium (now AT&T Stadium) in Arlington, Texas, enabling 108,713 people to attend, the biggest basketball crowd ever. I looked up to the top of the bowl in amazement a few times. I know I looked like an ant to the people up there.

We lost a defensive battle 141–139, and I fell to 0-4 in the All-Star exhibition, which bothered me not all. I was more a spectator than a coach in that game. The entire weekend played out in slow motion for me because I had much bigger things on my mind.

I made sure that all my kids and their mates attended the weekend of fun in Dallas. I wanted a little celebration: we had each other, we had the best team in the NBA, and I was the All-Star coach. And if the news was bad, they have parades for funerals in New Orleans. Some people see death as a beginning and not an end. Anyway, all of us were about to think about death, at least a little.

After the game, I gathered everyone together in my giant room at the Hyatt Regency. "Anyone need a drink?" I said. Then I told them that about six weeks before, I'd found out that a lump below my chin that I thought was just fat was really a tumor. And it was cancerous.

After Dr. Jacques Saari sent my cells to Johns Hopkins to confirm his diagnosis, he came to the house to make it official: I had HNSCC, a disease common enough for an acronym. Dr. Saari explained that treating my head and neck squamous cell carcinoma was not going to be as easy as fixing a diseased prostate. I'd have to survive radiation, chemo, maybe surgery. This was hard to hear.

Doc Jacques explained that squamous cells are normal; they're not cancer cells. Under a microscope they look a little like fish scales. We all have them in different parts of our bodies. But some of mine were mutating, and trying to kill me. My physician sat around with me for a while to sort of ease me into the bad news and to recommend some oncologists. He left and I went online.

Five-year survival rates were between 30 and 50 percent, making mine the eighth-most fatal cancer. *Shit.*

About half a million new cases develop every year throughout the world, which made HNSCC the sixth-most frequent cancer.

There'd been about 40,000 new cases in the United States in 2001, and 12,000 deaths from it.

Okay, why did I have this? I discovered that HSNCC is a potentially deadly side effect of smoking, but I've never smoked. Excessive drinking can be a factor but I rejected that as a cause, because I rarely drank anything stronger than beer, and I almost never had a hangover that indicated I'd been overdoing it. Google also told me that HNSCC can result from human papillomavirus, HPV, which is sexually transmitted. Michael Douglas, the actor, suggested he got his HSNCC this way.

My crappy diet seemed the likeliest culprit. I'd spent most of a lifetime eating too much red and processed meat, and not enough vegetables. So I never got enough vitamins A and B and zinc and I was way too heavy, close to three bills. Someone saw me at an All-Star game after not seeing me for quite a while. "You look like George Karl, only fat," said my friend.

As I mentioned before, more weight equals more cells equals a better chance for things to go haywire.

I told my family all this pretty quickly and as unemotionally as I could. It helped that some of them already knew about the diagnosis. Telling the team was much harder emotionally.

I dropped the bomb the next day, in our locker room during our first practice after the All-Star break. The players and staff were very caring and sympathetic and I think I hugged every one of them. Chauncey's comment to the media later was the right one, that basketball is unimportant compared to health.

"I want to stay with the team throughout my treatment," I said in the press conference the team set up. "I believe this is a championship team, and we're all after the same thing."

My voice cracked a couple of times during the announcement, and I sighed deeply once or twice. I fidgeted with my fingers. I mispronounced the word *squamous*—it rhymes with "calm us," not "tame us." I'm not after anyone's sympathy, I said, but I did ask for support.

Dr. Saari told the media that the chemo would weaken the

cancer cells so much that they'd get killed off easily by the radiation. I began treatments the next morning. They weren't so bad at first.

I'd joined the many thousands of people contending with life-threatening cancer. I don't want to make this seem more than it was or to paint myself as particularly brave. My journey was unusual only in that I'd try to coach an NBA team while suffering through the assaults to brain, breathing, mood, and diet.

In the end, and in keeping with my personality, I was pretty angry about the whole thing. I perceived the cancer industry to be not dedicated to curing the disease, but to making money while managing it. I came to believe that until the food industry gets cleaned up, we're just killing ourselves. The American diet is largely a mess. And cancer and diet are linked like a metal chain. And our cancer education is so poor. For example, did you know that the immune system runs on water, not on blood? So drink more water!

While I was getting thousands of dollars of synthetic morphine patches stuck to my skin, I wondered why no alternatives were presented to me. Where were the experts telling me about yoga, massage, tai chi, and acupuncture to relieve my pain? Or about meditation to combat the depression that fell on me like a load of bricks?

And where in our health-care system are the cash or tax incentives for staying healthy?

But what really chapped my ass was the stupid, *criminal* complication of the bill. Every day, it was: What's *this* (totally unexplained) bill for? Is this covered by insurance? Is that out of my pocket? Is this a scam? The bills seemed deliberately deceptive, jargon filled, and intimidating.

At one point, a demand for $70,000 arrived in the mail. I had Kim dedicating her sharp intellect and a lot of hours to sorting out our $470,000 bill, but what do people without a Kim do? I knew I wasn't going to be bankrupted by this but people with fewer means get an unwanted and unfair financial scare at the moment when they're fighting for their lives. I promised to do something about this when and if I could.

February, March: Five days a week for six weeks, Kim drove me through usually gray weather in our maroon SUV to the Swedish Medical Center in Englewood, Colorado. I'd lie down inside a big white machine that looked like a refrigerator bolted to a freezer. *Breathe normally, don't move.* The machine zapped my neck with gamma rays but it didn't hurt. In the middle of this period, the chemo started—eight sessions in seven days. That did hurt.

I watched an IV machine drip 5-fluorouracil, cetuximab, and platinum into my arm and tried to think of something else. The side effects were brutal. My throat was on fire. I couldn't swallow, a condition called dysphagia. Add mouth sores, and saliva as thick as chewing gum. I couldn't eat and I didn't want to. My voice became a raspy whisper. We had to go to the feeding tube.

Every day, Kim suctioned unspeakable stuff out of my throat with a vacuum hose. The bright red rash covering my hairless head and neck looked like really bad measles and made me look like a monster to our five-year-old. She asked her mom, "Is Daddy going to die?" Kim cried at that one.

Although I planned to stay with the team, I only made it three weeks. I coached some games feeling more weak than sick, but then I thought it would be better to stay away so everyone could focus on winning the game instead of worrying about me. I looked like hell and I was losing weight fast. I'd eventually drop about sixty pounds.

When friends and my assistants came out to the house, sometimes I'd answer the door and watch them try not to react to my shocking appearance. I was trying not to react, too, but the mirror told me how much I'd aged in a few months, how close to death I looked. I told my assistants to stop visiting; it was plainly making them too sad and worried.

As I said, depression hit me hard.

The interim head coach for the last quarter of the regular season was my top assistant, Adrian Dantley. AD, who'd been hired by the previous Nuggets coach, had a low-key, introverted style—my exact opposite. I don't know if my teams take on my personality, but at least they respond to my personality. But AD—a go-his-own-way guy—was not about to become a yeller or a motivator. To be honest, I wouldn't have hired him; he and I were just too different. With everything that was going on, including J.R. going crazy a little each day, replacing me was an unfair assignment for AD.

The Nuggets played about .500 ball under him. The fiber of our team fell apart.

"George has won over nine hundred games, man," Chauncey said when a writer asked him to compare Dantley and me. "AD's only been coaching about nine."

We limped into the playoffs as the number four seed. We played Utah, the number five.

I tried to help, but I didn't have the energy to go to the arena or to offer much insight on the phone. We lost the second game and home court advantage. Utah, incredibly, was outrunning us. We were down 3-1 when, for the second time, I had to be taken quickly to the emergency room: blood clots in my legs. I was supposed to be moving around a little to prevent them, but I got lazy. I was in the ICU between Games Five and Six with the game on a TV high on a wall opposite my bed. As we were losing Game Six and the series, I fell sound asleep from pain meds.

When I woke up, and heard that we'd lost, I doubted that I'd ever return to coaching.

But I went to the office a month later to help with the draft, then I rested and rehabbed. In July, at the ESPYs—ESPN's sports award show—I accepted the Jim Valvano Perseverance Award. Jimmy V, as you probably know, was the North Carolina State basketball coach who died after a gutsy fight with cancer. I used the occasion to thank my family and friends, to express my support for the St. Jude Children's Research Hospital in Memphis, and to urge any legislator listening to get behind a program of matching federal dollars with privately raised money for cancer research.

Believe me: I knew why I was on a stage in Hollywood. If I wasn't an NBA coach, I'd be one of the thousands of people facing cancer's brutal struggle without a huge salary or a speech or an award. Jocks like me may be fighters, but we can't claim to have more than ordinary courage.

I said: "Some of the people I sat with in chemotherapy and in radiation therapy are better competitors than any NBA player."

I walked off the stage, saw a buffet, and suddenly felt fed up with my feeding tube. I tore it out, and tried some food, some shrimp or cheese or something. Cardboard.

I had a sip of wine. Bilgewater.

———

If you've jumped ahead in this book, you know I returned to coaching. But I wasn't the same coach.

During the months of sitting alone with a nauseated stomach and a scorched throat, I read. Thank God one of those books was Amit Sood's *The Mayo Clinic Guide to Stress-Free Living*. I guess we all know that compassion, gratitude, and forgiveness are good things, but Sood lays out the scientific basis for their benefit. The book is so credible and so clearly written: it had a big impact on me.

One of my biggest takeaways was the absolute futility of trying to control other people—the truth is, few of us have a really tight rein on our *own* thoughts and actions. Attempting to control even your best friend means automatic frustration. So just help him enjoy what he does.

Dr. Sood also made me realize that in addition to searching for the physical reasons for my cancer, I should have thought a lot harder about the mental and spiritual causes. By which I mean:

stress. You may remember me saying how wins never felt as good as losses felt bad? By overreacting—by treating a bad game as a Negative Life Event like a tornado or a fire—I accelerated every unhealthy thing in my body. By not having a clue about good ways to relax, I overate and probably overdrank.

Another book that amounted to a lifeline during treatment and recovery was *Wisdom of the Ages*, by Wayne Dyer. I'm really skeptical of the canned inspiration some coaches depend on. Those "There's no 'I' in team" sayings had about a Cheetos' worth of value to me. But Dyer's book is a banquet.

Here are snippets of two longer quotations I've read over and over. The first is from the German poet and novelist Johann Wolfgang von Goethe:

Are you in earnest? Seize this minute
Boldness has genius, power, and magic in it
Only engage, and then the mind grows heated
Begin it, and then the work will be completed!

And here's Buddha, writing 2,500 years ago:

Do not believe what you have heard
Do not believe in tradition because it is handed down many
*   generations*
Do not believe in conjecture
But . . . when it agrees with reason and will benefit one and all,
*   then accept it, and live by it.*

Another book that replaced my usual thriller was *Finding Flow: The Psychology of Engagement with Everyday Life*, by Mihaly Csikszentmihalyi, who needs a rap name, like M-Zen or something.

The intellectual workouts and the nearness of death led to a profound change in my thinking. One of the first things I realized was that I had to break my pattern of feeling stress/ reacting to stress. I decided to make a point of *living* every day, instead of being a slave to the score of a basketball game and of my own bad habits.

Obviously, I'd have to handle defeat better, treat it a little more rationally. I decided to give the team and staff realistic goals for wins in a month, and sometimes—if we had a tough schedule or an injury—a 6-11 record might be our target. The old me would never have thought of eleven losses in a month as remotely okay.

And when I came back, I would definitely delegate. I simply didn't have the energy I had before. Instead of ten-hour days, I'd try to work six or seven. Coaches' meetings would no longer be a thirty-minute monologue from me and an amen chorus from them. Instead, we'd take sixty or ninety minutes, and we'd allow some argument. Sometimes I'd throw a log on the fire and let two guys chirp. I'd be more a discussion leader than a dictator. "What do you think, Chad Iske? Can Wilson Chandler defend Amar'e Stoudemire in the post? Should we go small if they're hitting threes?" And then I'd sit back and listen to my very smart assistants. I'd gone from dominant to democratic.

And instead of obsessing and worrying in the hours before a big game, I'd find a quiet place outside, if possible—a park bench, or under a tree—and just sit there. And think of nothing or everything.

Some big life changes occurred right away. As for what I put in my body, meat didn't go down my throat very well. So I became a juicer. I'm happy with a dinner of liquefied kale, carrots, ginger, celery, and a beet. I'm also dedicated to a kitchen sink version of guacamole. I'll put honey in there, and almost any vegetable to join the avocado and tomato, including more kale, peppers, onion, corn, beans, mushrooms, and broccoli. I eat a lot of salads and soup now. A big change for a cheeseburger man.

And as for drinking: when I resumed having "a" beer at the end of the day, I switched from Coors Light to Bud Light. Don't know why. But I hardly drink at all now compared to the old days. Wine tastes like crap and I've never been a mixed drink or straight whiskey guy. What I drink the most is ice water, gallons of it every day. The *agua* washes down a couple of handfuls of colorful pills: folic acid, vitamin C, turmeric, omega-3, probiotics, milk thistle, blood thinner, thyroid med, zinc, fish oil, coenzyme Q10, and maybe a few others.

I also came out of cancer treatment—maybe the books were part of this—with a renewed belief in God. Not the Christian God sitting on a throne in heaven, but God as a spirit of good, of love, and within us all.

Some balance had come into my existence. I'd been so stubborn and stupid that I had to have cancer twice before I woke up a little a bit. I ended the summer cancer-free, and weaker, but wiser, I think. So in early September, I told our owner: "I want to coach."

Two weeks later, Melo told our owner: "Trade me."

As you can imagine, or as you may remember if you're a Nuggets fan, my return and Carmelo's departure threw us into an uproar. But we kept playing pretty well, especially at home, where we were almost unbeatable. The constant questions about Melo almost made me scream, but we won 50 games, which to me is the gold standard.

Why did Melo want out? To start with the obvious: From even before we met, he and I had a little conflict bubbling. As I said before, I want as much effort on defense—maybe more—as on offense. That was never going to happen with Melo, whose amazing ability to score with the ball made him a star but didn't make him a winner. Which I pointed out to him. Which he didn't like.

But Carmelo hadn't just wanted a trade; he wanted a trade to New York—the Knicks, not the Nets, he hoped. LeBron had just taken his talents from Cleveland to Miami, and I think

Melo wanted to throw his weight around the same way. Part of that thinking had to have come from his wife, the former La La Vazquez, a native New Yorker, and a media star who had made the Vazquez-Anthony nuptial a five-part reality TV show called *La La's Full Court Wedding*. She wrote an advice book—a bestseller—that also had a little basketball in the title: *The Love Playbook*. Obviously, La La couldn't pursue her la-la career as well in Denver as she could in New York.

Some players at the top of the pyramid have so many people swirling around them—helpers and agents and advisors—that it's hard to get close to them. But far more often I've gotten really close with individual players on my teams, and I mentor their existence off the court, especially regarding girls and money. Carmelo was from the first group. He didn't need my help and we weren't close. Leaving me for another coach would not be a big deal for him.

One other thing: with his own expiring contract, and with Kenyon Martin, J. R. Smith, Chauncey Billups, and Marcus Camby's deals also about to end, the Nuggets looked to be falling into rebuilding mode in a year. Melo wanted no part of that. His analysis of the Nuggets may have been correct, by the way. But by pushing for this trade, and by making New York and its fans want him too much, we were able to get a hell of a deal. Rebuilding would not be necessary.

After the All-Star Game in February 2011, we sent Melo and Billups to the Knicks for Danilo Gallinari, Kosta Koufos, Timofey Mozgov, Ray Felton, and a number one draft pick in 2014.

"I'm gonna miss Chauncey," I said.

I think I used this phrase before, relative to trading Ray Allen: getting rid of Carmelo Anthony was a sweet release for the coach and the team, like popping a blister. I don't automatically hate a superstar, but he's got to buy in, he's got to play defense, and he's got to share the ball. And if his teammates and coaches don't like him, and *if* he doesn't help you win a championship . . . what good is he, except as bait?

We won this trade, definitely. Credit to our new GM, Masai Ujiri—a Nigerian, and a former international scout—and our new president and governor, the owner's son, Josh Kroenke. Our new players did not hold themselves apart and above, and they didn't care too much about the limelight, so they didn't annoy each other. They bought in; they played both sides of the ball. We had no stars, and we played a pretty rough, aggressive form of defense. I guess we hurt the feelings of some of the teams whose asses we beat, because our nickname was Thuggets.

As for our offense, I'd grown tired of teaching the same old shit. Many teams around the league were experimenting with playing the fast game—aka the passing game. But it takes a lot of energy. By the middle of the season, when the players' legs are starting to feel like lead, they all went back to possession basketball.

But I like a very aggressive offense. We played at a sprint in high school. We averaged 90 points a game at North Carolina without a three-point shot or a shot clock. And my coach in San Antonio was Doug Moe, who really pioneered the whole idea.

My assistant John Welch and I talked a lot about how to play fast but we really didn't have a system. "I got a guy," said John.

We brought in Vance Walberg, a former high school and college coach from Fresno. Over two weekends, he taught us the dribble-drive motion offense, which he had more or less invented. It involves spreading the floor—a lot—and is based on all five players reading the defense much more than set plays. If a player drives the ball but can't get a layup, he knows exactly where to pass it.

As for energy, after we traded Melo, we had all these young guys who were receptive to this new style of play. The ball rarely stopped for an isolation play, which was Melo's bread and butter. Our offensive game became better, faster, and easier. We hired Vance to be on our bench in 2012.

Chauncey's minutes went to our second-year point guard from the University of North Carolina. And Ty Lawson was a *blur*. Behind Ty and Andre Miller, we played fast and fun. We led the league in points and assists and home court record. Our fans absolutely loved us—until we lost in the first round of the playoffs again.

The next year was the same, only different, because of the extreme disruption of another lockout, including having some of our guys playing in foreign leagues in China, Lithuania, Italy, and Russia to begin the season. It was more arguments between millionaires over money, which causes fans to look elsewhere for entertainment.

But this strike didn't last as long as the previous one. We played our first game of the season on Christmas Day. Our 38-28 record in the shortened season was pretty good, but we lost Wilson Chandler, our starting power forward, to a hip injury just before the playoffs began. And we lost in the first round again, to L.A. in seven.

Rick Majerus occupied my mind a lot as the next season began. His friends were aware he was very ill but we were not allowed to call or visit him. He died on December 1, 2012, before he could get the heart transplant he needed. He was sixty-four.

Six days later after a game at Indiana, I flew to Milwaukee for my friend's funeral. It was a cold, clear Saturday morning. "When I got in trouble basketball-wise, I turned to three guys," I told a reporter outside the giant gray church on the Marquette campus. "Dean Smith, Del Harris, and Rick Majerus. We're here to say 'Thank you' to Rick and to celebrate our memories of him."

Church bells clanged and I went inside. The long funeral mass gave me plenty of time to think about life and death and my old friend. Through Rick, I'd met Don Nelson, Del Harris, and Senator Kohl, three of the most important people in my life. Coach Majerus had been my best friend in coaching. He was college and

I was pro. We argued as much as we agreed but I could always feel his love for the game and for me. I tried to express some of these sentiments when I spoke at the gathering we had after the funeral.

The 2012–13 season: It would sound like the premise of a sports movie to say that this year my team dedicated itself to finally getting a championship for their Cancer Comeback Coach. But as a matter of fact, it looked like it might happen. That Denver Nuggets team *perfected* shot prioritization, and its teamwork and cooperation made me proud to be their coach. The fast, thrilling game we played caused an emotional flow between the Nuggets and our fans in the arena and in the community. Only twice before—at North Carolina and at Seattle—had I been a part of this advanced level of team basketball.

With Kenneth Faried, Andre Iguodala, and Ty running their asses off, we won 15 in a row at one point and 21 straight at home. For the season, we won 57 games, the Nuggets' most wins since joining the NBA in 1977. We were 38-3 at home. This may have been the most fun I ever had in coaching.

We got Golden State in the first round. This would be the first-ever playoff series for their very young guards—Steph Curry and Klay Thompson—so we thought we had them. We thought so a little less after our equalizer, Danilo Gallinari, blew out his knee late in the season.

You may know the punch line. Thompson and Curry played great, and we lost in six. I was named NBA Coach of the Year in June, but with no deep playoff run, the Disney movie would have to wait.

———

his is very stupid," I told Josh Kroenke when he fired me a few weeks later. The calmness and acceptance I'd been working on boiled away in about ten seconds.

One writer described my dismissal as an NBA joke, but it was real enough. I cleaned out my desk, talked to agent LeGarie, informed my assistants, took calls from the Memphis Grizzlies and Los Angeles Clippers about their open head coaching jobs, and met the media.

I guess the worst part—and the biggest insult—was the complete lack of respect for the job we'd done. Getting so many pieces working together was an intricate process requiring eight and a half years of patience, experience, and hard work. Third place in the Western Conference? Fifty-seven wins? Fans, coaches, and players who were really happy with each other? Coach of the Fricking Year? I understood the rarity of the good thing we'd built, but Josh didn't.

"They think they can unplug us and plug somebody else in?" I said to the writers. "Wow, that is not respectful of the coaching profession."

Plenty of closed-door discussions had undoubtedly taken place between Stan Kroenke and his son. When Stan bought the St. Louis Rams in August 2010, the NFL had insisted he sell the Nuggets; he did, to Josh.

Thinkin' about firing George, Dad.

Josh, it's your team.

Josh could fairly point to our lack of success in the postseason as a reason to recycle the coaching staff. I heard he wasn't happy with JaVale McGee's slow progress, although I didn't think JaVale's lack of motivation was on me. My deal would have been up at the end of 2014. Some writers figured that I was clamoring for a new contract. I wasn't; in fact, I'd offered to negotiate the money and the number of years of an extension—in their favor—because I loved Denver and the Nuggets and I wanted to stay. But Josh wanted to prove he was in charge and firing me was a dramatic way of doing that.

The Nuggets sank like a stone under my plug-in replacement,

Brian Shaw, who had never been a head coach at any level. It was painful to turn on Channel 350 and watch my former team not play hard and not play together. The Nuggets went 36-46 in Shaw's first season. They started the next season 20-39. Then Josh fired Shaw, too.

As losses rose, attendance fell, from 14th best in the league when I left, to 19th, then to 27th—which meant about 5,000 empty seats every night in the Pepsi Center. T-shirt, beer, hot dog, and parking revenue declined, of course, so I'm tempted to say how much the cynical treatment of me and my staff cost the team. But, in reality—it didn't.

Just remember where the real money is in the NBA. With about half as many wins per year in the two years since getting rid of me, the value of Denver Nuggets Inc. almost *doubled*, to about $800 million. A big part of the increase came from the new TV deal. TNT and ESPN/ABC will pay the NBA $24 billion over nine years. With the money split evenly between the thirty teams, each team is awash in cash before the season even starts. Player salaries are skyrocketing, too.

In the modern NBA, prosperity is not exclusively linked to winning games.

Where did that leave me?

CHAPTER 12

BIG BROTHER

I've never been one to look back on my life and wish I had done things differently. What purpose would it serve? Life doesn't come with a mulligan.

—DEAN SMITH, *THE CAROLINA WAY*

The pool at the DoubleTree hotel in Bristol, Connecticut, is inside, where it has to be, because about half the year it's too cold to swim outside.

I put in many hours there. I'd haul my ass out of bed at 9 or 10 a.m.—I'd been working until 3 a.m.—and eat a depressingly healthy breakfast of fruit and juice. Then I'd limp on my replacement hips to the bright blue water in the L-shaped pool, where I did lap after lap—walking, not swimming. I'd walk slowly from one side to the other, then do more laps walking backward, then more back and forth using a shuffle step as if I were playing defense on a basketball court. My workout lasted about thirty exhausting minutes. Then I'd collapse my beat-up body into the whirlpool.

I never had any company at that hour. If I did, my fellow bathers could have observed the angry blue streaks on my legs, souvenirs from blood clots.

ESPN had hired me again soon after Denver cut me loose. I'd fly into town—Denver to Newark to Hartford—about every other week. From knowing the procedures and the people pretty well, my second tour as a commentator for Entertainment and Sports Programming Network had the feeling of ritual. Mornings were the pool and calls home to chat with Kaci and Kim. Afternoons always contained a salad bar somewhere, newspapers, and a nap. At about 5 p.m., I'd put on a suit and get a ride to the giant ESPN complex, which was virtually across the street—but given my hips and knees, and the snow, too far to walk.

ESPN headquarters looks like a college campus, only with twenty-seven satellite dishes and very tight security. It's also collegial, a fairly friendly atmosphere. The building I worked in was jammed with studios, offices, hallways, cafeterias, and tech people in dark clothes. Not much outside light.

Production meetings were held at a giant table, like in a company boardroom. There'd be about sixteen people around the table, with another half-dozen lower-status bodies in chairs by the wall. One big and maybe five smaller TV monitors hung on the walls. We'd go over the second-by-second plan for that night's episodes of *SportsCenter*, and for pregame, halftime, and postgame of the NBA games we were broadcasting. Very precise: ten seconds of this, eight seconds of that. Military time.

"A minute ten for George to talk about trades at 18:41:30," the producer, Bruce Bernstein, would say. "Coach, can Spencer Hawes help the Clippers? What are they thinking?" And I'd outline my scouting reports on Hawes and the Clippers—in effect a rehearsal for when they turned the cameras on.

There were two kinds of announcer/analysts at the table: the sort of recognizable ex-coaches and ex-players like me, Bruce Bowen, Tim Legler, and Jay Williams, and the professional broadcasters. The pros had perfect hair and big voices and looked like soap opera actors. I amused them; to them, I was an old-school coach from another century. I'd observe that someone's game was "too soft, too pretty" and they'd laugh as if I'd told a good joke.

I guess the outstanding thing about being on the air in the studio was the light, which is as bright as the surface of the sun. A few times it sort of stunned me. But you'd better be able to blink and think on your feet and forget that about 2.3 million people are watching during prime time. Or you're out of a job.

I liked ESPN, liked the people I got to know there, and I enjoyed having something to say and something to do. But it also felt like exile. I'm a coach. I needed to coach.

I had some new ideas about how to do it when I got another chance.

At my age, and after all I'd been through, I knew myself better than ever. I'd gained a lot of self-knowledge from many years as a coach and from 1,100-something NBA wins (and about 750 losses) and from looking over the edge when I had cancer.

I knew what I wanted.

———

*W*hat I wanted:

- More than anything I wanted to be back in a gym, building a team. I'm addicted to the camaraderie, the blending, and the improvement. It's a brotherhood when it all works. And I'm the big brother.
- A team that could win. I did not want to oversee a complete rebuilding project; merely improving a bad team would not float my boat. More than ever, I know I have to win to be happy. And I have to win now. The clock is ticking.
- A team loaded with guys who could rebound, run, shoot the three, attack the rim, and guard five, or at least three, positions.
- No stars. By which I mean no *selfish* stars. The Spurs of

David Robinson, Tim Duncan, Tony Parker, and Manu Ginobili are the kind of low-maintenance, team-first All-Stars most coaches would give a gonad to get. For years, with some of the young guys, all I'd hear was me-first: "I gotta get my money. I gotta get a max deal." I didn't want to hear that anymore.

• Fans ready to really get into it. Fans with so much energy they'd help us keep losing out of our building.

• A city I liked. Nothing against the Northeast, but I don't want to live in the old, cold cities in the Eastern Conference. A smaller city would be fine. Small markets have been very good to me.

• A respectable contract.

• A team leader, which would be nice, but I'd learned that they are not absolutely necessary. It's great when you have some coach-on-the-floor guys—I had Chauncey in Denver, Lonnie Shelton and Phil Hubbard in Cleveland, Chris Mullin and Sleepy Floyd at Golden State, and Gary Payton, usually, in Seattle—but it's so rare, you can't count on it. Ty Lawson in Denver didn't want the responsibility. I'd decided that leadership is overhyped and that good soldiers are undervalued. A connected, unified team is superior to a dissatisfied team with a great leader.

• 205 wins. I see nothing wrong with wanting to be the winningest coach in NBA history. I have the utmost respect for the five very competitive guys in front of me—Phil Jackson, Pat Riley, Jerry Sloan, Lenny Wilkens, and Don Nelson. As you know, I have a little personal history with a couple of them.

• To mentor more young coaches. I'm proud that seven current or recent NBA head coaches worked for me: Scott Brooks, Dwane Casey, Nate McMillan, Sam Mitchell, Vinnie Del Negro, Terry Stotts, and Mike Woodson. Helping a new generation along is the best kind of legacy.

- Vance Walberg, John Welsh, and Chad Iske to be my assistants.
- One thing I wasn't sure I could get: authority. I wanted Dean Smith–like power to set the tone and establish the culture, along with enough input on personnel decisions to get the kind of athletes who would listen to me and learn from me and play my way.

My years in the league taught me that winning requires harmony and orchestration between the basketball and the business sides. A sports club can have only one main goal. It should be to win a championship, not maximize profit and inflate the value of the franchise. Winning takes care of the money side eventually and everyone is happier rowing in the same direction.

In other words, the guy in charge of winning should guide the ship. Not sales, marketing, or the general manager. I said *should*.

———

So that's what I wanted, more or less. No one gets every item on his wish list, and you get plenty of stuff you don't want. I certainly hadn't asked for cancer, for example, or to be let go in Denver.

But things were heating up in the whirlpool at the DoubleTree as the 2014–15 season began. GMs were calling me and my agent, asking, "What does George want?"

The rumor mill had me coaching the Timberwolves, the Lakers, the Wizards, the Pelicans, the Jazz, and a few others. I was also supposedly being considered for president of basketball operations for the Cavs. I didn't discourage the speculation. It couldn't hurt me to have owners and GMs realize that I was in demand.

In December, another job opened up. Within minutes, maybe seconds, after the Kings fired Mike Malone, the Internet had me as the new guy in Sacramento. The bloggers gave me the job because Kings owner Vivek Ranadive wanted to run and I can coach that game, as you know. And they noted that I'd worked well with Pete D'Alessandro in Denver, and Pete had been the Kings' GM since June 2013. I also knew and respected Pete's assistant, Mike Bratz.

Both Pete and Mike called to say how great it would be to have me coach the Kings. Their interest in me made the idea more attractive. You want to go where you're wanted.

Sacramento didn't have everything I wanted, of course, but every NBA job is a good job. Friends asked why I didn't want to wait for a team that had been winning or had a better on-paper upside. But I don't think that you wait for an offer that might not come.

We did the deal over the All-Star break. For the first time in exactly a decade, I was once again singing "Getting to Know You" with a new team.

I showed them how I wanted to play, which was about twice as fast as they'd been playing. So I gave them half as much time to put up a shot. Scrimmaging with the shot clock at 12 seconds instead of 24 kind of blew their minds because they had no time for a buildup or a setup. Just pass, pass, pass and put the ball in the air. Rebound, run, repeat.

The players and I would have to get used to each other on the fly, which reminded me of something General George Patton said: "A good plan violently executed now is better than a perfect plan next week." So we improvised and did the best we could.

"Coaches are control freaks," I said as my half season began. "The other coaches in the league have one hundred percent control. I've got sixty percent. Maybe."

We won our first game, at home against the Celtics, and I got an embarrassing but gratifying standing ovation before the game began.

Big Brother

Over the next few months, I gave the impression that I'd mellowed. I almost never barked at the refs or my players. I didn't pace the sideline like I had before. Part of it was that my knees were killing me and needed to be replaced. But in the locker room at halftime it was a different story. You would have recognized the old George Karl.

———

And now, as I end this look back, I have to weigh my words very carefully. Because last year and this year isn't really the stuff of memoirs: it's current events.

The death of Donnie Wilson, my high school teammate, saddened me deeply. The other current event I'm still coming to grips with is the death of Dean Smith. He passed away in early February 2015, just before I took the Sacramento job.

He'd been ill with dementia for six, seven years, so we'd been seeing a diminished Coach Smith on our annual trip back to North Carolina for the Doug Moe Invitational. I think we all just wanted to hug his wife, Linnea, and to touch him and hope he remembered us, while we remembered him.

From the way he held his head or moved his eyes, one or two final times I felt the force of his personality. Although he didn't swear and didn't like to hear swearing, and he was obsessed with proper form in a hundred little things, Coach Smith wasn't one of those Bible-quoting pains in the ass who act like they own the moral high ground. I think his power came from how much he loved his players, from how much he respected the game, and from how well he taught it.

Four days after he died, I began remembering my coach in a very active way. Play hard, play smart, play together, I told the Sacramento Kings. We're not going to back off when an opponent has the last shot; we're going to trap and press and attack. When we have the ball with the shot clock off and the game on the line, we will win most of the time because we're going to practice that situation over and over.

Being late for a practice or a bus or a plane is the height of arrogance, I said. We're not going to allow that.

Practice is a privilege; if you're not going to concentrate and work, get lost, go bowling.

I won't take you out of a game for making a mistake.

A made shot doesn't mean it was a good shot.

Acknowledge the guy who threw you the pass after you score.

Pick up a fallen teammate.

Run to the bench when there's a timeout.

Although I didn't mention his name, all of the above was pure Dean Smith, a basketball idealist in a nonideal world.

I'm not Dean Smith and I never will be. But I was back, waving his flag. I was still a gym rat, still "the combative UNC point guard."

So in closing, I salute my mentors: Coach Smith, Larry Brown, Doug Moe, Rick Majerus, Don Nelson, Del Harris, and Gene Espeland; the assistants who made me look good and held me back when I wanted to tackle a ref; and the players who did the running, rebounding, winning, and losing. And the game itself. And my kids.

I think I'm going to win again. I think I'm going to help kick cancer's ass once and for all. I think I'm going to win an NBA championship. So I think the book of my life will have one more chapter, maybe two.

Let's talk again in a couple of years.

ACKNOWLEDGMENTS

'd like to thank my coauthor, Curt Sampson; Harper executive editor David Hirshey; and Byrd Leavell of Waxman-Leavell Literary Agency for making this book come to life.

Muchas gracias, señores.

My gratitude also extends to the following people:

Charles Barkley
Don Barr
Bob Bass
Mike Bratz
Rick Carlisle
Dan Coughlin
Coby Dietrick
Chad Forcier
World B. Free
Del Harris
John Hassan
Roy Hinson
Chad Iske
Michael Jordan
Coby Karl
Bob Lichter

Nancy Mancini
Kevin Melchionni
Doug Moe
Otto Orf
Gary Payton
Chris Redding
Kelci Karl Robinson
Campy Russell
Clay Sampson
John H. Sampson
John M. Sampson
John Strawn
Vance Walberg
John Welsh

ABOUT THE AUTHOR

George Karl, an All-American at the University of North Carolina and an original member of the San Antonio Spurs, is the fifth-winningest coach in NBA history. Karl lives in Denver, where his favorite pastime is watching his daughter Kaci play soccer and basketball. *Furious George* is his first book.

Curt Sampson played (actually, sat on the bench) for one year of D-1 basketball at Kent State University. His books *Hogan* and *The Masters* are *New York Times* bestsellers. He lives with his dogs in Bristol, Texas, near Dallas. *Furious George* is his fifteenth book.